WARRIORS
& CITIZENS

Edited by Kori Schake & Jim Mattis

WARRIORS
& CITIZENS

American Views of Our Military

HOOVER INSTITUTION PRESS

STANFORD UNIVERSITY   STANFORD, CALIFORNIA

www.hoover.org

Hoover Institution Press Publication No. 667

Hoover Institution at Leland Stanford Junior University,
Stanford, California 94305-6003

First printing 2016
21 20 19 18 17 16   7 6 5 4 3 2

Manufactured in the United States of America

The paper used in this publication meets the minimum Requirements of the American National Standard for Information Sciences—Permanence of Paper for Printed Library Materials, ANSI/NISO Z39.48-1992. ♾

Library of Congress Cataloging-in-Publication Data
Names: Schake, Kori N., editor. | Mattis, James N., 1950–   editor.
Title: Warriors & citizens : American views of our military /
    Kori Schake and Jim Mattis, editors.
Other titles: Hoover Institution Press publication ; 667.
Description: Stanford, California : Hoover Institution Press, Stanford
    University, 2016. | Series: Hoover Institution Press publication ; no. 667 |
    Includes bibliographical references.
Identifiers: LCCN 2016024317 | ISBN 9780817919344 (cloth : alk. paper) |
    ISBN 9780817919368 (epub) | ISBN 9780817919375 (mobi) |
    ISBN 9780817919382 (PDF)
Subjects: LCSH: Civil-military relations—United States. | United States—
    Armed Forces—Public opinion. | Public opinion—United States.
Classification: LCC JK330.W37 2016 | DDC 322/.50973—dc23
LC record available at https://lccn.loc.gov/2016024317

CONTENTS

Acknowledgments vii

1 A Great Divergence?
Kori Schake and Jim Mattis 1

2 Civil-Military Paradoxes
Rosa Brooks 21

3 Is Civilian Control of the Military Still an Issue?
Mackubin Thomas Owens 69

4 Thanks for Your Service: Civilian and Veteran
Attitudes after Fifteen Years of War
*Jim Golby, Lindsay P. Cohn,
and Peter D. Feaver* 97

5 Public Opinion, Military Justice,
and the Fight against Terrorism Overseas
Benjamin Wittes and Cody Poplin 143

6 Public Opinion and the Making of Wartime Strategies
Nadia Schadlow 161

7   Testing the "Flournoy Hypothesis":
    Civil-Military Relations in the Post-9/11 Era
    Thomas Donnelly   189

8   The "Very Liberal" View of the US Military
    Tod Lindberg   219

9   Young Person's Game: Connecting with Millennials
    Matthew Colford and Alec J. Sugarman   245

10 A Model for Connecting Civilians and the Military
    Jim Hake   265

11 Ensuring a Civil-Military Connection
    Kori Schake and Jim Mattis   287

    Contributors   327

    Index   333

ACKNOWLEDGMENTS

We are grateful to the Hoover Institution and in particular Robert and Marion Oster, who generously funded this project. Scholars could not ask for a more intellectually inviting environment than Stanford's Hoover Institution. It is an organization committed to developing and exploring ideas that define a free society. Few issues matter more to the preservation of a free society than the ability to keep it so, and sustaining a symbiotic relationship between our military and our public in America is essential. Hoover's official title is the Hoover Institution on War, Revolution, and Peace, and the institution commendably invests in serious scholarship on issues of warfare at a time when this is a rarity in academia. Bob and Marion championed this project—in fact, it was they who pulled us into undertaking it.

Our objectives for this project were twofold: to amass and disseminate research on public attitudes about military issues and to draw into the project leading thinkers on civil-military issues to reflect on different aspects of this data. We are deeply indebted to the people who did the real work of this project: the champion pollsters at YouGov and the authors who assessed the vast trove of data and wrote chapters for this book. Doug Rivers, Ashley Grosse, and Joe Williams at YouGov taught a couple of neophytes the basics of designing survey instruments and trained our judgment about where outcomes were consistent with broader trends in public opinion. It should go without saying that any remaining mistakes of survey design and interpretation are our fault, not theirs.

Our sorting criteria for authors was simple: we chose the people we learn from. The process of pleading with busy people long on competing obligations to carve out time to think and write about this subject was, we are still elated to admit, one hundred percent successful. Everyone we hoped might contribute did, an outcome so statistically improbable that we can only attribute it to the greed of smart people to get their hands on new data about an important issue in our field and make a contribution to the understanding of it. We thank them all.

Patrick Cirenza is the finest research assistant we could have hoped for and was a substantive contributor to our thinking about these issues. Curmudgeonly Dave Brady, Stanford's American politics ace, and Bill Whalen were very helpful in looking over the initial data and helping us understand whether we had anything interesting as we developed the second survey.

This book is dedicated to those who have served, serve today, and will serve tomorrow in the military as citizens who have carried the patriot's burden and committed all they have to protecting the country.

CHAPTER 1

A Great Divergence?

Kori Schake and Jim Mattis

We initiated this project out of curiosity about whether, after forty years of an all-volunteer force, a small force relative to our overall population, and twelve years of continuous warfare, the American public was losing connection to its military. Our concern was not loss of connection in the sense that preoccupies academic experts on civil-military relations in the United States—a military insubordinate to civilian control. We saw scant evidence of that in either our policymaking or military experience. Rather, with less than one half of one percent of the American public currently serving in our military (see figure 1.1) and with the high pace of deployments for significant elements of our fighting forces, we were interested in the cumulative effect of having a military at war when the broad swathe of American society is largely unaffected. Whether or not the different experiences of our military and the broader society amount to a "gap" and whether such a gap is adequately defined seemed worthy areas to delve into.

The untethering of our military from our society could be damaging to both in many ways. Some thought that our civilian society would become perhaps more willing to engage in wars and certainly

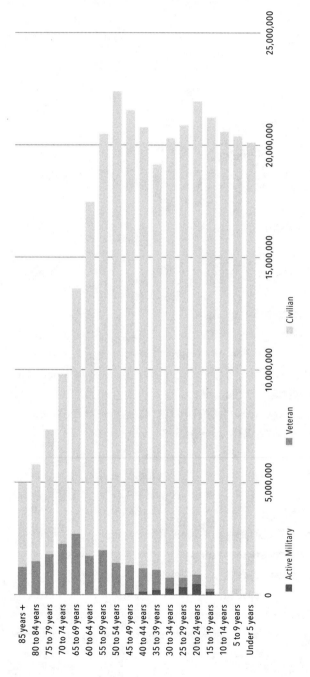

FIGURE 1.1 United States Civil-Military Population Pyramid

Courtesy of Tim Kane. (Data from United States Census Bureau, "Current Population Survey," 2012, http://www.census.gov/population/age/, http://www.census.gov/hhes/veterans/data/, and from Defense Manpower Data Center, *2014 Demographics: Profile of the Military Community*, 2014, http://download .militaryonesource.mil/12038/MOS/Reports/2014-Demographics-Report.pdf, p. 35.)

Source: Tim Kane, The Hoover Institution, based on US Census, ACS, and DMDC (most recent data as of 2015.

more hardened to the costs of warfare from which they have the luxury of being insulated. Anecdotes indicated that public inexperience with veterans could complicate their reintegration into society, even cause them to be perceived as a threat to the broader society. With little experience of warfare in the general population, the public may have scant appreciation for what is needed to win our wars or become contemptuous of the military virtues necessary for winning on the battlefield when those virtues are out of synch with the values of our civil society. Elected political leaders without military expertise may have trouble crafting strategies for the successful conduct of our wars. The military could even come to consider itself a society apart, different from, and more virtuous than, the people they commit themselves to protecting, like praetorian guards at the bacchanalia, as one soldier described it. Or our military could begin to feel that society "owes them something," fostering entitlement attitudes that would chip away at the culture essential to retaining warriors in our military forces. We were concerned above all about suggestions that the rest of society has simply become apathetic to the issues that dominate the consciousness of those who have been putting their lives on the line for the rest of us in the wars our country is fighting.

While major surveys of public attitudes occasionally focus series on veterans' issues and include some questioning in these areas, we were surprised at the dearth of systematic data or quantifiable indicators to gird analysis about the American public's understanding of, and relationship to, its military. After two extensive polls and cross-disciplinary exploration, we are greatly relieved to say that the concern about the American public losing connection to its military was not substantiated by research conducted for this project. The common perception of divergence is wrong. Public opinion surveys conducted as part of this study strongly suggest that while the American public is not knowledgeable about military issues, its judgment is fundamentally sound, and its concern is unabated for the soldiers, sailors, airmen, coastguardsmen, and Marines who fight the nation's wars.

Whatever they think of the wars our country is fighting, Americans no longer blame their military as many did during the Vietnam War. The enormous respect Americans have for our military is obvious in ways large and small throughout society: the near-universal convention of thanking men and women in uniform for their service; the now-standard practice of tributes to our military during major sporting events; airlines' policy of boarding military passengers first (without apparent exasperation by other travelers); and—especially—the overwhelming support in Congress for increasing military pay and benefits, even when the military services themselves would like to curtail the rate of growth. No one gets elected in America running against the troops. Foreign troops serving in America are often amazed at the affection Americans demonstrate for our military personnel.

In this way, the broader society reflects the distinction prevalent in the military itself between personal judgments about a war and the commitment to fighting it. Choosing war is the business of elected politicians in America; fighting war is the business of our military. The sturdiness of this principle on both the civilian and military sides of the equation goes a long way to explaining the affection Americans now have for their military, even though less than 16 percent of Americans served or had a family member serve since 9/11.

The American military's continuing function as a conveyor belt into the middle class is another strong source of public affection. Strong majorities of both the public and elites consider the American military one of the few remaining reliable means of economic advancement, especially for minorities and the poor. As an institution, it is also considered fairer than virtually any other: it clearly defines and rewards merit. Our research revealed that these long-standing conventions still have powerful resonance with the American public.

The surveys identified, however, many gaps between the American public and its military. We wondered whether some of these gaps make public support for the military broad but shallow. In other words, support for the military is an easy social convention because it demands little from the broader populace. We also explored whether some gaps could in time erode important elements of America's beneficial civil-military relationship. Moreover, some operant gaps appear not between civilians and the military but between civilians and civilian elites or between civilians and governmental elites, with concomitant effects for the military.

Research Questions

Reviewing the literature on civil-military relations and utilizing our experience in defense policy and the military, respectively, we identified several initial concerns for exploration in the surveys.

Ignorance

Does the public have a basic working knowledge of the military? Does their lack of knowledge lead to worrisome misconceptions—for example, that all veterans suffer from post-traumatic stress disorder (PTSD), making them potentially dangerous? Knowledge differences could also affect recruitment and make the public less empathetic about the demands of military life. Does the differential level of knowledge cause the public to be too deferential to military views or cause the public to believe the military is insufficiently deferential to civilians on issues properly decided by suits rather than uniforms?

Public ignorance could also affect the choices political leaders make about warfare: whether to use military force at all, whether to adopt an approach of overwhelming or incremental force, how much political capital to expend on war efforts, whether they face political reversals for escalating costs or failure to achieve their war aims. It can also lead to dramatic and rapid collapses in public support for war efforts. The relationship is interactive: the less informed the public, the greater latitude governmental elites have to avoid electoral consequences for the material and human cost of strategic failure and the more likely public support is to be erratic and quickly eroded.

Strategy Differences

Is there a different approach to making strategy as the result of fewer military veterans' involvement at high civilian policymaking levels? Before 9/11, it was believed that civilians have a more relaxed view of threats than does the military; since 9/11, scholarly concern has shifted to the way civilians can be too willing to use military force while policymakers focus on civilian opinion and may not understand how to use military force effectively.

Several studies suggest a "veteran advantage" in the making of policy; namely, that veterans are believed to be more hesitant to use military force than civilians. Civilians tend to overstate what military force can achieve, to assume a wider margin for error than those with knowledge and experience from military service, and to lack the analytic discipline essential to developing clear and achievable war aims. Moreover, in a political culture with wide acceptance for the use of military force, veterans are better positioned politically to withstand public pressure favoring it. But military leaders often try to leach the politics out of political decision making in order to better analyze problems and develop strategy; this can lead to "perfect" solutions impractical for consideration by elected officials whose portfolios are broader than the military mandate alone.

Isolation

Because of its smaller size and how little the wars affect the general public, is the military growing more distant from society? Some of the impediments to routine interaction between civilians and the military are the result of budget or operational choices, such as consolidating military forces on fewer larger bases. Some are a consequence of base security or convenience. The result is seclusion for many military families from nearby support in the broader community and less understanding of the demands of military life by civilians.

Most civilians, for example, would have little idea of how to comfort a military family grieving a loss—something that was a much more common experience when our military was larger and service compulsory. Many well-intentioned Americans cannot even find a thread of conversation when discussing military service with a veteran other than asking about PTSD or sexual harassment in the case of female vets. This is potentially a two-way problem: veterans may not want to dwell on their wartime experiences or let such experiences define them in the eyes of society.

Cultural Differences

There is a fundamental difference between military rank structure and the egalitarian culture of America. This sometimes leads civilians without personal familiarity with the military to believe military service is "only about following orders." There is also among some civilians the temptation to treat warfare as just another arena of politics, with public indifference giving latitude for the imposition of social choices—conservative or progressive—uninformed by the grim exigencies and atavistic demands of warfare. This can translate into a perceived lack of respect by civilians in a military culture steeped in respect.

The culture gap can also lead to difficulties in military recruitment and the reintegration of veterans. Is the public sensitive to the military's concern that too great a focus on benefits may not bring into the military the types of people the military believes it needs? It can also lead to service members and their families undervaluing the well-intentioned gestures civilians make toward them (for example, yellow ribbons or verbal thank-yous), mistaking unfamiliarity for empty tokenism.

The perception is widespread in the military that civilians are insensitive to its culture—more than insensitive: intolerant. Is our military ideologically and socially out of step with the rest of society? Does the public appreciate that values and practices in the military considered old-fashioned and even out of step with the broader society are considered by many in the military to be integral to their fighting functions in defense of that society? Will a progressive society continue to invest in and connect itself to a military whose requirements for success on the battlefield demand attributes fundamentally at odds with those of the society it protects? If not, is a war-winning military sustainable in a society in which war's gruesome realities must be reconciled to an operant degree with the larger society's human aspirations?

Undermining Military Effectiveness

Many of the policies civilians are most eager to change about the military are perceived by civilians as social in nature: the inclusion of women in the infantry, and allowing homosexuals and transgender people to serve openly in America's military forces, for example. The public may perceive them as civil rights issues; the military by and large does not. In fact, there is concern in the military both about distrust among junior ranks toward their seniors for not defending the military's prerogatives and about losing those people we most need to draw to and keep in our fighting ranks. Are civilians intruding into healthy and necessary functional practices by the military? Are there social pressures on the military to adopt a victim mentality? How committed is the public at large to effecting these changes? Do they perceive trade-offs with military effectiveness? Is the public open to military arguments or do gaps in understanding prevent the arguments from gaining traction? Are uninformed civilian leaders viewing military leaders in political terms, leading them to dismiss as partisan sound military advice or to vet military leaders by their perceived politics rather than military qualifications?

Changed Civil-Military Relationships

Far down in our list is the issue that predominates in academic inquiry: diminishing loyalty to civilian leaders. We see little evidence of this in today's American military, but serious people worry about commitment on the part of the military to upholding the principle that elected leaders have a "right to be wrong"—to go against military advice because civilian leaders have to aggregate societal preferences and make decisions about how much to commit to war efforts.

It is currently more common to hear complaints that the military is too deferential to its political leadership, but might there eventually develop a counterpressure in the military to insist rather than advise? Are changes in public attitudes about elected leaders eroding restraints that the professional ethos of the American military imposes on itself? These pressures could push the military into politicized roles, something it is deeply uncomfortable with, or cause cynicism about civilians for hiding behind the military to avoid taking responsibility for their political choices. Perceptions of politicization by civilian leaders can also lead to vetting military nominees for political pliancy.

The Grief Gap

The American military feels its casualties deeply and has rituals and ceremonies to grieve losses and bind military units and communities together. The public is largely unaffected by deaths and wounds from the wars, and we have few public rituals beyond Veterans Day and Memorial Day to involve the public and pull the military into the broader society in times of grief. This can lead to a perception by the military that broader society does not understand their losses. There also seems to be an atrophying in the broader society of understanding and willingness to bridge the gap of grief and meaningfully engage Gold Star families. What had been a more common experience of loss in previous wars now tends to be an isolating experience for military families. Are there practices that can be promulgated throughout society, as has been the practice of routinely thanking our military for its service, to better get our civilian arms around our military in times of loss?

Military Entitlement

Another azimuth of potential concern is whether civilian society has begun to think about the American military as, and the military has come to behave like, just another interest group in our national political scrum. Is there tension between a self-regarding "only 1 percent serve" attitude among the military and a "you signed up for this" attitude among the public? Are choices by the military leadership about when and how to engage in public debate over spending or policy issues delegitimizing? Is the political activism of veterans' organizations and retired military officers shading perceptions of the active-duty military? Will the national indebtedness lead to trade-offs between public beneficiaries that stoke resentment about veterans' preferences? All of these things could portend a diminished demonstration of respect for the military by American society. And while it would take a cataclysmic collapse to bring regard for the military down to the levels of public distrust encountered by every other organ of the federal government, this diminishment would still represent a significant change in the relationship the American public has had with its military since the Vietnam nadir.

Civilian-Military versus Elite Civilian Categories

There is a widespread (although possibly outdated) perception that our soldiers, sailors, airmen, Marines, coastguardsmen, and their families tend to be more religious and hold more politically conservative views than the rest of society. This tendency may also be true of the general population of our country as compared with elites. Which of the many ways to define elite—advanced education, high income, skilled profession, community stature, policy influence—have relevance for civil-military issues? Do elites accurately understand public attitudes about the issues? Are elites of some stripes less appreciative of martial values than the rest of civilian society?

The public may share the military's views but not know, or care, whether the military is allowed to preserve them. Are elites responding to public pressure for social change in the military? Or are they seeking to utilize the military as a laboratory for social change, capitalizing on the lack of connection between the military and general public and making the military lead (instead of follow) the broader society's trends? Sensing that the military speaks for the public could lead elites to distrust military advice, or the advisors themselves, for having a court of appeal in the public if their advice is rejected by elected leaders.

Nonmilitary Purposes

Americans like our military partly because it is good at its job. Does that incline policymakers to utilize the military rather than other national tools to achieve their objectives? Many of our current national security challenges require developing cultural expertise about societies becoming threats to us because of their weakness—not obviously a military task. The past decade has been a long slog of mastering (or remastering) counterinsurgency, and inherently civilian functions have migrated to the military because as a country we keep selecting strategies that rely on "whole of government" capacities our government manifestly lacks. Put another way, if only our intelligence agencies and military are organized to compete in a globalized world, do our national leaders fail to use traditional diplomacy and instead reach too often for the military instrument?

Has the nature of contemporary national security threats seemed too elusive for military force to effectively combat? Has observing our military at war for the past decade affected public confidence in its central obligation of winning the nation's wars? Has the tendency among elected officials to talk of all veterans as though they are disabled and to represent all trauma as weakening rather than strengthening diminished public confidence in our fighting forces?

Familiarity

Lastly, we were interested in whether the panoply of civil-military issues could be addressed by fostering simple familiarity. Earlier studies have found the strongest correlate of shared civilian and military attitudes to be personally knowing someone who is or has been in military service. With the smaller size and professionalization of our military is that familiarity being lost? If so, does that lead to "brittle and shallow" public support? Does knowing someone in the military make the public more or less likely to give the benefit of the doubt on issues where the public is not fully informed? Is the American system of national security policymaking, designed for dialectic discussion at high levels between elected leaders and the military, so brittle that it requires heroic effort to function?

Methodology

We did not address all of these questions, but they provided the universe of inquiry in which we thought about the issues, developed polling questions to probe for public attitudes, and looked for interesting answers among the data. Many of them touch on related phenomena.

Most of these issues were identified in the seminal Triangle Institute for Security Studies (TISS) project of 1998, which, it turns out, is the last systematic research about civil-military relations conducted on a large scale. Much of our understanding was shaped by it, and many of our survey questions were cribbed directly from it. This pilferage not only represents the highest academic compliment but also was intended to provide a second set of data points on these issues following over a decade of war with our all-volunteer military—a first in our history. We anticipate future studies will continue this practice so that trend analysis will become possible. It would be a great benefit to scholarship for such data collection to become routine across decades.

This study attempts to accomplish five objectives:

- collect data on American public attitudes toward the military;

- identify those gaps between civilian and military attitudes on issues central to the military profession and the professionalism of our military;

- determine which if any of these gaps are problematic for sustaining the traditionally strong bonds between the American military and its broader public;

- analyze whether any problematic gaps are amenable to remediation by policy means; and

- assess potential solutions.

Much of the debate about civil-military issues is driven by anecdotal or impressionistic evidence. Experiential data is valid but may not be generalizable. We sought the ability to determine whether the concerns were systemic. In order to explore these questions, we designed and conducted two extensive surveys of public attitudes. Public opinion research is, of course, not definitive, and we can only make limited claims on the basis of two studies. But there is no knowing what the public thinks without asking the public, and we wanted to start the exploration with at least some data on which to base analyses by a cadre of thinkers.

We attempted across the two surveys to ask questions differently in order to get some sense of the degree to which responses were sensitive to wording. In developing the surveys we were guided by the experts at the internet-based market research firm YouGov. We began with a baseline survey, to identify general issues, train our judgment on the tradecraft of survey design, and gauge whether potentially interesting attitudes might merit further and more detailed research. Our initial, baseline survey suggested that surprising and interesting variations may exist between elites and the general public on these issues. We designed the second, much larger survey to test that proposition across a wide array of substantive issues.

Coming up with a robust definition of "elite" proves surprisingly difficult. Separating wealth from political affiliation, and in some cases profession from political affiliation, turns out to be tricky. The Triangle study from 1998—far and away the most important survey of public attitudes—was criticized by Andrew Kohut of the Pew Research Center for a selection bias that, he believed, called some of the study conclusions into question. The wizards at YouGov puzzled over this for us and developed a methodology, described thus via email, that we hope will prove useful:

> The dataset includes 500 interviews with a sample of elites designed to represent opinion leaders in 10 professional areas of expertise—media, business and finance, state and local government, nongovernmental organizations (NGOs), think tanks and academia, religious organizations, and congressional staff. The elite sample was randomly drawn from leaders in the sectors of business and finance, academia, and religious organization using publicly available lists of leaders. Academics were selected from members of the National Academy of Sciences, executives from the largest 500 US companies ranked by total annual revenue as of June 1 of the current year, journalists from the 2013 list of best state-based political reports, religious organizations from a database of religious institutions compiled from the Pluralism Project at Harvard University. Congressional staff, NGO leaders, and think tank staff were recruited via YouGov's DC Insider recruiter.

We sought out experts to apply their perspectives to the YouGov data. Our sorting criteria for authors was simple: we chose the people we learn from. We wanted a host of scholars to sort out what it all meant, for, as with picking raspberries, we would miss a lot if the data were examined from a single perspective. Rosa Brooks, Georgetown University law professor, defense policy analyst, and military spouse probes the paradoxes of public attitudes. Mackubin Thomas Owens, editor of *Orbis* and author of *US Civil-Military Relations after 9/11,* considers how the data challenge or reaffirm his thinking. Peter Feaver, Duke University professor of political science who ran the 1998 Triangle study, Major Jim Golby, and Lindsay Cohn explore the differences in findings between that study and our data. Benjamin Wittes, founder of the Lawfare blog, and Cody Poplin of the Brookings Institution examine perceptions of the military justice system. Nadia Schadlow, from the Smith-Richardson Foundation, reflects on executive branch difficulties putting military force into broad and effective national security strategies. Tom Donnelly, director of the Marion Ware Center for Defense Studies at the American Enterprise Institute, gives his insights on how changing public attitudes affect Congressional action in defense policy. Tod Lindberg, Hoover fellow and author of *The Heroic Heart: Greatness Ancient and Modern* (2015), looks across the political spectrum for similarities and differences in our cultural attitudes about the military. Matthew Colford and A. J. Sugarman, recent Stanford graduates now both working in policy jobs in Washington, suggest ways to better connect young Americans with the military. Jim Hake, founder and CEO of the nongovernmental organization Spirit of America, also picks up the theme of how to better connect Americans to the nation's war efforts. In concluding, we try to sift through the issue of whether the public attitudes displayed in the surveys conducted for this project are consistent with preserving dominant military power for the United States.

Main Findings

Rosa Brooks explores a series of paradoxes in American attitudes toward their military: enthusiasm for our military coupled with ignorance about it; mistrust with awe; belief that our military is the world's best with opinion that it is incapable of addressing today's most pressing threats; appreciation for our military's professionalism with decrying of its institutional differences from broader civilian society. She perceives a "pernicious gap between elite civilian political leaders and elite military leaders: a gap of knowledge, and a gap of trust," arguing that "if we want a military that is strong, capable and responsive to America's changing needs, we will need to rethink many of our most basic assumptions about the military and its role."

Mackubin Thomas Owens gives an overview of civil-military frictions in America, emphasizing that current levels fall well within historical norms and that the bargain between the American people, the president, the Congress, and their military is always being renegotiated. He illustrates that our system of military subordination to civilian control with wide latitude for military input in advance of policy decisions relies fundamentally on mutual trust between civilian officials and military leaders. He believes the YouGov data show a worrisome trend toward distrust of the military among elites—especially self-described "very liberal" elites—as well as a growing political partisanship in the military that augur greater civil-military friction. Moreover, he considers the uninformed public gives political leaders wider latitude to impose "transmutation" of progressive cultural values over the functional imperatives of the military for success on the battlefield.

Jim Golby, Lindsay Cohn, and Peter Feaver explore the ways fighting extended wars our all-volunteer force was not designed for, and without the other resources of a full wartime mobilization of society, have affected civil-military relations since the seminal 1998 Triangle study. They find a striking continuity in public attitudes and are reassured the all-volunteer force has not become dangerously isolated from the rest of society. They do identify a large increase in civilian ignorance or apathy about military issues and also in civilian deference to the military on conduct of the wars, which they consider may be connected to decline in trust of civilian leadership. They see in the YouGov data a disturbing public acceptance of norms for military behavior improper in the American civil-military model, belief that the military has different values than the rest of society, and decline in familiarity with our military. They offer several recommendations to shore up important elements of American civil-military relations, including better scholar and journalist policing of politicization of the military by politicians and veterans' groups, and caution against policy remediations such as the draft, which they consider "a cure that is worse then the disease."

Benjamin Wittes and Cody Poplin emphasize the volatility and contradictions in public attitudes about the wars our country is fighting, noting that, while pessimism Americans have about the policies being pursued stokes support for stronger actions, the public's ignorance about military issues precludes them from developing stable views on the complex issues of current conflicts where military operations are tightly integrated with issues more often associated with law enforcement and justice. They worry that this combination will lead to ineffectual counterterrorism policies, policies that symbolize toughness without achieving lasting effects, unless political leaders engage the public more substantively. They also highlight the fact that, while Americans generally support the military having different standards from those in our broader society, there is significant public opposition to specific applications by the military of those different standards.

Nadia Schadlow suggests that public attitudes are much less a constraint on the making of strategy than civilian leaders attest. She emphasizes that engagement of the public has substantial effects on public attitudes, especially given the high frequency of "don't know" responses in the YouGov surveys. The nature of the war, its anticipated costs, strong civil-military leadership, and the coherence of strategy weigh heavily in public consideration. By failing to engage the public on its strategy, civilian leaders may be creating the constraint of public disapproval that they argue is determining their policy choice.

Thomas Donnelly believes that, while scholars of civil-military relations advocate energetic civilian management of military policy—and politicians even believe they practice that supreme command—in reality, we have a rigid distinction between military and civilian spheres of competence and high levels of civil-military tension that are debilitating to our national security policies. He argues for a Janowitzian approach, with greater blending of civilian and military perspectives. Donnelly also believes the familiarity gap between civilians and the military has led to pity rather than respect for the difficulties service families undergo on our behalf. He concludes, "It's only a little hyperbolic to conclude that some Americans—those who feel most removed from military life—see the service as an experience leading to pathological behavior."

Tod Lindberg is, by contrast, sanguine about the state of civil-military relations, drawing from survey data that a high level of trust in the military is "a bedrock component of the American social compact." He emphasizes the distinction of self-described "very liberal" Americans in their attitudes toward the military as compared with those in every other political category, for example in debates over the movie *American Sniper* and with regard to their confidence that the military can be made more like the rest of society without negative repercussions in their ability to win our nation's wars. He notes that the 4.8 percent of Americans who hold these views are considerably fewer than often have held a skeptical view of our military yet they wield a disproportionate cultural influence that can alienate civilians unfamiliar with the military, and that can often impose policy changes on social issues within our military.

Matthew Colford and A. J. Sugarman modeled a greater civilian effort to connect with our military, designing and teaching a course on civil-military relations while still undergraduate students at Stanford University. They point out that "young Americans between 18 and 29 have made the transition into adulthood during the single longest period of continuous war in American history," and YouGov survey data illustrate that their attitudes are indeed different from their elders. Colford and Sugarman note that young Americans' attitudes toward the military actually accord most closely with those over 65, the last generation to have experienced our country being at war for an extended duration. But given the smaller size of our contemporary American military and policies by universities that still in effect restrict ROTC programs, young Americans are significantly less informed. Colford and Sugarman offer several suggestions for ways the military could interact more with young Americans and open itself up to greater involvement by young Americans.

While most scholars of civil-military relations place the burden of reconnecting the civilian and military spheres of American civic life on the military, Jim Hake shows that "the resources and brainpower of our citizens—unfettered by bureaucracy and the inevitable restrictions on the use of taxpayer funds—can have an off-scale impact" on military operations. His chapter describes creating an organization that crowd-funds support to the mission needs of deployed troops, a venture capital model of giving civilian America a participatory role in projects to assist military missions and thereby reconnecting them directly with the war effort and deployed servicemen and women.

In conclusion, we explore some possible consequences of two themes that emerged strongly for us from the data: public disengagement and the effect of high levels of public support for the military combined with very low levels of trust in elected political leaders. The pervasiveness of "don't know" responses across the breadth of survey questions indicates a public largely uninformed about military issues. In all but the arena of social issues, the public defers to military judgment—and familiarity with the military tends to erase even this exception. This deference contrasts starkly with the decline in public respect for, and trust in, its elected leaders, which has the potential to shift toward the military the balance of responsibility properly tilted toward elected civilian leaders.

We also reflect on whether American society is becoming so divorced from the requirements for success on the battlefield that not only will we fail to comprehend our military, but we also will be unwilling to endure a military so constituted to protect us. In particular, we are concerned that civilians believe the military can sustain a war-winning force without the values our military inculcates in order to produce success on the battlefield.

Because we believe complacency about military requirements could lead to terrible outcomes for our country, we also venture some recommendations for remediation of this gap in cultural appreciation appropriate in a nation whose military is under civilian control. Most of the weight of these recommendations falls to civilians, not the military. Many of them focus on the responsibility of elected leaders. All of them seek to foster greater familiarity that will ensure our military are braided tightly to our broader society in a manner that will keep alive our experiment in democracy.

CHAPTER 2

Civil-Military Paradoxes

Rosa Brooks

Civil-military relations in modern America are characterized more by paradox than by consistency: ordinary Americans support the military more than ever but know less about it than ever. In Washington, senior government policymakers simultaneously overestimate the military's capabilities and mistrust the military leadership. The US military is widely viewed as the strongest military in the history of the world, but military leaders view conventional military tools as less and less useful for dealing with the complex security threats we face today. Meanwhile, although the military itself is more professional than ever, its internal structures—from recruiting, training, and education to personnel policies—lag badly behind those in most civilian workplaces, making it difficult for the military to change from within.

Portions of this chapter draw on several columns published in *Foreign Policy* over the last few years. I am deeply grateful to *Foreign Policy* for providing me with an early venue to work through some of the ideas discussed here and to the New America Foundation and Arizona State University for providing financial support for my work.

These paradoxes both reflect and contribute to an underlying conundrum. In today's world, where security challenges increasingly stem from nonstate actors, the cyber domain, the diffuse effects of climate change, and similar nontraditional sources, it is growing ever more difficult to clearly define the US military's role and mission. We no longer have a coherent basis for distinguishing between war and "not war," or between military force and other forms of coercion and manipulation. In such a context, we no longer know what kind of military we need, or how to draw sensible lines between civilian and military tasks and roles. The resulting confusion is a recipe for tensions between civilian and military leaders, challenges to military morale, and, in the end, poor policy decisions.

Paradox One:
Enthusiasm and Ignorance

Most Americans know roughly as much about the US military as they know about the surface of the moon. It is not that Americans dislike the military—most of us support it wholeheartedly. It is just that we do not have a clue who is in it, what it does, what it costs those who join it, or what current US military policies cost us—as a nation or as a democracy.

Manifestations of public support for the military are everywhere in post-9/11 America. Troops are treated to special discounts at chain stores and a constant barrage of "Thank you for your service!" Airlines invite military personnel to board before other passengers, schools arrange for children to send greeting cards to "wounded warriors," and employers tout their commitment to hiring military veterans at "Hire a Hero" job fairs.

But though support for "the troops" has become a kind of American civil religion, these ritualized gestures sometimes seem only to emphasize the distance between the military and civilian society. As James

Fallows noted in a 2015 *Atlantic* article titled "The Tragedy of the American Military," nearly 10 percent of the US population had been in uniform by the end of World War II.[1] Today, it is quite different.[2] Speaking at Duke University in 2010, former defense secretary Robert Gates was blunt: "For a growing number of Americans," he said, "service in the military, no matter how laudable, has become something for other people to do."[3]

The majority of living veterans served in wars that most Americans now consider part of our history, not part of our present.[4] Not coincidentally—and despite nearly fifteen years of war—younger Americans are far less likely than older Americans to have a member of their immediate family in the military. More than 75 percent of Americans over sixty have had a member of their immediate family serve in the military, compared to 40 percent of Americans under forty, and only 33 percent of Americans under thirty.[5] Looking only at more recent periods of military service, the numbers tell a story of dwindling civilian connections to the military: in the 2014 YouGov survey population, only 19 percent of Americans said they had served themselves or had an immediate relative who served in the military after 1991, and only 15.6 percent had served or had an immediate relative serve after September 11, 2001 (CM2T 1–2).[6]

What is more, military service has largely become a hereditary profession in modern America: the children of military veterans join the military at a significantly higher rate than those without a parent who served do. The essay in this volume by James Golby, Lindsay Cohn, and Peter D. Feaver provides a thorough discussion of how a parent's veteran status affects his or her children's decisions about whether to join the military.

Meanwhile, base-relocation policies have isolated many military personnel and their families in a small number of US states and regions. Half of all active-duty military personnel are now stationed in only five states: California, Texas, Virginia, North Carolina, and Georgia.[7] Partly as a consequence of these policies, over the last few decades the military has become more southern, less urban, and more politically conservative than American society as a whole.

Certainly, many military personnel feel ignored or misunderstood by their civilian compatriots. In its 2012 annual survey, the Military Times found that more than 75 percent of all active-duty personnel and reservists agreed with the statement, "The military community has little in common with the rest of the country and most civilians do not understand the military."[8] There is substantial truth to the latter clause, at least: ask the average American to describe the basic structure of the military, estimate its size and budget, guess the locations of "forward deployed" military personnel, or describe the military's activities, and you will get a lot of sheepish shrugs. Although nearly 70 percent of all YouGov respondents claimed to be "very" or "somewhat" familiar with the military (CM1T 39), when asked to estimate the number of people currently serving in all five branches of the military, the YouGov respondents were strikingly wrong: on average, their guesses were off by some five million people. Guesses on the size of specific branches of the military, such as the U.S. Army and Marine Corps, were incorrect by hundreds of thousands of people.[9]

While a near majority of YouGov respondents say they think the military is not isolated and a substantial number are "not sure" if it is isolated (CM2T 23), majorities across all demographic groups in the YouGov survey, both military and civilian, agreed that "military culture and way of life . . . is very different from the culture and way of life of those who are not in the military" and that "the military has different values than the rest of society," as Golby, Cohn, and Feaver observe. Speaking to West Point cadets a few years ago, Admiral Michael Mullen, former chairman of the Joint Chiefs of Staff, expressed a similar sentiment: "Our work is appreciated, of that I am certain. There isn't a town or a city I visit where people do not convey to me their great pride in what we do. But I fear they do not know us. I fear they do not comprehend the full weight of the burden we carry or the price we pay when we return from battle."[10]

The price paid by those who go into battle has certainly been high: more than 7,000 American military personnel have given their lives in Iraq and Afghanistan, and more than 30,000 have been wounded.[11] Deployments also bring countless intangible costs: damaged or broken marriages, children growing up with absent parents, and the psychological strain of separation, hardship, and danger.

Even within the military, however, these costs are unevenly distributed. In 2003, for instance, enlisted personnel in combat occupational categories (such as infantry, armor, artillery, or Special Forces) made up less than 13 percent of the active-duty force; the remaining 87 percent were in support services, public affairs, transportation jobs, medical and scientific jobs, human resources, engineering and construction, and so on.[12] By 2013, even after two lengthy wars, the percentage of enlisted personnel in combat specialties had inched up to 15 percent. For officers, the percentage held steady at 15 percent over the decade from 2003 to 2013. The percentage of personnel in combat occupations varies substantially by service, as well: 28 percent of enlisted army personnel serve in jobs classified as combat positions, for instance, compared to only 3 percent of navy enlisted personnel.[13]

To be sure, many military personnel in noncombat positions end up in combat anyway: a truck filled with supply clerks can be ambushed or hit with an Improvised Explosive Device (IED) as easily as a truck full of infantrymen can. But even when deployed in combat zones, most members of the military are not tasked with fighting: instead, their jobs are to maintain vehicles, enter data into computers, write articles for the base newsletter, monitor satellite imagery, make sure the right number of Meals, Ready-to-Eat (MREs) have been ordered, and so on.

A solid third of military personnel have never deployed at all to the Iraq or Afghanistan theaters, though deployment rates also vary substantially by branch of service. As of 2011, the most recent year for which there are statistics available, some 27 percent of active-duty army personnel had never deployed to either of these conflicts, nor had 34 percent of navy personnel, 41 percent of air force personnel, and

39 percent of Marines.[14] Army personnel were also far more likely than personnel in any other service to have endured multiple deployments to combat theaters: 25 percent of army personnel in 2011 had been deployed to Iraq or Afghanistan for three or more years, compared to fewer than 7 percent of sailors, airmen, or Marines. Unsurprisingly, the army has also taken the lion's share of the casualties from these wars: of the roughly 0.6 percent of military personnel deployed to Afghanistan and Iraq who were killed in action in the decade after 9/11, more than two thirds were army soldiers, and most of the rest were Marines.[15]

Still, the sacrifices borne by all members of the military community are substantial. Even personnel who never see combat face the risk of doing so, and face a punishing and often unpredictable training and rotation schedule. Military families too must make substantial sacrifices: they are constantly uprooted, with consequent costs to friendships, children's performance in school, and the ability of military spouses to build their own careers. War or no war, life in the military is full of difficulties and disruptions of a type born by few civilians with comparable education and income levels.

There are plenty of dangerous civilian jobs—construction workers, truckers, loggers, miners, and fishermen all have rates of fatal accidents approaching those of military personnel—but tough as these jobs are, civilians can always quit. A logger who does not like his odds can decide from one day to the next to become a realtor; a miner ordered into a situation he deems dangerous can tell the foreman to go to hell. His pay may be docked—he may be fired and face consequent economic hardship—but he will not go to prison for his refusal to risk his life.

This is not the case for service members. Yes, America has a volunteer military, but once you sign up, there is no changing your mind until you have fulfilled your service obligation. A soldier assigned to Fort Hood cannot decline the assignment because he does not think much of the Texas public schools; a financial clerk ordered to deploy to Iraq can not politely decline. Under the Uniform Code of Military Justice, disobeying a lawful order will land you behind bars—and desertion in wartime is still punishable by death. The Declaration of Independence tells us that all men have the right to life, liberty, and the pursuit of happiness, but those who volunteer for military service effectively give up those rights. Once in the military, their lives belong to the nation.

Perhaps to their credit, polls suggest that a fair number of American civilians are aware of their ignorance of military matters. Golby, Cohn, and Feaver note that current polling shows a "surprisingly large increase in the number of 'don't know' and 'no opinion' responses from nonveterans when asked about issues related to the military," compared to responses to similar poll questions a decade and a half ago. Among nonveteran nonelites, the rate of "don't know" and "no opinion" answers was a consistent 25 percent to 30 percent.

The diminishing percentage of Americans who serve or have family members who have served taken together with the shared military and civilian sense of being separate cultures are usually viewed as indicative of a large civilian-military "gap." But despite distinct differences in the experience of civilians and of those within the military community, today's military is far less different from the general public than many Americans tend to assume.

Before going further, it is useful to look at a quick snapshot of today's military. Start with the basics, courtesy of the Department of Defense's annual report on military demographics: there were roughly 1.4 million active-duty military personnel in fiscal year 2013, along with 843,000 reservists. The army is the largest service (it is almost as large as the navy and air force put together, though it is currently drawing down; at the end of fiscal year 2014 there were 508,000 active-duty army personnel).[16] The Marine Corps is the smallest service, with just under 190,000 active-duty personnel.[17] More than 14 percent of active-duty personnel are women, and 30 percent self-identify as members of minority populations.[18]

Today's military is relatively mature compared to the military of the Vietnam War or World War II. The average age of active-duty personnel is 28.6 years, and more than a quarter of officers are over the age of 40. More than half of active-duty personnel are married, and 36 percent are married with children. (In contrast, only 48 percent of all US households are made up of married couples, and only a fifth of US households are made up of married couples with children.[19]) Altogether, there are roughly three million military dependents (mostly spouses and children), and roughly 30 percent of military personnel and their families live in military housing.[20]

Today's military personnel are more likely than comparable age groups in the civilian population to have graduated from high school (with rare exceptions, military recruits must have high school degrees or General Education Development [GED] degrees to be eligible to serve). Military officers, meanwhile, are substantially better educated than civilians: only 30 percent of the overall population over age 25 have bachelor's degrees,[21] compared to more than 80 percent of officers.

Commentators often complain that "elites" (however you choose to define them) are underrepresented within the military. In 2010, for instance, only about 1 percent of students commissioned through ROTC came from Ivy League schools.[22] But since the eight small Ivy League schools confer less than 1 percent of all bachelor's degrees granted in the United States, this is not particularly telling.

Today's military is distinctly middle class. In part, this is because military requirements render many of the nation's poorest young people ineligible: the poorest Americans are the least likely to finish high school or gain a GED, for instance, and poverty also correlates with ill health, obesity, and the likelihood of serious run-ins with the criminal justice system, all of which are disqualifying factors for the military. Individualized data on the economic backgrounds of military personnel are not available, but several studies have looked at the income levels in the zip codes new military recruits give with their home addresses. A 2008 Heritage Foundation study found that a quarter of new recruits came from neighborhoods in the highest income quintile, with only 10 percent coming from neighborhoods in the lowest quintile.[23] A 2010 study by the National Priorities Project examined slightly different data and found a less top-heavy distribution, but the largest share of recruits came from the middle-income quintile nonetheless, with numbers in the top and bottom quintiles roughly even.[24]

People join the military for many reasons. Some people sign up because—reared on old World War II movies, or maybe just on first-person-shooter video games—they want to "go to war." Others dislike the idea of going to war but believe that a strong military will prevent war by deterring potential adversaries and want to be part of such a deterrent force. Others still join up for reasons that do not have much to do with the nature of the military: they are attracted by the military's excellent educational benefits and free heath care, they are looking for opportunities to travel and learn, or they simply view the military as a relatively stable job with benefits during economic hard times.

A 2011 Pew Research Center survey asked post-9/11 military veterans to list the most important factors that had motivated them to join the military. Nearly 90 percent listed serving the country as an important reason for joining, and 77 percent listed educational benefits as important. Upwards of 60 percent said they wanted to "see more of the world," and 57 percent said that learning skills for civilian jobs was an important factor. In contrast, only 27 percent said that difficulty finding a civilian job had been an important factor in the decision to join the military.[25]

That said, the military remains an important source of upward mobility for many Americans, and particularly for women and minorities. Contrary to much popular mythology about dysfunctional vets, most veterans do pretty well economically—better than comparable nonveterans. Overall, veterans are less likely than nonveterans to be unemployed, are less likely than nonveterans to live below the poverty line, and have higher median incomes than nonveterans.[26]

This doesn't mean that specific subsets of the veteran population don't struggle. Veterans are overrepresented among the homeless, for instance, and post-9/11 veterans have above-average unemployment rates—though this may simply reflect transition issues.[27] Transition issues are, unfortunately, common: according to the 2011 Pew survey, 44 percent of post-9/11 veterans say the transition to civilian life was difficult for them.[28]

Overall, however, post-9/11 veterans are a surprisingly contented group. Across the board, Pew found: "Veterans who served on active duty in the post-9/11 era are proud of their service (96 percent), and most (74 percent) say their military experience has helped them get ahead in life. The vast majority say their time in the military has helped them mature (93 percent), taught them how to work with others (90 percent) and helped to build self-confidence (90 percent). More than eight-in-ten (82 percent) say they would advise a young person close to them to join the military."[29]

Given all the recent media attention to military sexual harassment and assault rates, it is worth noting two things: first, though any amount is too much, rates of sexual assault and harassment do not appear to be higher in the military than in comparable civilian settings such as universities.[30] Second, Pew found that post-9/11 female veterans were "just as likely as their male counterparts to say they have experienced the positive benefits of military service." Seventy-nine percent of women veterans believed their military service had "helped them get ahead in life," 87 percent said that serving in the military had built their self-confidence, and 93 percent felt the military had helped them "grow and mature as a person."

Politics

Most people consider the military a politically conservative institution. But although a majority of surveyed military personnel self-identify as "conservative" in the much-cited annual Military Times poll, the reality is more complex. Most polls that purport to show "military opinions" suffer from various flaws. The Military Times poll, for instance, relies on voluntary responses to surveys sent by email to subscribers—and, as the editors note, a disproportionate number of the respondents are white, male, and older than average. What is more, many polls fail to differentiate between career military personnel and short-timers, or between officers and enlisted personnel.[31]

Perhaps the best recent study of military attitudes comes from Jason Dempsey, a U.S. Army lieutenant colonel and veteran of West Point's social science faculty. Overall, he found that social and political attitudes of army personnel track fairly closely with the views of the civilian population. On certain issues, he found, army personnel are in fact decidedly more *liberal* than the general population: in 2004 (the most recent year for which he found hard data), for instance, civilians were substantially more likely than army personnel to oppose abortion under all circumstances, and large majorities of army personnel supported increasing domestic government spending on education, health care, Social Security, and environmental protection.[32] Demspey's findings track those of other studies, which suggest that military officers "support civil liberties at significantly higher rates than . . . the general public" do; they also more strongly support stringent gun control.[33]

To a significant extent, the perception that members of the military are "right wing" is a holdover from the post-Vietnam era. In 1976, a study by the Foreign Policy Leadership Project found that only 33 percent of military officers identified with the Republican Party. But the end of the draft and the advent of the all-volunteer military dramatically changed the military's character, making it smaller, more professionalized, and more isolated from mainstream civilian society. After Vietnam, many of those who remained in the smaller force felt "abandoned" by the civilians who had sent them to war. By 1996, the percentage of officers identifying with the Republican Party had climbed to 67 percent (the same period saw only a slight rise in Republican Party identification among civilian elites).[34]

But today, the US military is a different animal than it was in the 1980s and early 1990s. The majority of senior officers continue to self-identify as conservative, but they make up only about 6 percent of the overall army population. And Dempsey's research found that they are more conservative (and more Republican) than junior officers and dramatically more conservative than enlisted personnel, whose views tend to more closely track those of the general population. Given this, it seems likely that future studies of the officer corps will find fewer self-identified conservatives, as today's most senior officers—who entered the military in the seventies and eighties—retire and are replaced by a new generation.

Dempsey's most interesting finding, perhaps, is that self-selected political labels are extremely poor predictors of actual views on social, political, and economic issues. On the whole, officers' views on specific issues ranging from abortion to government spending on social programs tended to be moderate to liberal, while the views of enlisted soldiers tended to skew liberal.

The notion that "the military" is homogeneous and inherently right wing is out of date. "On the whole, military opinions tend to parallel civilian opinions," concludes Dempsey. "The idea that service members have a distinctly different worldview (that is, a 'military mind')—conservative and dramatically out of step with the rest of society—is a myth that must be constantly debunked." Tellingly, post-9/11 veterans have only slightly more positive views of recent wars than the general population. In a 2011 survey, only 28 percent of civilians and only 34 percent of veterans said that both the war in Afghanistan and the war in Iraq had been worth it. Asked whether "relying too much on military force creates hatred that leads to more terrorism," the attitudes of post-9/11 veterans and the public were virtually identical, with, respectively, 51 percent and 52 percent agreeing.[35]

Geography

Many assume that military personnel are drawn disproportionately from stereotypically "red" states. It is true that the "red" South, the Southwest, and the mountain states are overrepresented within the military, while the "blue" Northeastern states are underrepresented, relative to their overall populations.[36] In and of itself, this helps account for why the military might still skew a bit conservative. But as with other assumptions about the military and politics, there is a more complicated picture lying beneath these broad-brush statements. To some extent, the demographics of military recruitment tell a story that is less about ideology than about economics, geography, and population density—and the natural tendency of people to gravitate towards the familiar and away from the unfamiliar.

Consider this: the state of California, which is hardly known for its homogeneous population or its right-wing politics, hosts the single largest concentration of active-duty military personnel in the nation. Meanwhile, the dark-blue state of Maine, which ranks forty-first in population size, sends a higher percentage of its young people into the military than any other state.[37] A simple red state/blue state model does not account for this.

The demographic makeup of today's military is probably best understood as a product of two somewhat related phenomena: population density and the location of large military installations, which create, in effect, self-replicating military clusters. Members of the military are disproportionately likely to come from nonurban areas,[38] and, if we break out recruitment by state, states with high population densities have, on average, lower per capita military recruitment than states with low population densities. (In 2010, the ten most densely populated states produced 1.8 recruits per thousand 18- to 24-year-olds, while the ten least densely populated states produced 2.4 recruits per thousand.[39])

To some degree, this is a story of economic and cultural opportunity: an 18-year-old from sparsely populated Maine or Wyoming does not have as many options for employment or seeing the world as does an 18-year-old from more densely populated regions. But new military recruits are also likely to come from areas that already have large military populations, and for this reason decisions about where to locate large military installations are a major driver of military demographics. For complex historical reasons—including the post–Civil War occupation of the American South by federal troops and the Mexican and Indian Wars of the nineteenth century—the South and Southwest have long hosted a disproportionate share of America's major military bases. This pattern has been exacerbated by base closure and realignment policies, which in recent decades have consolidated military bases into a relatively small number of states. Of the roughly 1.2 million active-duty service members stationed in the United States, 49 percent are stationed in only five states: California, Texas, Virginia, North Carolina, and Georgia.[40]

To a significant extent, base-location decisions create self-fulfilling prophesies: young people's career choices are profoundly influenced by the career choices of the adults around them, so it is not surprising that those who grow up in communities with high military populations end up joining the military in higher numbers than those who grow up far from large military bases, just as the children of military personnel are themselves more likely to join the military. (This is equally true for most professions: a disproportionate number of lawyers are the children of lawyers, for instance.)

When it comes to the military, the tendency for people to follow career paths familiar to them as a result of their communities is apparent. Look at the list of the one hundred US counties that produce the highest number of military recruits each year; to a great extent, it is a list of the counties that house the largest military installations. High recruit-producing counties include, for instance, Cumberland County, North Carolina, home to Fort Bragg; El Paso County, Texas, home to Fort Bliss; San Diego County, California, home to Naval Base Coronado and Naval Base San Diego; Montgomery County, Ohio, home to Wright-Patterson Air Force Base; Bell County, Texas, home to Fort Hood; El Paso County, Colorado, home to Fort Carson; Pierce County, Washington, home to Fort Lewis; Maricopa County, Arizona, home to Luke Air Force Base; Muscogee County, Georgia, home to Fort Benning; Honolulu County, Hawaii, home to Joint Base Pearl Harbor-Hickam, and so on.[41]

If Americans want a more geographically diverse military (and a military that would arguably become more ideologically diverse as a result), there is a simple solution: redistribute military installations with an eye to equalizing recruitment across the nation's major geographic regions. Want more liberals in the military? Put some more bases in Massachusetts, sit back, and let nature take its course. Of course, it would be expensive to move bases around to ensure a military population that is completely representative of the overall population. If we wanted more liberals in the military, for instance, we would want bases in the nation's major urban areas, which, regardless of state, tend to be more liberal than rural areas. But just try finding thousands of square miles of unoccupied land to train in the Boston metro area. To some degree, low regional population density correlates with the presence of large military bases: with the exception of some older bases, military installations tend to be located where land is plentiful and cheap.

But it is a useful thought experiment to imagine what the military would look like with a radically different base location pattern. It is common to hear people insist that only a draft would give America a truly representative military, but this is probably not so; recruitment priorities, for instance, have a profound effect on military demographics. The military pours money into ensuring a steady stream of high-caliber minority recruits, for a simple reason: as a society, we have decided it is important to have a military that is as ethnically and racially diverse as the overall population—and, by and large, we have succeeded in making the military a diverse and hospitable place for people of all races and ethnic backgrounds. Similarly, if we are worried about urban-rural divides or ideological divides, tinkering with base-location decisions is an obvious way to make the military more geographically and ideologically representative of American society. Sure, it would cost money, just like many other important but difficult things—but if Congress made it a priority, it could be done.

In many ways—despite the end of the draft and the advent of the all-volunteer army—the US military remains extraordinarily diverse. As an institution, it has unique strengths, as well as some unique weaknesses, and it is far from homogeneous: the services vary substantially in their cultures, and the military experiences of different subgroups (minorities, women, officers, etc.) can differ very significantly from the experiences of those in other subgroups.

This suggests that the first apparent paradox I highlighted—that Americans love the military more than ever but know less about it than ever—should not automatically be viewed as a cause for concern. Arguably, this particular manifestation of a civilian-military gap is more a matter of perception than reality: though many civilians and military personnel perceive themselves as belonging to distinct and profoundly different communities, they are in fact more interconnected and less different than many might assume.[42]

Nevertheless, the question that should concern us is not whether there are distinctive differences between military and civilian communities. The question that should concern us is this: When and how do civilian-military differences make a difference? In other words, Does "the civilian-military gap" matter? In what ways does it matter, and for whom?

Admiral Michael Mullen thinks the gap matters. As he puts it, "a people uninformed about what they are asking the military to endure is a people inevitably unable to fully grasp the scope of the responsibilities our Constitution levies upon them."[43] In a deep sense, this is surely true—but not necessarily more true for issues relating to the use of force than for any other issue. Poll after poll tells us that the American people are dismayingly ignorant across a wide range of issues. If this translates into superficial opinion formation, it is an equal opportunity cluelessness, not reserved solely for military issues.

More to the point, there is little clear evidence that reduced public knowledge of the military translates predictably and reliably into differences of opinion on important policy matters. Intuitively, it makes sense to think that those with little military knowledge will have different attitudes towards the use of force than those with more experience do, but the evidence cuts in multiple different directions. Thus, in this volume Golby, Cohn, and Feaver observe that both current and older surveys suggest that "veterans are more reluctant about the use of force but favor fewer restrictions on its employment, whereas non-veterans are supportive of more wide-ranging use, but favor greater restrictions." Whether this has any systematic impact on US policy is anyone's guess; as noted earlier, civilians with no military connections show attitudes towards the wars in Iraq and Afghanistan similar to those of veterans.

Certainly, civilian-military gaps have not stopped military budgets from expanding since 9/11, even as budgets for most nonmilitary foreign-affairs-related government agencies and institutions (such as the State Department and the U.S. Agency for International Development [USAID]) have been stagnant, and domestic spending on civilian social welfare programs has been slashed. After 9/11, the defense budget skyrocketed to levels not seen since the immediate post–World War II era. Today, despite current budget cuts, the defense budget remains at a historically high level, and even in this period of fiscal austerity, proposing drastic cuts to military compensation and benefits is still considered political suicide for national politicians.

Perhaps spending money on military personnel and their families makes it easier for civilians not to feel guilty about the disproportionate sacrifices they make. Before 9/11, civilian and military benefits and compensation were, on average, about the same. Today, it is different: the average member of the military is now paid more than civilian federal workers with comparable experience,[44] and members of the military and their families can also lay claim to some of America's most generous (though arguably unsustainable) social programs. The military offers free health care to service members and their dependents, discount groceries, subsidized child care, tuition assistance that can be transferred to spouses and children, and a host of other services.

This creates numerous strange ironies: even as the post–New Deal welfare state continues its slow collapse, the military has become a substitute welfare state for a large swathe of small-town America. In a sense, the military—despite its reputation for political conservatism—has become the last outpost of "big government" paternalism in Tea-Party-dominated "red" America. On the whole, Americans seem to accept this. The YouGov survey shows that most Americans are aware of the benefits that accrue to those in the military but continue to view the military as fairer and more meritocratic than the rest of society: strong pluralities of YouGov respondents believe that the military is fairer than civilian society in terms of promotions and recognition, the opportunity to excel, and the opportunity for self-improvement (CM2T 26–28). Majorities or strong pluralities of respondents also believe that the military provides more opportunity than society does for the poor, minorities, and immigrants (CM2T 31, 33–34).

In a world in which fewer and fewer government institutions seem capable of performing with even minimal competence, Americans also consistently say they trust the military more than any other public institution: in a 2015 Gallup poll, for instance, 72 percent of Americans expressed "a great deal" or "quite a lot" of confidence in the military compared to 33 percent expressing confidence in the presidency, 32 percent expressing confidence in the Supreme Court, 31 percent with confidence in the public schools, and 23 percent with confidence in the criminal justice system. Only 8 percent of Americans expressed any confidence in Congress.[45] Little wonder, then, that Americans throw money at the military: we may not understand it, but we recognize that it is the only reasonably well-functioning public institution we have these days.

But once again: if the civilian-military gap *does not* seem to lead directly to different policy views, reduced financial support for the men and women in the military, or reduced confidence in the military as a public institution, why does it matter?

Paradox Two:
Mistrust and Awe

Civilian-military gaps do matter, but not in the ways we usually think they do. Lying beneath the gaps reflected in public polls are less obvious but more pernicious gaps between elite civilian political leaders and elite military leaders: a gap of knowledge and a gap of trust.

I am speaking here not of "elites" as defined in public opinion polls, but of the tiny decision-making elite that runs the nation's capital: the few hundred people—certainly less than a thousand—who occupy senior positions in the White House's West Wing, the Old Executive Office Building, the State Department's 7th Floor, and the Pentagon's E-Ring: the service chiefs and their senior deputies, the president's top national security staff, the cabinet secretaries and their senior deputies. In Washington-speak, these are the principals and the deputies, together with a handful of influential advisors without line positions.

If there is any venue where civilians and military personnel work together side by side, day after day, it's in Washington's national security establishment. In theory, this constant interaction ought to breed respect and mutual understanding. In practice, it often produces the opposite: a mixture of mistrust and almost willful ignorance.

In Washington, top civilian policymakers often simultaneously mistrust the military leadership and overestimate the military's capabilities. Too frequently, the favor is returned by military leaders, who dismiss civilians as "politicians" and are sometimes unwilling to accept their concerns as legitimate. Too many senior civilian officials know virtually nothing about the structure of military organizations, the chain of command, or the military planning process, while some senior military officers have forgotten that there are other ways to run an organization and think about problem solving.

Most fundamentally, civilian and military leaders often think of themselves and their roles in quite different ways, though the differences are generally unarticulated. Their experiences and training have led them to think differently about what it means to plan, to evaluate risk, and to define problems in the first place. As a result, they frequently talk past each other, using the same words to mean quite different things.

During my time serving in civilian jobs at the Pentagon and the State Department, I watched numerous interagency discussions devolve into exercises in mutual misunderstanding and frustration. Some of these discussions—such as Pentagon–White House squabbling over troop levels in Afghanistan and the split-the-baby outcome—were public. Others never came close to registering in the public consciousness, but rankled for those involved.[46]

Take a small but not atypical example. In the spring of 2010, a small crisis unfolded in Kyrgyzstan. Several hundred people were killed by police and ethnically aligned mobs, many more were wounded, and thousands of refugees (mostly from Kyrgyzstan's Uzbek minority population) fled their homes.[47] Within the White House, these events triggered fears of a possible ethnic cleansing campaign to come, or even genocide. At the time, I was serving as an advisor to the Undersecretary of Defense for Policy, and one day I received a call from a member of the White House's National Security Staff (NSS). With little preamble, he told me that U.S. Central Command (CENTCOM) needed to "move a surveillance drone over Kyrgyzstan, ASAP, so we can figure out what's going on there."

In many ways, this was a creative idea. Drones and other intelligence, surveillance, and reconnaissance (ISR) assets have the potential to be powerful tools in human rights monitoring. The ability to watch troops or mobs or refugees move in real time, to see weapons being stockpiled or mass graves being filled, could potentially help the United States take timely and appropriate action to stop a genocide before it gets off the ground. But there was one enormous problem with my NSS colleague's request: neither of us had any authority to order CENTCOM to immediately shift a potentially vital ISR asset from wherever it was currently being used to the skies over Kyrgyzstan.

"It's an interesting idea," I told him. "Has the president discussed it with [Defense] Secretary Gates?"

"We don't have time to spin up a whole bureaucratic process," he responded irritably. "The president doesn't want another Rwanda. This is a top priority of his. I need you to just communicate this to CENTCOM and get this moving."

But the chain of command does not go from a director at the NSS to an advisor to the undersecretary of defense to CENTCOM—and the military does not put drones into foreign airspace without a great deal of planning, an enormous amount of legal advice, and the right people signing off on the whole idea. Where would this drone come from? What was it doing now, and what could not be done if it was shifted to Kyrgyzstan? Which personnel would control it, from what air base in what country? Whose airspace would it fly over? What budget would support the shift? What would the political consequences be if it fell or was shot down? Exactly where would it go? What would it be looking for? Who would receive and analyze any imagery or other intelligence it gathered? How long would it stay? And so on.

My NSS colleague was incredulous. "We're talking about, like, *one drone*. You're telling me you can't just call some colonel at CENTCOM and make this happen? Why the hell not? You guys [by which he meant the Pentagon writ large] are always stonewalling us on everything. I'm calling you from the *White House*. The president wants to prevent genocide in Kyrgyzstan. Whatever happened to civilian control of the military?"

He, I had to explain, was the wrong civilian.

This turned out to be a minor issue, in many ways, but the exchange was far from unusual. My White House colleague—a smart, energetic, dedicated professional—went away angry, convinced that "the military" was refusing to take atrocity-prevention issues seriously (an attitude that soured many later interagency discussions about Sudan, Libya, Syria and more).

My military colleagues reacted to the request, when I relayed it, with equal frustration: How could a senior White House official fail to understand why sensitive, expensive military assets could not instantly be moved from a war zone to foreign airspace via a simple phone call from a director at the National Security Council to a Pentagon acquaintance? If the president wanted to make this happen, he could call the defense secretary and direct him to have CENTCOM undertake such a move (though he would be unlikely to do so without plenty of discussion at lower levels first), but the chain of command cannot be accessed midway down and more or less at random. My military colleagues were insulted by what looked, to them, like civilian arrrogance and ignorance.

Some months later, similar misunderstandings plagued interagency planning on Sudan. With a referendum on South Sudanese independence in the offing, officials at the White House and the State Department were concerned about a resurgence of ethnic violence in the wake of a pro–independence vote. The Defense Department was asked—this time more formally, at the assistant secretary/deputy assistant secretary level—to produce plans for preventing or responding to mass atrocities, to "give the options" in the event of a rapidly deteriorating humanitarian situation.

Once again, the response from the Pentagon's military planners was to express polite frustration. What assumptions and constraints should guide planning? What kind of plans did the White House want? To respond to what kind of mass atrocities, against whom, and in what likely places? Respond for how long and through what means, and to what ultimate end: peace in Sudan? peace on earth? Would this mean fighting Sudanese government forces on northern Sudanese soil? going to war with a foreign (and Muslim) state? If so, it was hard to imagine the president signing off on such a thing—the United States already had two ongoing wars, plus, it would be a foolish waste of scarce planning resources to plan for something that was never going to happen.

Or maybe the goals were narrower? Should the military be planning to evacuate displaced people? Where to? Should they just focus on protecting a humanitarian corridor? Where? For how long? Was the White House prepared to have boots on the ground, with the inevitable risk that events could easily spiral out of control if US troops were attacked? Did they want planning for targeted strikes designed to degrade the military capacity of the bad guys, whoever they might be? Did they even have a theory about who the bad guys would be?

The ensuing back and forth was tense and occasionally broke out into open expressions of anger and mistrust. At best, White House staff members considered their military counterparts rigid, reductionist, and unimaginative. At worst, they were convinced that the Pentagon was just being difficult—that the military "didn't care" about Sudan or about atrocity prevention and was determined to flout the president's wishes by stonewalling and foot dragging at every turn instead of getting down to work.

The military representatives involved in the discussions were equally exasperated. What was wrong with these civilians? Didn't they know what they wanted? Were they too naive—or uncaring—to understand that the potential mobilization of thousands of people and millions of dollars of equipment required greater specificity in terms of assumptions, constraints, and desired end-states? Without that specificity, the range of possibilities was endless. The United States could use nuclear weapons against the Sudanese regime; the United States could withdraw all forces from Afghanistan and shift them to Sudan, or do nothing whatsoever, or do a great many things in between. But unless the president wanted to move into crisis-planning mode, ginning up serious plans for any of these options would require months, not days or weeks, and planning for all of them just was not realistic.

In a sense, this situation was a civil-military version of the chicken-and-egg problem. White House staff wanted to be able to give the president a sense of his options: In the event of mass atrocities, what was it realistic for him to consider doing? How complicated, time-consuming, risky, expensive, and effective would it be to protect a humanitarian corridor, as opposed to engaging in limited military strikes to degrade the capacity of those committing atrocities?

Without help from military planners, White House staff could not properly advise the president. But without political and strategic direction from the White House (How much money are we willing to spend? How many troops are we willing to move? What trade-offs are we willing to make in terms of other ongoing operations? What constitutes success?), military personnel could not properly advise their civilian counterparts.

Eventually, the issue got semiresolved. The White House staff was forced to get more specific; the Pentagon was forced to let go of the elaborate planning process it preferred and cough up some back-of-the-envelope assessments. Fortunately for all, the feared genocide in Sudan did not happen.

At the national level, however, the costs of the civil-military gap are real, and high. Such mutual ignorance—and such systematic cultural differences in how to think about problems and solutions—leads frequently to misunderstanding, inefficient decision making, and, too often, bad policy.

There's an irony here: at the senior policymaking level, much of the civilian mistrust of the military derives from an exaggerated estimate of military capabilities. From the outside, the US military appears able to do magic: get the combat elements of a full division deployed overseas in a single week, see in the dark, eavesdrop on global telecommunications, and fire missiles from invisible unmanned drones that strike only designated individual targets, leaving nearby structures undamaged.

Few outsiders understand just how much time, money, and effort lies behind these astonishing capabilities (indeed, today's military is so specialized and high-tech that even most military personnel see only a small piece of the puzzle).[48] As a result, civilian leaders often find it difficult to comprehend military claims that a particular task is too difficult, or will take longer than desired, or require more troops or other resources than expected. If your starting assumption is that the military can do anything, any pushback is apt to seem like stonewalling.

Consider a final example of high-level civil-military misunderstandings: the 2009 debate about troop levels in Afghanistan. As a presidential candidate in 2008, Senator Barack Obama had promised to "finish the job" in Afghanistan,[49] and in early 2009, the newly inaugurated president got to work. He commissioned a sweeping interagency review of US policy in Afghanistan and announced that, as an interim measure, he had authorized the deployment of an addition 17,000 US troops to Afghanistan in response to theater commander General David McKiernan's request.

By the end of February 2009, the president had adopted the new strategic objectives recommended by his review team (led by diplomat Richard Holbrooke, former CIA official Brice Reidel, and the Pentagon's Michele Flournoy, whom the president appointed as undersecretary of defense for policy): henceforth, that the United States would seek to disrupt terrorist networks in Afghanistan and Pakistan, thus degrading al Qaeda and its associates' ability "to plan and launch international terrorist attacks." To that end, the US would promote "a more capable, accountable and effective government in Afghanistan" and "develop increasingly self-reliant Afghan security forces" capable of operating with "reduced U.S. assistance."[50]

These new strategic objectives proved easier to articulate than they were to achieve. By mid-May, General McKiernan had been ousted from his position—becoming the first of several Afghanistan-theater commanders to discover just how elusive "finishing the job" would turn out to be.

McKiernan was succeeded by General Stanley McChrystal, who was in turn assigned the job of undertaking a sixty-day review of the situation in Afghanistan, with a view towards determining what changes might be needed to achieve the president's new strategic objectives. McChrystal completed his review on schedule, but when word spread that he intended to propose a substantial troop increase—potentially as high as 70,000 to 80,000 additional troops—Pentagon officials asked that he hold off on submitting his assessment for several weeks: even the rumor of such a large troop request had sent waves of dismay through the White House. In any case, it was late summer by then, and everyone from the president on down was taking a vacation.

Much behind-the-scenes skirmishing ensued, and in mid-September, a preliminary copy of General McChrystal's assessment was leaked to the *Washington Post.* Although the leaked version of the report contained no numbers, the bottom line was clear: if the United States did not pour additional resources, including troops, into Afghanistan, McChrystal warned, the likely result would be "mission failure."[51]

Furious at the leak, which they blamed on the Pentagon, and unwilling to accept McChystal's gloomy conclusions, senior White House staff engaged in strategic counterleaks. In their version of the story, McChrystal and the Pentagon were trying to "box in the president" by pushing tens of thousands more troops and "refusing" to consider other approaches.[52]

Eventually, a compromise was reached: 30,000 more US troops would be sent to Afghanistan. But the episode left scars. Senior White House officials suspected the military of exaggerating Afghanistan's problems and inflating their estimates of required troop numbers, viewing the military as having a vested interest in continuing a conflict the president had vowed to end. Civilian officials felt manipulated. Less than a year later, General McChrystal was out of a job, forced to resign after a *Rolling Stone* profile quoted his senior aides speaking mockingly of several senior civilian officials.

Of course, the military's take on the 2009 debate about Afghan troop levels was quite different—and it points to the real gulf between the military and its civilian leadership, a gulf that has more to do with differing perceptions of roles and missions than with the near-insubordination some White House officials suspected. As one former senior Pentagon official told me, "The [military's] general stance is 'We can do this, but we want you to acknowledge the mess, cost and complexity.'"[53] To many in the military, General McChrystal fell victim in 2009 to a White House unwilling to acknowledge any of these factors and equally uninterested in understanding the military's methods, capabilities, or limits. To many military leaders, the White House appeared to be constantly demanding contradictory and impossible things but refusing to resource them.

From the Pentagon's perspective, the White House's refusal to accept the costs of its own ambitious Afghan strategy was either naive or hypocritical. After all, the White House had not asked General McChrystal if he thought the president's strategy in Afghanistan was a *good* strategy, or if he thought long-term US interests might be better served by pursuing a radically scaled down counterterrorism mission, or even by withdrawing US forces altogether. McChrystal was instead told to address a rather narrow question: What resources were required for the existing strategy to succeed?

In response, McChrystal gave an equally narrow answer: to succeed in the mission as defined by the White House itself, many more troops would be required. If the president wanted a different answer, he needed to ask a different question. If he did not feel like sending thousands more troops, that was his prerogative—but then he needed to scale down his strategic goals.

The 2009 debate over Afghanistan troop levels both typified and further fueled the mutual mistrust between the White House and senior military officials. Senior civilian leaders often lack the time or inclination to learn more about the military. "They don't want to take the time to go through the slide deck, or get the full briefing," a former Pentagon official who also had White House experience told me. "They're intimidated by the acronyms, and they don't understand the military's structure or planning process. Basically, they don't want to know. They'll never cross the river and set foot in the Pentagon." With little comprehension of the complexities of military planning and operations, senior civilian leaders often wildly overestimate military capabilities. In consequence, military hesitation or requests for more time, information, or resources can look like foot dragging.

Meanwhile, military leaders often have only limited understanding of the political constraints within which civilian leaders must operate and can be quick to dismiss the concerns of policymakers as "shallow" or "politically driven." Today, many senior military officials complain of feeling baffled and shut out by a White House that combines micromanagement with a near total inability to articulate coherent strategic goals. "The NSS wants to run the show, day to day and minute to minute," one former senior military official told me, "so they have no time—they're almost incapable of strategic thinking. It's often just crisis *du jour* over there." Meanwhile, military recommendations go unheeded because senior White House staff have come to assume that a risk-averse Pentagon exaggerates every difficulty and inflates every request for troops or money.

This assumption can turn every discussion into an antagonistic negotiation session. "Sometimes you want to tell them, this isn't a political bargaining process," another retired senior military official told me ruefully. "Where the military comes in high, they counter low, and we settle on an option that splits the difference. Needless to say, the right answer is not always in the middle."

Over time, of course, the tendency to split the difference creates perverse incentives, and mutual mistrust becomes self-reinforcing. If military leaders "believe the mission truly requires 50,000 troops and 50 billion dollars but you know that the White House is going to automatically cut every number in half, you'll come in asking for 100,000 troops and $100 billion dollars," a Pentagon insider told me. "The military eventually starts playing the very game the White House has always suspected them of playing," the former senior official added.

If any civil-military gap matters, it is this one. Cultural or opinion gaps between the general public and the military community worry us, but there is little evidence that they cause actual harm. The mistrust and mutual ignorance that often characterizes relations between high-level civilian and military decision makers is another story: here, misunderstandings and mistrust lead to arbitrary decisions and can do genuine harm both to the military and to US interests.

Paradox Three:
The Best Tools for the Wrong Problem

Lying at the heart of the high-level civil-military tensions described above is another paradox: the United States has what President Obama has called "the strongest military in the history of the world,"[54] but that same military seems increasingly incapable of addressing many of today's most pressing threats.

In many ways, the US military is a victim of its own success: our conventional military dominance makes direct challenges nearly suicidal for other states, pushing adversaries towards asymmetric strategies designed to neutralize our strengths and play on our weaknesses. Thus, we handily defeated Saddam Hussein's armies in 1991 and again in 2003—but were caught flat-footed by the rise of terrorism and insurgency inside Iraq and by the challenges of postconflict stabilization and reconstruction. In Afghanistan, CIA and Special Forces advisors plus American air power helped the Northern Alliance gain rapid victory over the Taliban—but top al Qaeda leaders slipped across the porous Pakistani border, the US occupation helped the Taliban generate new recruits, and our troops were frequently confounded by an invisible enemy that left IEDs in roadways and then melted back into the civilian population.

Conventional US military force, designed to combat the militaries of peer and near-peer states, has only limited value when it comes to many of the more distributed and complex challenges we currently face. Tanks and fighter jets cannot stop disaffected teenagers in Birmingham or Paris or Detroit from being inspired by al Qaeda or ISIS; they cannot stop ISIS from posting gruesome footage of beheaded hostages on YouTube, or halt the spread of Ebola, or prevent cyber espionage and attack.

None of this stops us from trying, however. As I noted earlier, the American public may know little about the military, but we recognize that it is the only reasonably well-functioning public institution we have these days. We do not trust Congress, and the budgets of civilian foreign policy agencies have taken a beating, along with their capabilities. Faced with problems, we send in the troops—after all, who else can we send? Unlike any other part of the government, the US military can be relied on to go where it is told and do what it is asked—or die trying.

As a result, we increasingly treat the US military as an all-purpose tool for fixing anything that happens to be broken. Terrorists and insurgents in Syria are beheading journalists and aid workers? Afghanistan's economy is a mess? An earthquake in Japan has endangered nuclear power plants? The Egyptian military needs to be encouraged to respect democracy? Call the military. We want our military busy here at home, too, protecting us from cyber attack, patrolling New York's Grand Central Station, stopping illegal immigration in Arizona, and putting out summer forest fires.

But we are trapped in a vicious circle: asking the military to take on more and more nontraditional tasks requires higher and higher military budgets. Higher military budgets force us to look for savings elsewhere, so we freeze or cut spending on civilian diplomacy and development and cut domestic social programs. As budget cuts cripple civilian agencies and programs, they lose their ability to perform as they once did, so we look to the military to pick up the slack, further expanding its role in both foreign and domestic activities. This requires still higher military budgets, which continues the devastating cycle.

If your only tool is a hammer, everything looks like a nail. The old adage applies here as well. If your only functioning government institution is the military, everything looks like a war—and when everything looks like war, the military's role expands.

Here's the deep problem: we are no longer sure what a military is *for*. We do not know what we want our military to do and oscillate between asking it to do everything and demanding tighter but often quite arbitrary limits on its use. Asked for definitions, we end up going in circles: the military is the institution that fights wars, and wars are conflicts in which we use the military. If we can imagine "cyberwar," cybersecurity must be a military task; if cybersecurity is a military task, then cyber attacks must be a form of warfare.

For most of recorded history, humans have sought to draw sharp lines between war and peace. Until less than a century ago, for instance, most Western societies insisted that wars should be formally "declared," take place upon clearly delineated battlefields, and be fought by elaborately uniformed soldiers operating within specialized, hierarchical military organizations.

In different societies and earlier times, humans developed other rituals to delineate war's boundaries, including complex initiation rites preceding wars and the elaborate painting and costuming of warriors. In nineteenth-century Liberia, warriors wore special masks during raids, and war was prohibited while "bush school" was in session for boys and girls.[55] In the American Southwest, Navajo warriors literally spoke a different dialect after setting out on raids, using what they called a "twisted language" with a special vocabulary. The Navajo also sought to carefully maintain the spatial boundaries between war and nonwar: "On the way home from a raid," noted anthropologist D.W. Murray, "a symbolic line would be drawn in the desert, the men would line up facing the enemy country, and as they sang they all turned toward home and the common language was resumed."[56]

We modern Americans are not all that different from the Liberians or the Navajo. We prefer to think of "war" as a distinct and separate sphere, one that should not intrude into the everyday world of offices, shopping malls, schools, and soccer games—and we prefer to relegate war to the military, a distinct social institution that we can simultaneously lionize and ignore. For the most part, we prefer to believe that both war and the military can be kept in tidy little boxes: war, we like to think, is an easily recognizable exception to the normal state of affairs, and the military an institution easily defined by its specialized, war-related functions.

We are wrong on both counts.

Two years before the 9/11 terrorist attacks shattered American illusions of safety, two colonels in China's People's Liberation Army published a slender little book called *Unrestricted Warfare.* Historically, wrote colonels Qiao Liang and Wang Xiangsui, "the three indispensable 'hardware' elements of any war" have been "soldiers, weapons and a battlefield."[57] This, they warned, will soon cease to be true: humans are now entering an era in which even these most basic "hardware" elements of war will be transformed beyond recognition.

In the wars of the coming decades, predicted the two Chinese officers, the "soldiers" will increasingly be computer hackers, financiers, terrorists, drug smugglers, and agents of private corporations, as well as members of organized state militaries. Their "weapons" will range from "airplanes, cannons, poison gas, bombs, [and] biochemical agents" to "computer viruses, net browsers, and financial derivative tools." Warfare, wrote Qiao and Wang, will soon "transcend all boundaries and limits. . . . [T]he battlefield will be everywhere . . . [and] all the boundaries lying between the two worlds of war and non-war, of military and non-military, will be totally destroyed."

When *Unrestricted Warfare* was first published in 1999, its dystopian predictions received little attention beyond a small circle of military and intelligence officials. Seen from the vantage point of today, however, the two Chinese officers look chillingly prescient. The accelerating pace of technological advances in the last few decades has enabled information, people, money, and materiel to move across national borders with unprecedented speed and ease.

These changes have created astonishing new opportunities: today, ordinary Americans can take vacations in Thailand or Botswana, invest money instantly in foreign stock exchanges, consult by email with medical specialists half a world away, or share favorite music videos with fellow fans in Berlin and Bombay. But our increasing dependence on the Internet and other forms of electronic communication also creates new vulnerabilities, as does our increasing global interconnectedness. Syrian hackers can now bring down major US media websites; terrorist ideologues in Yemen can use the Internet to disseminate bomb-making instructions to extremists in Boston or London; Mexican drug cartels can launder money through a series of nearly instantaneous electronic transactions; financial meltdowns in one market can lead to rapidly cascading crises in other markets; and everything from pollution to bioengineered viruses can be spread rapidly around the globe.

As a result, states and their traditionally organized militaries are facing more and more competition from small, decentralized, nonhierarchical organizations and networks. In 1941, it took a coordinated attack by 350 Japanese military airplanes to kill 2,403 Americans at Pearl Harbor. Six decades later, nineteen men from four different countries—armed only with box cutters—hijacked four civilian jets and caused the deaths of nearly 3,000 Americans. Nonstate actors—even one or two individuals—can increasingly compete with states when it comes to using physical force to cause large-scale death and physical injury.

What is more, the use of physical force *itself* has more and more competition. War, wrote the nineteenth-century Prussian military strategist Carl von Clausewitz, is "an act of violence to compel our opponent to fulfill our will."[58] But our increased interconnectedness and dependence on interlinked electronic technologies has created new means for clever actors—be they states or individuals—to achieve war's traditional ends. Imagine a cyber attack that brought down the electrical power grid in a major population center for weeks, or a significant cyber disruption of the nation's financial infrastructure: either could rapidly cause massive economic damage and lead, albeit indirectly, to significant death and suffering.

The 9/11 attacks made it clear that the changes described by Qiao Liang and Wang Xiangsui did not lie off in the distant future. As the nineteen al Qaeda plotters made their unimpeded way through airport security, the era of unrestricted warfare was already well under way, though few of us knew it at the time.

The US response to the 9/11 attacks moved us still further into the era of unrestricted warfare. Just days after the attacks, the Bush administration declared that the United States was launching a "war on terror," and that was no mere metaphor: more than a decade later, the United States still regards itself as being in an "armed conflict" with "Al Qaeda and its associates." But just as Qiao and Wang predicted, this armed conflict bears little resemblance to what we traditionally think of as war. Our enemies wear no uniforms and are loyal to no states; many of those we consider "enemy combatants" do not even seem to be part of any organized group.

In the years since 9/11, it has grown steadily more difficult to define our enemies (the United States will not define or list al Qaeda's "associates"). The "battlefield" keeps shifting, too: it has ranged from Afghanistan and Iraq to Pakistan, Yemen, Somalia, and the Philippines, with forays into Syria, Mali, Nigeria, and elsewhere. What counts as a "weapon" or an "attack" in this war is also murky: the United States has detained and killed alleged terrorist planners, recruiters, and financiers working to disrupt everything with means ranging from planned bombings to cyber attacks. But when you wage war against a nameless, stateless, formless enemy—an enemy with goals as protean as its methods—how can that war ever end?

The US government has also made it clear that it views cyber threats primarily through the lens of "war." In 2011, the White House released an "International Strategy for Cyberspace," declaring that the United States would "respond to hostile acts in cyberspace as we would to any other threat to our country."[59] In 2012, the State Department's top lawyer announced that as a legal matter, the United States believed that "cyber activities may in certain circumstances constitute uses of force," triggering the law of armed conflict and giving rise to a right to respond with traditional physical force.[60]

War has burst out of its old boundaries—and as the lines between "war" and "nonwar" grow blurry, the role and mission of the US military have grown similarly blurry. Today, as the US military struggles to respond to novel threats from novel quarters, its once straightforward *raison d'etre*—defending America from armed attack by foreign states—is no longer clear-cut. This has had a negative effect on the public's perception of the military's effectiveness. Some 50.6 percent of YouGov respondents believe that the military getting too involved in "non-military" affairs hurts military effectiveness (CM2T 58). Just twenty-five years ago, most US military personnel understood their role in a manner that would have been equally familiar to Alexander the Great or Ghengis Khan: the military's job, to put it bluntly, was to "kill people and break stuff." But today's military has vastly expanded its sphere of activities.

American military personnel now operate in nearly every country on earth. While in some places, they "shoot, move and communicate" just as soldiers have been taught to do in basic training for generations, they also analyze lines of computer code in Virginia office buildings, build isolation wards in Ebola-ravaged Liberia, operate health clinics in rural Malaysian villages, launch agricultural reform programs and small business development projects in Africa, train Afghan judges and parliamentarians, develop television soap operas for Iraqi audiences, conduct antipiracy patrols off the Somali coast, monitor global email and telephone communications, and pilot weaponized drones from simulated airplane cockpits thousands of miles away.

These and a thousand other activities now performed by the US military are intended to "shape the battlespace," prevent and deter future conflict, and disrupt or destroy the capabilities of potential adversaries, whomever—and wherever—they may be. Why wait passively for the next terrorist attack—or nuclear missile launched by a rogue state, or cyber attack emanating from China—when we could be eliminating the root causes of conflict by fostering economic development and good governance, building relationships, creating networks of agents and allies, collecting data, promoting "new narratives," or striking likely future enemies *before* they can develop the ability to harm us?

To the military, it is all about staying "left of boom." Imagine a timeline running from left to right, with potential calamity looming somewhere in the hazy future. "Boom" might be the IED buried under the road, a radioactive "dirty bomb," an aerosol canister filled with a bioengineered virus, or a computer worm that shuts down the New York Stock Exchange. You always want to stay left of boom—and as the varieties of "boom" expand, the military has expanded correspondingly.

Paradox Four:
The Best and the Worst

Here's the final paradox: the US military is today more professionalized and better educated than ever before—certainly far more healthy than most other US government institutions—but at the same time, it is increasingly hamstrung by its own organizational rigidities. The US military has increasingly been locked into a defensive crouch, semiparalyzed by interservice rivalries, dysfunctional budget politics, and personnel and acquisition systems that seem diabolically designed to discourage creativity and innovation.

Virtually every military leader understands that as an institution, the US military still lacks many of the core skills and attributes that are essential to addressing today's security challenges—but though military leaders universally proclaim the need for flexibility, adaptability, decentralization, and creativity in today's military personnel, our recruiting system has changed little in the last century. Similarly, military training and education remains focused primarily on skills that are relevant only in a diminishing number of situations. The acquisitions process is cumbersome, slow, and often held hostage to political considerations. Meanwhile, the military personnel system makes it difficult to bring in new skills or allow personnel to specialize, and a zero-defect internal culture rewards conformity and punishes creativity. In all, as the Defense Science Board declared in a 2010 review, "DOD's processes are complex, time consuming, and often do not align well with the timeframes dictated by today's operational environment."[61]

Take just a few examples, starting with recruiting. In some ways, much has changed in recent decades: seventy years ago, the United States had a segregated military, but today people of every race, color, and creed train and fight side by side. Twenty-five years ago, women were excluded from half the occupational specialties in the army and 80 percent of Marine Corps jobs; today, women can serve in almost every military job. Just a few years ago, gay and lesbian service members risked discharge; today, they can serve openly.

But there is one thing that has changed hardly at all. Each year, the overwhelming majority of new military recruits are young and male. In that sense, the American military of 2012 still looks a great deal like the American military of the 1970s, the 1940s, the 1860s, or the 1770s. For that matter, it still looks a lot like virtually every group of warriors in virtually every society during virtually every period of human history.

For millennia, having an army full of young men made sense. As soldiers, young males have had two things going for them, historically speaking. First, they are usually stronger, on average, than any other demographic group: they can run fast and carry heavy loads. Second, they are biologically "expendable": from a species-survival perspective, women of child-bearing age are the limiting factor in population growth. A society can lose a lot of young men without a devastating impact on overall population growth.

Today, though, these characteristics do not matter as much as they once did. Overall birthrates are much lower in modern societies than they were during earlier periods, but life expectancy is much longer. Early societies worried about sustaining their populations; today, we worry less about ensuring population growth than about over-burdening the planet's load-bearing capacity. Simple brawn also offers far less advantage in our high-tech age. In modern warfare, brutal hand-to-hand combat is no longer the norm, and warfare is no longer a matter of sending out wave after wave of troops to overwhelm the enemy through sheer mass. Increasingly, much modern warfare involves a mixture of high-tech skills and low-tech cultural knowledge rather than "fighting" in the traditional sense.

Being young, male, and strong thus offers no particular advantage to an air force remote-drone pilot, an army financial services technician, or a "cyber warrior" assigned to the National Security Agency or Cyber Command (CYBERCOM). Even for service members in combat positions, the physical strength that young men are more likely to possess no longer offers as much of an advantage: even the most impressive musculature is no match for an IED.

I do not mean to suggest that the physical strength of soldiers has no further military relevance. Notwithstanding all our high-tech gadgets, military personnel—particularly in the infantry—often still find themselves doing things the old-fashioned way: hauling heavy equipment up a winding mountain trail or slugging it out hand to hand during a raid. The infantry, along with specialized groups such as Navy

SEALs, will continue to view strength and endurance as essential to their mission. But for increasing numbers of military personnel, the marginal benefits of sheer physical strength and youth have plummeted relative to earlier eras—and this trend seems likely to continue.

Meanwhile, an increasing number of tasks we now assign to the military require quite different skills and attributes: technical experience; scientific know-how; foreign language and regional expertise; an anthropological cast of mind; media savvy; maturity and good judgment.

If military recruiting were better calibrated towards ensuring the mix of skills we need, we might make an effort to recruit far more women, greater numbers of older personnel and college graduates, and many more immigrants with vital language skills and cultural knowledge. Not everyone will have the physical strength and endurance needed for certain combat jobs, but, as noted earlier, 85 percent of military personnel serve in noncombat positions. If we truly want a military that is adequately prepared for today's challenges, why not differentiate in recruiting and focus on ensuring a better match between recruits and the positions they will have to occupy?

We might also look for ways to make it easier for Americans to move back and forth between the military and civilian worlds. At the moment, it is virtually impossible to move laterally into and out of the military. CYBERCOM's commander cannot decide to bring on a dozen top experts from Google for five-year stints at ranks commensurate with their experience: if a 45-year-old top technical expert at Google wanted to join the military, he would need an age waiver and would have to start as a first lieutenant (with a commensurate salary), making it impossible for him to hold positions of authority for years to come. Nor can CYBERCOM's commander decide to send his ten brightest young officers off to work in Silicon Valley for a few years: by doing so, they would put promotions within the military at risk. As it is, many military officers fear that taking "broadening" assignments will work against them when it comes to promotion and command opportunities: despite rhetoric from senior military leaders about the value of gaining diverse experiences, it is often those who have followed the straight and narrow path who end up in top positions.[62]

The current all-or-nothing approach to military careers does not serve the nation well. It keeps talented people out of the military and makes it risky or impossible for military personnel to branch out and then return without career penalties.

Granted, there are military positions that require substantive skills that can be gained only by many years in the military itself—civilian life, no matter how rich and varied, does not tend to give people the ability to operate tanks in close formation in a combat setting while coordinating air support. But there are many other military positions for which this is far less true, particularly in technical areas and areas in which new skills are needed, be they technical or linguistic. You cannot learn combined arms maneuver in civilian life, but you *can* learn to be a computer programmer, a medic, an agricultural expert, or an Arabic interpreter. At the moment, the near impossibility of lateral moves between the military and civilian worlds forces an overreliance on contractors. This is one way to bring in skills but probably not the best way, and it carries with it risks of its own.

During World Wars I and II, the urgent need for officers led the military to grant temporary wartime commissions to lawyers, doctors, and others deemed to possess valuable skills; those with comparable civilian experience could enter the military at ranks commensurate with their civilian career levels. Today's military urgently needs to experiment with similar flexible programs, both to bring in outside talent and to permit talented military personnel to gain new skills in the civilian world and then return without career penalties.

Similarly, the nature of military evaluations and promotions boards makes officers only as good as their last evaluation report; a zero-defect culture discourages risk taking and pushes out many talented officers.[63] Shifting from one occupational specialty to another is difficult, and transcending poor evaluations in one area is next to impossible, even if ratings are exceptionally high in other areas.[64] I recall a three-star general with responsibility for cyber operations lamenting that his most talented aide was likely be involuntarily separated from the army because he had a mediocre record as an infantry officer. Despite his talents in the cyber domain, even his three-star mentor could not save the young officer's career.

Meanwhile, rigid bureaucratic rules also push out many of the military's best and brightest. Tim Kane, the author of *Bleeding Talent* and a vocal critic of the military personnel system, notes that "talented senior officers [are often] badly mismatched with . . . optimal jobs because the Pentagon continue[s] to use a command-and-control personnel system right out of a Soviet playbook, rather than trusting the voluntary nature of their volunteers. Surveys reveal that the main drivers of attrition [are] not high op-tempo but frustration with the personnel bureaucracy."[65] If you speak Korean and want to be stationed in Korea, you may find yourself posted involuntarily to Kuwait, while an Arabic speaker is sent off to Korea. Your kids may have one more year of high school and your spouse may need one more year to finish her nursing degree at the local university, but none of this matters to the military; you can still be shipped off posthaste to Germany, even though someone else might be better suited to your assignment in any case. You may be an expert in nuclear engineering, but that will not necessarily stop the military from plunking you down in a Pentagon job where you will spend your days on counterinsurgency planning.

When rigid bureaucracy drives out many talented people, you are left mainly with people who are not bothered by rigid bureaucracy—but these may not be the right people to lead the military through uncharted waters.

In a 2013 study, Stephen J. Gerras and Leonard Wong of the Army War College examined some of the reasons the military is often resistant to change and transformation. They evaluated the degree to which some of the Army's most successful officers exhibited "openness," which "is manifested in a strong intellectual curiosity, creativity and a comfortable relationship with novelty and variety. . . . People with low scores on openness tend to have more conventional, traditional interests, preferring familiarity over novelty. They tend to be conservative and resistant to change. . . . Leaders high in openness . . . solicit alternate points of view and are comfortable debating with those whose perspectives differ from their own. They are generally more receptive to change."[66]

Senior military personnel did not score very high on "openness," Gerras and Wong found: "Personality data gathered at the US Army War College from lieutenant colonel and colonel students show that the most successful officers score lower in openness than the general US population. Upon reflection, this makes sense. People with lower openness scores would probably be more inclined to join the Army in the first place. . . . To make matters worse, though, those Army War College students selected for brigade command"—a traditional indicator of success for full colonels—"score even lower than the overall Army War College average. This raises an interesting paradox: the leaders recognized and selected by the Army to serve at strategic levels— where uncertainty and complexity are the greatest—tend to have lower levels of one of the attributes most related to success at strategic level."[67]

Overall, "[c]areers of the Department's military personnel, active and reserve, are currently managed within a restrictive set of laws, regulations, and policies, all reinforced by culture and tradition," notes a 2010 Defense Science Board report. "Many of these laws and regulations have been in force fifty years or more. They all may have been sensible fifty years ago, but the DSB believes they certainly have the effect today of inhibiting the Department's flexibility and adaptability, lessening its ability to use and deploy people efficiently, and ultimately wasting human capital."[68]

It is well beyond the scope of this chapter to examine the numerous ways in which today's military, impressive though it is, holds itself back through anachronistic internal policies. Some of these policies are dictated by Congress, but many could be changed internally. The trouble is, the nature of the system itself creates strong disincentives for those inside to change it.

Conclusion

Today's military is a strange sort of animal. It is at once idealized and ignored, celebrated and mistrusted. It is the most impressive public institution we have, but it is increasingly unsure of its own *raison d'etre*—and increasingly ill equipped, despite a wealth of internal talent and external support, to tackle today's most pressing challenges.

If we want a military that is strong, capable, and responsive to America's changing needs, we will need to rethink many of our most basic assumptions about the military and its role. In a world in which the contours of war and warfare are no longer clear, and many tasks assigned to the military seem increasingly "nonmilitary," we need to consider whether we are distributing authorities and funding in a sensible way. If our political leadership is unwilling or unable to rebuild the capabilities of the civilian foreign policy sector, we need to accept that our military will probably be in the business of development, diplomacy, and governance for the long term, whether we like it or not—and we will need to adapt recruitment, training, education, and everything else along the DOTMLPF (doctrine, organization, training, material, leadership, personnel, and facilities) spectrum accordingly.

If we cannot meaningfully draw lines between "military" and civilian tasks, we need to rethink our assumptions about the nature and purpose of civilian control of the military, the relationship between civilian and military leaders, and the accountability mechanisms designed to ensure the responsible use of power. We will also need to consider how to maintain a sense of military identity and morale in a world in which roles have grown increasingly blurry.

The paradoxes characterizing modern US civil-military relations will not be easily resolved, and debates about the nature and consequences of civil-military gaps will surely continue. Some will demand that the military change to become more like civilian society; others will demand that civilian society become more like the military. Regardless, we should never forget a basic truth: love it or hate it, the US military does not exist in a vacuum but is a product of our culture and our collective decisions.

Whatever it is, it is what we have made it.

Notes

1. James Fallows, "The Tragedy of the American Military," *Atlantic,* January–February 2015, http://www.theatlantic.com/features/archive /2014/12/the-tragedy-of-the-american-military/383516.
2. Sabrina Tavernise, "As Fewer Americans Serve, Growing Gap Is Found between Civilians and Military," *New York Times,* November 24, 2011, http://www.nytimes.com/2011/11/25/us/civilian-military-gap-grows-as -fewer-americans-serve.html?_r=0.
3. Quoted in Thom Shanker, "At West Point, a Focus on Trust," *New York Times,* May 21, 2011.
4. While Americans over sixty account for less than 20% of the general population, roughly half the US veteran population is over sixty. U.S. Dept. of Veterans Affairs, "Living Veterans by Age Group/Gender, 2010–2040," http://www.va.gov/vetdata/docs/demographics/new_vetpop_model/1l _vetpop2014.xlsx.
5. Pew Research Center, "The Military-Civilian Gap: Fewer Family Connections," November 23, 2011, http://www.pewsocialtrends.org/2011/11 /23/the-military-civilian-gap-fewer-family-connections.
6. References to the YouGov data by question number appear in parentheses throughout this essay with the abbreviations CM1T and CM2T indicating the 2013 and 2014 surveys, respectively. The complete results are available at http://www.hoover.org/warriors-and-citizens-crosstabs-1 (CM1T) and http://www.hoover.org/warriors-and-citizens-crosstabs-2 (CM2T).
7. U.S. Dept. of Defense, "2012 Demographics: Profile of the Military Community," http://www.militaryonesource.mil/12038/MOS/Reports/2012 _Demographics_Report.pdf.
8. Military Times, Poll, 2012, http://militarytimes.com/projects/polls/2012 /results/politics.

9. Compare CM1T 56–58 with U.S. Dept. of Defense, "Active Duty Military Strength by Service," https://www.dmdc.osd.mil/appj/dwp/dwp_reports.jsp.

10. Quoted in Kellie Lunney, "America's Other 1%," Government Executive, September 1, 2013, http://cdn.govexec.com/interstitial.html?v=2.1.1&rf =http%3A%2F%2Fwww.govexec.com%2Fmagazine%2Fbriefing%2F2013 %2F09%2Famericas-other-1-percent%2F69797%2F.

11. "Iraq Coalition Military Fatalities by Year; Afghanistan Coalition Military Fatalities by Year," http://icasualties.org/; "Iraq Coalition Casualties: U.S. Wounded Totals," http://icasualties.org/Iraq/USCasualtiesByState.aspx.

12. "Military Enlisted Personnel by Broad Occupational Category and Branch of Military Service," June 2003, http://www.globalsecurity.org/military/agency /mos.htm.

13. U.S. Dept. of Labor, Bureau of Labor Statistics, "Military Careers: What They Do," http://www.bls.gov/ooh/military/military-careers.htm.

14. Dave Baiocchi, "Measuring Army Deployments to Iraq and Afghanistan," Rand Corporation, 2013, http://www.rand.org/content/dam/rand/pubs /research_reports/RR100/RR145/RAND_RR145.pdf.

15. Nese F. DeBruyne and Anne Leland, "American War and Military Operations Casualties: Lists and Statistics," Congressional Research Service, report no. RL32492, January 2, 2015, http://www.fas.org/sgp/crs/natsec/RL32492.pdf.

16. "In 2015, Army Will Lose Nearly 20,000 Soldiers in Drawdown," *Army Times,* December 27, 2014, http://www.armytimes.com/story/military/careers/army /2014/12/26/2015-drawdown-year-ahead/20860491.

17. Sandra I. Irwin, "Marine Corps Leaders Warn Troop Cuts May Go Too Far," *National Defense,* January 15, 2015, http://www.nationaldefensemagazine.org /blog/Lists/Posts/Post.aspx?ID=1714.

18. U.S. Dept. of Defense, "2013 Demographics: Profile of the Military Community," http://www.militaryonesource.mil/12038/MOS/Reports/2013 -Demographics-Report.pdf.

19. Ibid.

20. U.S. Dept. of Defense, "Military Families and Their Housing Choices," report no. HCS80T2, by Kristie L. Bissell et al. for LMI Government Consulting, February 2010, http://www.acq.osd.mil/housing/FH%20Choices.pdf.

21. Richard Pérez-Peña, "U.S. Bachelor Degree Rate Passes Milestone," *New York Times,* February 23, 2012, http://www.nytimes.com/2012/02/24/education /census-finds-bachelors-degrees-at-record-level.html?_r=0.

22. Jim Michaels, "ROTCs Return to Ivy League," *USA Today,* August 2, 2011, http://www.usatoday.com/news/education/2011-08-02-ROTCs-return-to-Ivy -League_n.htm.

23. Shanea Watkins and James Sherk, "Who Serves in the US Military? The Demographics of Enlisted Troops and Officers," Heritage Foundation,

August 2008, http://www.heritage.org/research/reports/2008/08/who-serves-in-the-us-military-the-demographics-of-enlisted-troops-and-officers.

24. National Priorities Project, "Military Recruitment 2010," June 2011, http://nationalpriorities.org/analysis/2011/military-recruitment-2010.

25. Pew Research Center, "War and Sacrifice in the Post-9/11 Era: The Military-Civilian Gap," October 5, 2011, http://www.pewsocialtrends.org/2011/10/05/war-and-sacrifice-in-the-post-911-era.

26. U.S. Dept. of Veterans Affairs, "Profile of Veterans, 2011," March 2013, http://www.va.gov/vetdata/docs/SpecialReports/Profile_of_Veterans_2011.pdf.

27. U.S. Dept. of Veterans Affairs, "Profile of Sheltered Homeless Veterans," September 2012, http://www.va.gov/vetdata/docs/SpecialReports/Homeless_Veterans_2009-2010.pdf.

28. Pew Research Center, "War and Sacrifice."

29. Ibid.

30. Rosa Brooks, "Is Sexual Assault Really an 'Epidemic'?" *Foreign Policy,* July 10, 2013, http://foreignpolicy.com/2013/07/10/is-sexual-assault-really-an-epidemic.

31. Rosa Brooks, "Red Herring: The Myth of the Republican Military Voter," *Foreign Policy,* November 1, 2012, http://foreignpolicy.com/2012/11/01/red-herring-2.

32. Jason K. Dempsey, *Our Army: Soldiers, Politics, and American Civil-Military Relations,* Princeton: Princeton University Press, 2009.

33. See the chapter in this volume by Golby, Cohn, and Feaver.

34. See Kent Friederich, "Strange Bedfellows: The American Public and Its Military in the Aftermath of September 11th," *US Army War College Strategy Research Project,* April 7, 2003, http://www.dtic.mil/dtic/tr/fulltext/u2/a416089.pdf.

35. On a related note, only 34.4% of YouGov respondents strongly or somewhat supported continued military involvement in Afghanistan after 2014 (CM2T 72).

36. Heritage Foundation, "Military Enlisted Recruit-to-Population Ratios, by Region in 2007," http://www.heritage.org/static/reportimages/E8F05D884C7E78E45A200DC953ED3854.gif.

37. U.S. Dept. of Defense, "2013 Demographics"; see also National Priorities Project, "Military Recruitment 2010."

38. Tim Kane, "The Demographics of Military Enlistment after 9/11," November 2005, http://www.heritage.org/research/reports/2005/11/the-demographics-of-military-enlistment-after-9-11.

39. National Priorities Project, "Military Recruitment 2010."

40. U.S. Dept. of Defense, "2012 Demographics."

41. National Priorities Project, "Military Recruitment 2010."

42. Some civilians recognize this. In the YouGov survey, 43.6 percent of respondents agreed that the US military has different values from those of the rest of American society, while 38.8 percent disagreed and 17.5 percent were unsure (CM2T 18). Similarly, only 32.5 percent of respondents agreed that the military is isolated from American society, while 46.2 percent disagreed and 21.3 percent were not sure (CM2T 23).

43. "Joint Chiefs Chair to Graduates: 'I Fear They Do Not Know Us,' " CNN, May 21, 2011, http://www.cnn.com/2011/US/05/21/new.york.mullen.military.

44. Terry Howell, "Report Compares Military and Civilian Pay," January 27, 2011, http://militaryadvantage.military.com/2011/01/report-military-paid-more -than-federal-workers.

45. Cited in Jeffrey M. Jones, "Confidence in US Institutions Still below Historical Norms," 2015, http://www.gallup.com/poll/183593/confidence-institutions -below-historical-norms.aspx.

46. See generally Rosa Brooks, "Thought Cloud," *Foreign Policy,* August 8, 2011, http://foreignpolicy.com/2012/08/02/thought-cloud.

47. International Committee for the Responsibility to Protect, "Crisis in Kyrgyzstan," http://www.responsibilitytoprotect.org/index.php/crises/crisis -in-kyrgyzstan.

48. See, e.g., Robert Killibrew, "Rapid Deployment: The Army and American Strategy," *War on the Rocks,* December 9, 2013, http://warontherocks.com /2013/12/rapid-deployment-the-army-and-american-strategy.

49. Barack Obama, "Barack Obama's New Hampshire Primary Speech," Transcript, *New York Times,* January 8, 2008, http://www.nytimes.com/2008 /01/08/us/politics/08text-obama.html?pagewanted=all.

50. "White Paper of the Interagency Policy Group's Report on U.S. Policy toward Afghanistan and Pakistan," 2009, http://www.whitehouse.gov/assets /documents/Afghanistan-Pakistan_White_Paper.pdf.

51. Bob Woodward, "McChrystal: More Forces or 'Mission Failure,' " *Washington Post,* September 21, 2009, http://www.washingtonpost.com/wp-dyn/content /article/2009/09/20/AR2009092002920.html.

52. Peter Baker, "How Obama Came to Plan for 'Surge' in Afghanistan," *New York Times,* December 5, 2009, http://www.nytimes.com/2009/12/06/world /asia/06reconstruct.html?pagewanted=all.

53. Notes on file with author for all personal interviews cited in this chapter.

54. DoD News, "Carter 'Will Help Keep Our Military Strong,' President Says," February 12, 2015, http://www.defense.gov/news/newsarticle.aspx?id =128174.

55. See George W. Harley, *Masks as Agents of Social Control in Northeast Liberia,* 1950.

56. See D.W. Murray, "Transposing Symbolic Forms: Actor Awareness of Language Structures in Navajo Ritual," *Anthropological Linguistics,* vol. 31, no. 3/4 (Fall–Winter 1989), pp. 195–208.

57. Qiao Liang and Wang Xiangsui, *Unrestricted Warfare* (1999), available at http://www.cryptome.org/cuw.htm.

58. Carl von Clausewitz, *On War* (1832), available at http://www.clausewitz.com /readings/OnWar1873/BK1ch01.html.

59. "International Strategy for Cyberspace," May 2011, http://www.whitehouse .gov/sites/default/files/rss_viewer/international_strategy_for_cyberspace.pdf.

60. Harold Hongju Koh, "International Law in Cyberspace," September 18, 2012, http://www.state.gov/s/l/releases/remarks/197924.htm.

61. Defense Science Board, "Enhancing Adaptability of US Military Forces," 2011, http://www.acq.osd.mil/dsb/reports/ADA536755.pdf.

62. Leonard Wong, "Fashion Tips for the Field Grade," Carlisle, PA: Strategic Studies Institute, U.S. Army, 2009.

63. Amy Schafer, "What Stands in the Way of the Pentagon Keeping Its Best and Brightest?" July 14, 2014, Defense One, http://www.defenseone.com/ideas /2014/07/what-stands-way-pentagon-keeping-its-best-and-brightest/88630 /?oref=d-channelriver.

64. Tim Kane, "An Army of None," *Foreign Policy,* January 10, 2013, http://foreignpolicy.com/2013/01/10/an-army-of-none.

65. Ibid.

66. Stephen J. Gerras and Leonard Wong, "Changing Minds in the Army, Strategic Studies Institute," October 2013, http://www.strategicstudiesinstitute .army.mil/pdffiles/PUB1179.pdf.

67. Ibid.

68. Defense Science Board, "Enhancing Adaptability of U.S. Military Forces."

CHAPTER 3

Is Civilian Control of the Military Still an Issue?

Mackubin Thomas Owens

During the early 1990s, a number of influential observers argued that civilian control of the military was eroding. A serious "gap," they contended, had opened up between the uniformed military, which was becoming more alienated from liberal civil society, and the civilians, who did not understand or respect the military and its nonliberal virtues. The military clashed repeatedly with the Clinton administration over the integration of openly homosexual recruits and the use of force for "constabulary" operations in the Balkans and elsewhere.[1]

Civil-military tensions did not end with the Clinton presidency. Although George W. Bush told the US military that help was on the way, the uniformed military and civilian leaders, especially Secretary of Defense Donald Rumsfeld, were constantly at odds over everything from "transformation" to the conduct of the wars in Afghanistan and Iraq. Many high-ranking officers opposed the "surge" in Iraq.[2]

Problems have continued during the administration of President Barack Obama. Most, if not all, military officers opposed the precipitous reduction of US forces in Iraq and Afghanistan and the failure to reach a status of forces agreement (SOFA) with the Iraqi government, which would have allowed the United States to exert more influence in the country. An article in *Rolling Stone* led to the high profile resignation of the US commander in Afghanistan, General Stanley McChrystal.[3] Observers were shocked when Marine General James Mattis, commander of U.S. Central Command, was relieved in March of 2013, several months before he was scheduled to retire.[4] In April of 2014, Lieutenant General Michael Flynn, the director of the Defense Intelligence Agency, announced that he would retire a year before he was scheduled to leave his post, reportedly due to serious disagreements with his civilian superiors.[5]

Declining budgets exacerbated the tensions between a military that believed the administration was hostile to the military and an administration that seemed not to trust the uniformed military. In September of 2013, retired Army Major General Robert Scales penned an op-ed for the *Washington Post* claiming that serving officers "are embarrassed to be associated with the amateurism of the Obama administration's attempts to craft a plan that makes strategic sense. None of the White House staff has any experience in war or understands it."[6] The public largely concurs. Fifty-two percent of Americans believe that political leaders are not very or not at all knowledgeable about the modern military (CM2T 15).[7]

These sorts of events led the eminent military historian Richard Kohn to observe in 2002 that "in recent years civilian control of the military has weakened in the United States and is threatened today" to the point "where it could alter the character of American government and undermine national defense."[8] Kohn's claim raises several questions. First, is civil-military tension in the United States only a recent phenomenon? Second, is civilian control threatened to the extent that Kohn claims? And finally, what are the future prospects for civil-military affairs in general and civilian control of the military in particular?

Poll data support public unease about these questions. Americans are concerned about the military's lack of confidence in the country's political leadership. Some 68.4 percent believe that it is hurting effectiveness while only 3.2 percent believe that it is not happening (CM2T 65). However, significant majorities of Americans also support the idea that the military should be able publicly and privately to voice their concerns with the president's Afghanistan policy to Congress and the public if it disagrees (CM2T 76–78). Additionally, a majority of Americans support the idea that military leaders, when faced with an order that they perceive to be unwise, should be permitted to attempt to persuade civilian leaders to change their minds, inform other civilian or military officials who disagree with the policy about the order, or appeal the matter to a higher authority even if it means circumventing the chain of command (CM2T 82, 83, 86).

This chapter seeks to demonstrate that US civil-military tensions are nothing new. Instead they are the result of a civil-military bargain that is being constantly renegotiated as circumstances change. Civilian control of the military is indeed still an issue but one whose resolution will depend on the respective attitudes of civilians and the uniformed military. Too often during both the Bush and Obama administrations, civilians and soldiers have demonstrated a profound lack of trust in one another. History demonstrates that, ultimately, healthy civil-military relations depend on mutual trust.

Civil-Military Relations and Civilian Control of the Military

Civilian control of the military is an important aspect of civil-military relations, although not the only one.[9] The term "civil-military relations" refers broadly to the interaction among the armed forces of a state as an institution, the government, and the other sectors of the society in which the armed force is embedded and has much to say about the allocation of responsibilities and prerogatives between the civil government and the military establishment. Civil-military relations can be seen as "two hands on the sword": the military hand, which keeps the sword ready for combat and wields it during war, and the civil hand, which draws it in pursuit of the policy goals of the state.[10]

Civil-military relations as a whole can be viewed through two lenses. The first is an institutional lens, which draws a clear line between elected and appointed civilian leaders on the one hand and the uniformed military on the other. The institutional lens is the perspective of the political scientist. In this view, the purpose of the state is to protect the individual rights of its citizens and the purpose of the military is to protect liberal society. The institutional lens characterizes the view of the late Samuel Huntington and his many followers.[11]

A competing perspective, prominent in the work of Morris Janowitz and his followers, is the "sociological" lens, which studies the relations between individuals and groups in both civil society and the military. The normative quest of those who favor the sociological lens is toward "civic virtue," engaging citizens in the activity of public life, hence their emphasis on the citizen soldier.[12]

Elsewhere I have argued that civil-military relations can be seen as a *bargain,* the goal of which is to allocate prerogatives and responsibilities between the civilian leadership on the one hand and the military on the other.[13] There are three parties to the bargain: the American people, the government, and the military establishment. Periodically, the civil-military bargain must be renegotiated to take account of political, social, technological, or geopolitical changes.

For much of its early history, the military was a peripheral institution in the United States. It was mobilized for war but was kept small in size during peacetime and deployed away from the view of most Americans, either on the frontier or abroad. It was not until World War II that the US military became a central institution in America. Another renegotiation of the civil-military bargain occurred with the onset of the cold war. As nuclear weapons and deterrence moved to the forefront of US security policy, the uniformed military for the most part was displaced by civilian strategists, who placed limits on military action in both Korea and Vietnam. As the flaws in deterrence theory became more apparent, the uniformed military made its presence felt in developing realistic conventional warfighting options designed to prevail at the operational level of war, for example, the army-air force doctrine of follow-on-forces attack and AirLand Battle for dealing with the Soviet conventional superiority in Europe and the navy's maritime strategy.

Another renegotiation took place after the cold war and the first Persian Gulf War, which validated the US military's operational doctrine. But in the 1990s, the US military reluctantly took on more and more constabulary operations, for example, in the Balkans, even as it preferred to focus on a quick victory in a conventional war. Arguably 9/11 led to another civil-military debate as the United States entered a period of protracted conflict in Afghanistan and Iraq.

Some have expressed concern that, as efficient and effective as the US all-volunteer force has been on the battlefield, it constitutes a small percentage of the population that is culturally distinct from America at large. Indeed, 82.3 percent of Americans and their immediate family members have not served since 9/11; thus, the tenor of the debate will be different from previous renegotiations (CM2T 2). The question today is whether there will be another renegotiation of the civil-military bargain in America.

Some may question whether the idea of a civil-military bargain is compatible with what most Americans, including the uniformed military, understand to be civilian control. Is the military not subordinate to civilian decision makers? Is such subordination not at odds with the idea of negotiating a civil-military bargain? Eliot Cohen, a student of Sam Huntington and one of the most influential writers on civil-military relations, has called American civil-military relations an "unequal dialogue,"[14] by which he means that civilian policymakers ultimately have the final say. And Peter Feaver, another prominent expert on civil-military relations has argued that civilian leaders have "the right to be right"—and, by extension, the right to be wrong.[15]

In the main, both Cohen and Feaver are correct. But as Andrew Bacevich has argued, "the dirty little secret of American civil-military relations, by no means unique to the [Clinton] administration, is that the commander in chief does not command the military establishment; he cajoles it, negotiates with it, and, as necessary, appeases it."[16]

Richard Kohn has echoed this point. He writes, "In theory, civilians have the authority to issue virtually any order and organize the military in any fashion they choose. But in practice, the relationship is much more complex. Both sides frequently disagree among themselves. Further, the military can evade or circumscribe civilian authority by framing the alternatives or tailoring their advice or predicting nasty consequences; by leaking information or appealing to public opinion . . . or by approaching friends in Congress for support."[17] But these sorts of actions do not signal a crisis in civilian control as much as the sort of renegotiation that has characterized US civil-military relations since the beginning of the Republic. In addition, the idea that there is something inappropriate about the military appealing to Congress ignores the point that the legislative branch is a central component of civilian control.

The key to healthy civil-military relations is trust on both the civilian and military sides of the negotiation: the civilians must trust the military to provide its best and most objective advice but then carry out any policy that the civilian decision makers ultimately choose. The military must trust the civilians to give a fair hearing to military advice and not reject it out of hand, especially for transparently political reasons. Civilians must also understand that dissent is not the same as *disobedience*.

Unfortunately, data about elite civilian opinion regarding military advice do not bode well for such trust. For example, the YouGov data suggest that the civilian elite population has a significant distrust of the military. Some 43.4 percent of elites believe that the US military has different values from the rest of the American public; 61.7 percent believe that the military's increasing involvement in nonmilitary affairs hurts effectiveness; and only 13.3 percent believe that there is not a lack of public trust in the uniformed leaders of the military (CM2T 18, 56, 58).

Civilian Control: Theory and Practice

How do we ensure civilian control of the military establishment? In his watershed study of civil-military relations, Samuel Huntington identified two broad approaches, "subjective" and "objective" control.[18] The first approach advocates controlling the military by maximizing the power of civilians, be it by means of authority, influence, or ideology. Subjective control can be achieved through government institutions, social class, or constitutional form, for example, democracy. But totalitarian regimes have controlled the military by pitting one part against another: the SS versus the Wehrmacht in Nazi Germany; "political" officers in the USSR. While civilian control is maximized, the military may be weakened to the point that its effectiveness is adversely affected.

Huntington preferred the second approach, which maximizes military professionalism. On the one hand, civilian authorities grant a professional officer corps autonomy in the realm of military affairs. On the other, "a highly professional officer corps stands ready to carry out the wishes of any civilian group which secures legitimate authority within the state." Eliot Cohen calls this the "Normal" theory of civil-military relations but notes that this approach is by no means the norm in American history, even in recent times.[19]

Although the debate over civilian control entered the public consciousness in the 1990s, civil-military tensions in the United States are nothing new. Just because the United States has never suffered a coup does not necessarily mean that civil-military relations are healthy. This has been true from the very beginning of the Republic. For instance, in 1783 with the Continental Army encamped at Newburgh, New York, some officers attempted to persuade others to take unspecified actions against the Continental Congress in response to the failure of that body to pay the soldiers. When George Washington got wind of the plot, he unexpectedly confronted the dissatisfied officers during a meeting. His demeanor defused the near mutiny and—along with his return of his commission after the end of the war—helped to cement in the minds of American officers ever since the sacred idea of civilian control.

Such tensions continued during the early Republic. After the American Revolution there was a spirited debate between Federalists and Republicans regarding the desirability of a permanent military establishment. Prominent Federalists including Washington, Alexander Hamilton, and Henry Knox favored a standing army or at least a uniformed militia, but the "genius" of the people made such an establishment impossible. It was a matter of faith for Americans that standing armies were a threat to liberty and that the militia in the form of a "people numerous and armed" was the only acceptable way to defend a republic. This vision of the militia was never completely true, but it took the debacle of the War of 1812 to disabuse the American people of their attachment to a militia.[20]

In 1818, Creeks, Seminoles, and escaped slaves launched a series of attacks on Americans from sanctuaries in Spanish Florida. General Andrew Jackson, acting on the basis of questionable authority, invaded Florida, not only attacking and burning Seminole villages but also capturing a Spanish fort at St. Marks. He also executed two British citizens whom he had accused of aiding the marauders. Most of President James Monroe's cabinet, especially Secretary of War John Calhoun, wanted Jackson's head, but Secretary of State John Quincy Adams came to Jackson's defense, contending that the United States should not apologize for Jackson's preemptive expedition but insist that Spain either garrison Florida with enough forces to prevent marauders from entering the United States or "cede to the United States a province . . . which is in fact derelict, open to the occupancy of every enemy, civilized or savage, of the United States, and serving no other earthly purpose than as a post of annoyance to them." As Adams had written earlier, it was his opinion "that the marauding parties . . . ought to be broken up immediately."[21]

During the Mexican War, President James Polk, a Democrat, feuded constantly with his generals in field, both of whom were Whigs with presidential aspirations. Both Major General Zachary Taylor and Major General Winfield Scott did not hesitate to criticize the president's policy, strategy, and leadership while conducting the military operations in Mexico.[22] Such behavior on the part of general officers would be unthinkable today. Their public criticism of Polk adumbrated Major General George B. McClellan's similar public denunciations of Lincoln during the Civil War.[23]

Civil-military tensions persisted into Reconstruction and the era of westward expansion of the United States. During the election of 1920, General Leonard Wood, who had already served as general in chief of the army, campaigned for the Republican presidential nomination while in uniform.

Of course, we are much more familiar with the problems of civil-military relations during the Truman administration, with the firing of General Douglas MacArthur, and the recent events during the Clinton, Bush, and Obama presidencies. So in fact, civilian control does continue to be an issue, but it is far from a recent problem, reflecting the fact that while the uniformed military has internalized the concept of civilian control, the actual "line" between civilians and the military is itself an issue for negotiation.

Any discussion of civilian control must take into account that it involves not only the executive branch but Congress as well. The fact is that the two branches vie for dominance in the military realm. While the president has constitutional authority as commander in chief of the military, Congress retains the power of the purse and is therefore the "force planner of last resort." Nonetheless, the decentralized nature of Congress gives the president and the executive branch an advantage when it comes to military affairs. Ironically, Congress further strengthened the executive's hand by enacting the Goldwater-Nichols [Department of Defense Reorganization] Act in 1986.[24]

In addition, any discussion of US civil-military relations must recognize that historically, civil-military disputes usually do not pit civilians per se against the military. Instead, these disputes involve one civil-military faction against another.[25] For instance, shortly after World War II, civil-military tensions were inflamed by the debate between the newly established air force and the navy regarding long-range air power, in particular, strategic bombers. On the one hand, Harry Truman, his secretary of defense, Louis Johnson, and certain members of Congress favored the air force's long-range B-36 bomber. On the other hand, the navy and its supporters in Congress and the press advocated on behalf of that service's proposed supercarrier, the USS *United States.*

These sorts of factional debates have persisted into our own time. For instance, the choice of the air force's A-10 Warthog land-attack aircraft over its competitors pitted the congressional delegations of several states and both the civilian and uniformed leadership of the three military departments against one another. A similar situation arose in the case of the Marine Corps's V-22 Osprey, with the Marines, the Department of the Navy, and several congressional delegations arrayed against very powerful opponents within the Office of the Secretary of Defense (OSD). The creation of Special Operations Command (SOCOM) also occurred despite strong opposition from the services as well as OSD. It was an alliance between an assortment of "guerrillas" within the Department of Defense and some very dedicated congressional advocates that saw the reorganization come to fruition.[26]

As budgets decline, such disputes among various factions are likely to be the main arena of civil-military discord. Although it is common to attribute the decline in interservice disputes to the passage of the Goldwater-Nichols Act in 1986, the more likely reason is that as defense budgets increased beginning in the early 1980s, each of the services got most—if not all—of what they requested. We should hope that declining defense budgets do not presage a return to the "bad old days" of the late 1940s and early 1950s.

Even the alleged textbook case of a civil-military crisis, Truman's firing of MacArthur, is more complex than it appears at first sight. In fact there was military support for the firing: both George Marshall and Dwight Eisenhower urged Truman to fire him, while Republicans in Congress supported MacArthur.

The Character of Military Advice and the "Calculus of Dissent"

The uniformed military is obligated to provide its best professional advice to civilian policymakers. Officers are obligated to offer this advice forcefully, but this does not mean they have the right to *insist* that their advice be followed. History shows that the military is not always right, even regarding strictly military affairs. Moreover, officers are not elected, whereas political leaders who are have legitimacy in making trade-offs for society. Nonetheless, dissent is not disobedience: there must be a "calculus of dissent."[27]

Americans largely understand and support this calculus. The public—and perhaps surprisingly elites even more so—supports the concept of officers dissenting from orders that they deem unwise in a variety of manners, including trying to convince superiors to change their minds and referring the matter to an inspector general (CM2T 82, 83, 87). However, this support is not without reservations; in cases where the officer leaks the matter to the press or refuses to carry out the order even when faced with a court-martial, the public does not approve and elites are less supportive than the general public (CM2T 85, 88).

Healthy civil-military relations involve a trust relationship between civilians and the uniformed military, at least when service in the military is a true profession worthy of being granted significant autonomy and a unique role in its relationship with civilian policymakers due to specialized knowledge and expertise. Otherwise, the military is little more than just one more obedient bureaucracy within the executive branch. The difference between a profession and a merely obedient bureaucracy is important when we consider the character of military dissent.

A member of a bureaucracy has no legal right to dissent. The choice in a disagreement is either "salute and obey" or resign. But a profession must provide a set of alternatives beyond either "loyalty" or "exit." As Albert Hirschman argues, the institutionalization of greater "voice," that is, dissent, can help stem massive exits. If the military is truly a profession, then dissent—although not disobedience—is necessarily an option when an officer disagrees with the policies of civilian leaders.[28] But such dissent should take place during the debate leading up to a final decision. Once a decision is made, the military is obligated to abide by it.

Several years ago, Lieutenant General Greg Newbold (Ret.) of the U.S. Marine Corps, wrote: "I offer a challenge to those still in uniform: a leader's responsibility is to give voice to those who can't—or don't have the opportunity to—speak. . . . It is time for some military leaders to discard caution in expressing their views and ensure that the President hears them clearly."[29] Of course, many observers pointed out that Newbold's advice would have been more persuasive had he offered it while still on active duty.

Newbold's op-ed was a part of an episode dubbed "the revolt of the generals" in the spring of 2006, which saw a number of retired army and Marine Corps generals publicly and harshly criticize the Bush administration's conduct of the Iraq War and call for the resignation of Secretary of Defense Donald Rumsfeld.[30] Following the 2006 election, President Bush asked for Rumsfeld's resignation and opted to change course in Iraq, initiating what came to be known as the "surge."

What about resignation in response to a policy with which an officer disagrees? Many argue that resignation was the proper response of the Joint Chiefs of Staff who disagreed with the policy and strategy of the Vietnam War pushed by Secretary of Defense Robert McNamara. This is the purported lesson of the very influential book by H. R. McMaster, *Dereliction of Duty.*[31] Many serving officers believe that this book makes the case that the Joint Chiefs of Staff should have more openly voiced their opposition to the Johnson administration's strategy of gradualism during the Vietnam War and then resigned rather than carry out the policy.

But the book says no such thing. While McMaster convincingly argues that the chiefs failed to present their views frankly and forcefully to their civilian superiors, including members of Congress when asked for their views, he neither says nor implies that the chiefs should have obstructed President Lyndon Johnson's orders and policies through leaks or public statements, or by resigning.[32]

Richard Kohn has made the strongest argument against resignation as a legitimate response to a policy disagreement between the uniformed military and civilians, contending that "personal and professional honor do not require a request for reassignment or retirement if civilians order one's service, command, or unit to act in some manner an officer finds distasteful, disastrous, or even immoral. The military's job is to advise and then execute lawful orders. . . . If officers at various levels measure policies, decisions, orders, and operations against personal moral and ethical systems, and act thereon, the good order and discipline of the military would collapse."[33] However, a plurality of Americans disagree with Kohn: 43.9 percent believe that it is appropriate to retire or leave the service in protest, while 26.9 percent believe it is inappropriate and 29.2 percent are unsure (CM2T 84).

But what alternatives are available? Several commentators, including Leonard Wong, Douglas Lovelace, and Don Snider, have provided some thoughtful guidance on the issue. Wong and Lovelace contend that the proper response depends on two variables: the magnitude of the threat to national security resulting from the disputed policy and the degree of civilian resistance to military advice.[34] Snider offers a similar but broader array of variables: the gravity of the issue; the relevance of one's expertise to the dissent; the degree of sacrifice that one's dissent entails; the timing of the dissent; and the dissenter's authenticity as a leader.[35] Obviously, resignation must remain an option, although one that should never be orchestrated for political reasons.

Public Attitudes and Implications for Civilian Control of the Military

In *The Soldier and the State,* Samuel Huntington argued that a source of civil-military tensions is the clash between the dominant liberalism of the United States, which tends toward an antimilitary outlook, and the "conservative" mind of military officers.[36] Part of this conservative mindset is a focus on military effectiveness or what Huntington calls the *functional* imperative, which stresses virtues that differ from those favored by liberal society at large—which he called the *societal* imperative. Huntington further argued that while American liberalism accepted the need for an effective military during wartime, it tended to turn against the military during peacetime, trying to force it more into line with liberal values. He contended that in peacetime the dominant liberalism of the United States sought *extirpation* of the military but, recognizing that even liberal society needs a military, liberal civilians would settle for *transmutation,* which seeks to supplant the functional imperative with the societal one.[37]

It is clear that the American military must take account of societal considerations, no matter the demands of the functional imperative. We return to the idea of civil-military relations as a bargain that must periodically be renegotiated. Thus, in 1993, President Bill Clinton's proposal to permit military service by openly homosexual recruits was rejected by Congress, indeed, a Congress controlled by his own party. The legislative branch accepted the view of the uniformed military that service by those who are openly homosexual would undermine the military's functional imperative. The result was a veto-proof law prohibiting such service. But two decades later, Congress repealed that same law, reflecting the case that the attitude of Americans regarding this issue had clearly changed in the interim, as evidenced in the YouGov poll in which 54.5 percent of Americans strongly or somewhat agreed with homosexuals serving openly in the military (CM2T 54). Some 46.1 percent say it is relevant if most men in the infantry oppose homosexuals serving openly in the military, 34.5 percent say it is irrelevant, and 19.4 percent are unsure (CM2T 55).

In November of 2015, Secretary of Defense Ashton Carter announced that all military specialties, including the infantry and special operations, are open to women. American public opinion is generally supportive of the move. Some 58 percent of Americans currently somewhat or strongly disagree with excluding women from serving in the infantry (CM2T 52). Yet 45.8 percent believe that it is relevant if most men in the infantry oppose women joining the infantry, 31 percent believe it is irrelevant, and 23.2 percent are not sure (CM2T 53).

Clearly, the outcome of the civil-military bargain depends on the contrasting attitudes of the military and civilians. Until recently, the best available data regarding such attitudes came from a 1993 survey conducted by the Triangle Institute for Security Studies (TISS) in North Carolina. This study was undertaken in response to the claim that a serious "gap" between civilian and military attitudes had arisen, making the US military dangerously alienated from the society it served.[38]

The study confirmed the fact that civilians and members of the uniformed military possessed different views of the world and that the military's had diverged considerably from those of civilians over a twenty-year period. For instance, by 1993, the officer corps had become less politically liberal and more conservative than in the late 1970s. In 1976, 16 percent identified themselves as either somewhat or very liberal. In 1993, only 3 percent of officers identified themselves as somewhat liberal. Meanwhile, the percentage of officers identifying themselves as conservative increased from 61 percent to 73 percent. According to the recent YouGov poll, only 11 percent of Americans think that people serving in the military are somewhat or much more likely to vote Democratic in elections (CM1T 40). On the civilian side, a smaller percentage had any awareness of, or experience with, the military. At present, only 7 percent of the public say that they are not at all familiar with the military and 23 percent say not very familiar (CM1T 39).

Of more concern is the increase in partisanship. The percentage of officers calling themselves independents declined while those identifying themselves as Republicans increased. In 1976, the figures were independents 46 percent and Republicans 33 percent. Two decades later the numbers had flipped: only 22 percent identified as independents while 67 percent identified as Republicans.[39] Of course, there is a reason for this: the perception that liberals and Democrats were antimilitary, a theme that can be traced to the aftermath of the Vietnam War. Since the TISS survey, the number of civilian veterans who self-report as Republicans has remained relatively stable (36.95 percent to 33.06 percent), according to the YouGov results. At the same time, there has been a decrease in the number of Democrats (31.03 percent to 18.55 percent) and an increase in independents (27.59 percent to 39.52 percent). However in terms of ideology, the number of veterans who self-report as conservative has increased (33.16 percent to 45.16 percent) and so has the spread between veterans and nonveterans (4.63 percent to 28.49 percent).

The origins of a growing partisanship on the part of the military notwithstanding, many observers have expressed the fear that the result of this increasing partisanship will be an officer corps that sees its role as going beyond merely *advising* civilian decision makers to instead *insisting* that its recommendations be followed. An example is the very public "warning shot" that General Colin Powell, then chairman of the joint chiefs of staff, fired regarding the Clinton administration's potential involvement in the Balkans and the army's purported resistance to constabulary operation in the Balkans and elsewhere.[40] Indeed, one of the TISS study's major findings confirmed this view. There have been no studies of military attitudes since the TISS study, but anecdotal evidence, for example, the aforementioned revolt of the generals, suggests that this attitude has only hardened in response to the impact of fifteen years at war. The problem of this trend among military officers clearly has implications for civilian control of the military.

What of the civilian side? What are civilian attitudes toward the military after two wars and what do they portend for civilian control in the future? Surveys conducted by YouGov provide data that offer some interesting possibilities, especially in light of Huntington's discussions of the clash between the "conservativism" of the military officer, on the one hand, and American liberal society, on the other, and how this plays out in terms of "extirpation" and "transmutation," both of which seek to reshape the military along the lines of Huntington's "societal" rather than "functional" imperative. Huntington's discussion strongly suggests that tensions between the military and civilians will be greater the more liberal the civilians.

For instance, the data from the YouGov survey is instructive. A majority of those who self-identify as "very liberal" do not believe that military leaders share the same values as the American people at large. For "liberals" the percentage of individuals who believe that they do not is nearly the same. Nearly a half of "moderates" and a substantial majority of both "conservatives" and the "very conservative" do believe that military leaders share the same values as the American people (CM2T 16). It also reveals that over a third of those that call themselves "very liberal" believe the military gets more respect than it deserves (CM2T 14).

Answers to question 19 reveal that "liberals" see the values of the military as being less progressive than those of the society at large. This is true of "conservatives" as well but they no doubt see this as a virtue rather than a vice, presumably because conservatives tend to oppose service by those who are openly homosexual and access to such military specialties as infantry and special operations forces for women (CM2T).

The survey also shows shows that nearly a third of all those who believe that military values are less progressive than those of the American people at large attribute it to the sort of people that the military attracts: those with less progressive views (CM2T 20). This in some respects validates Huntington's idea of a conservative military mindset. Critics of the military often contend that people join the military because they have no other economic options, but it is more likely the case that most in the military are motivated by some degree of patriotism and a sense of service. Those who do are more likely to possess or seek the traditional virtues normally associated with military service in the public mind: discipline, loyalty, courage, honor, and self-sacrifice.

This seems to be the consensus of survey respondents, large majorities of whom, both "liberals" and "conservatives," see the military as socially conservative (CM2T 21). Yet answers to question 24 illustrates that by large majorities all ideological groups, including the most liberal and conservative segments of the population, believe a military isolated from America at large is a bad thing (CM2T).

There is a divergence of opinion between "liberals" and "conservatives" when it comes to the issue of "fairness" towards women, with liberals seeing the military as treating women less fairly than American society at large does (CM2T 25). Surprisingly, there are no data regarding the question of fairness with respect to minorities, although the survey shows that all groups, but especially "conservatives," believe that there are more opportunities for minorities in the military than elsewhere in American society. Significantly more than 50 percent of African-Americans, Hispanics, and other minorities believe that the military is either more, or about as, fair as the rest of society in terms of promotions and recognition, the opportunity to excel, the opportunity for self-improvement, the opportunity for respect, and middle-class status.[41] Some 48.7 percent of Americans believe that the military offers more opportunity than the rest of society for minorities while 34.3 percent say about the same, 6.9 percent say less, and 10.1 percent are unsure (CM2T 33).

Huntington's thesis suggests that the more politically liberal an administration is, the more likely it will be to favor the societal over the functional imperative. The implication of this thesis is that the attitudes toward the military of those in power will be reflected in policies toward the military. The more liberal an administration, the more likely its policies will tend toward "extirpation"—severely cutting force structure—in peacetime and severe "transmutation"—trying to force the military more into line with liberal values—during wartime, which will engender some degree of military pushback against that policy.

Most people would regard the Obama administration as very liberal. In light of Huntington's categories, the data from the YouGov survey suggest that with such an administration, civil-military relations in general and civilian control of the military in particular will be problematic, and this indeed seems to be the case.

A very liberal administration is likely to base its military and security policies on ideas that the uniformed military will find hard to accept. Based on Huntington's thesis, one would postulate that an administration that shares the "very liberal" attitudes reflected in the data from the YouGov survey is likely to pursue a policy of extirpation in its approach to the military. This seems to be borne out by the evidence. On the one hand, the Obama administration has failed to develop a strategy for dealing with events in the world, including the emergence of ISIS, Iran's nuclear ambitions and its quest for regional hegemony, Russian aggression against Ukraine, and a rising China (the so-called Asia Pivot has not materialized for lack of resources and events throughout the rest of the world). On the other hand, the defense budget has declined precipitously, and force structure has contracted to levels not seen in decades.

Contending that it has ended two wars and that the world has little need of US military force, the Obama administration has made its real push for extirpation in the realm of social change. Its first success was in the repeal of the law banning service by those who are openly homosexual. Of course that action reflected changes in public opinion regarding homosexuality. The Obama administration has now begun to open all military specialties to women, who were excluded from service in the infantry and special operations forces. In one respect, this is a continuation of a trend that has been at work for some time. The military has been providing more and more opportunities for women, but the line has traditionally been drawn at the infantry and special operations forces.

While there have been calls to open these specialties for some time now, those urging such steps were always seen to be on the margins of the debate, for example, feminist academics waging a war on military culture, decrying its "masculinist military construct" that favors the "hypermasculine male." For instance, in her article "By Force of Arms: Rape, War and Military Culture" for the February 1996 issue of the *Duke Law Review*, Madeline Morris wrote that there was much to be gained and little to be lost by "changing this aspect of military culture from a masculinist vision of unalloyed aggressivity to an ungendered vision."[42]

But in early 2013, former defense secretary Leon Panetta set a deadline of January 2016 for the services to integrate women fully. Critics of the mandate are concerned that this full integration of women will be achieved only by lowering standards. The services most affected by the mandate, the U.S. Army and Marine Corps, have stated that they will not lower the standards, but the chairman of the Joint Chiefs of Staff, General Martin Dempsey, opened the door to double standards when he said in January 2013, "if we do decide that a particular standard is so high that a woman couldn't make it, the burden is now on the service to come back and explain to the secretary, why is it that high? Does it really have to be that high?"[43]

The issue of women in the infantry has already generated pushback from military officers who believe that their leaders may succumb to political pressure rather than defending what they believe to be the traditional virtues of the military. The Marine Corps in particular was very vocal in its opposition to opening infantry positions to women. This affair will be a major test for civilian control on both the civilian and military side. Will the military simply acquiesce in establishing double standards, violating a key component of military culture—fairness? Will officers either salute and obey or leave the service, or will they exercise a "calculus of dissent?" Will the civilian leadership accept the advice of those who object to the elevation of the societal imperative over the functional; who believe that the full integration of women into the military will be counterproductive if standards are compromised?

The answer will ultimately be decided by the third party to the civil-military bargain: the American people. History has shown that the military can defend its prerogatives only to the extent that they are not completely at odds with public opinion. As Abraham Lincoln remarked in his first debate with Stephen Douglas (1858), in a republic such as ours, public opinion is everything: "He who moulds public sentiment, goes deeper than he who enacts statutes or pronounces decisions. He makes statutes and decisions possible or impossible to be executed."

But it is possible that the military's increasing isolation from civilian society, combined with a high level of public ignorance regarding the military,[44] gives political leaders greater latitude in this realm, independent of public opinion. This is further exacerbated by political leaders who do not engage the public on security affairs.

The Future of Civilian Control of the Military in America

Civilian control of the military is safe in America, mainly resulting from a combination of institutional and normative constraints and military professionalism. There is no danger of anything approaching a military coup in the United States, and many of the concerns that

commentators raised beginning in the 1990s were not so much indications of a crisis in civil-military relations as they were manifestations
of the reality that the civil-military bargain in America is frequently
renegotiated. In addition, most of the concerns projected in the 1990s
are not borne out by the data in the YouGov polls. But a potential danger arises from the combination of the military's isolation from civilian
society and the possibility that more and more officers will see their
role as insisting that civilians follow their advice.

The main change in circumstances that has led to civil-military
tensions since the election of Barack Obama in 2008 is that his administration reflects the attitudes of what the YouGov survey labels the
"very liberal." It is to be expected that the conservative mindset that
Huntington attributed to the military would be at odds with the very
liberal Obama administration over issues from the use of force to the
integration of women.

While relations between the uniformed military and the Obama
administration are very likely to remain strained, the military will
make its case to its other civilian master, the Congress. Despite the fact
that Congress itself strengthened the hand of the executive by passing
the Goldwater-Nichols Act, the military has the right to make its case
to the legislative branch and it no doubt will, very strongly. Of course,
this assumes that Congress actually provides a balance to counter a
liberal administration. But even with Republican majorities in both
houses of Congress after the 2014 election, this has not proven to be
the case.

A danger for the military, of course, is that officers who dissent will
be pushed aside for those who are more compliant. Those who argue
that healthy civil-military relations are characterized by comity and a
low number of disagreements between civilian and military decision
makers ignore or discount the possibility that this may be the result
of promoting yes men who are politically safe and who will not really
fulfill their obligation to provide their best military advice as forcefully
as possible.

The Obama administration has demonstrated that it is willing to curtail independence on the part of its high-ranking officers. Of course, a president has every right to choose the generals and admirals he wants, but it is also the case that he usually then gets the generals and admirals he deserves. If a president indicates by his actions that he does not want smart, independently minded generals who speak candidly to their civilian leaders, the message that generals and admirals may receive is that they should go along to get along. Nothing could be worse for the health of US civil-military relations.

It is undeniable that American civil-military relations have been healthiest when there is a high level of trust between civilian and military leaders, that is, when there is mutual respect and understanding between them that leads to the exchange of candid views and perspectives between the two parties as part of the decision-making process. Examples of healthy US civil-military relations include Lincoln and Grant during the Civil War, Franklin Roosevelt and George Marshall during World War II, and the tenure of Robert Gates during the last part of the George W. Bush administration.

On the one hand, the military must have a voice in strategy making, while realizing that politics permeates the conduct of war and that civilians have the final say, not only concerning the goals of the war but also how it is conducted. On the other hand, civilians must understand that to implement effective policy and strategy requires the proper military instrument and therefore must insist that soldiers present their views frankly and forcefully throughout the strategy-making and implementation process. This is the key to healthy civil-military relations.

A number of factors will influence US civil-military relations in the future. One is the participation gap, the fact that less than one percent of the population now serves in the military. It is unlikely that the military will return to being a "peripheral" institution in America, its status before World War II. But of all the civil-military "gaps" that observers have identified over the past two and a half decades, the participation gap is by far the most consequential.

The US military is a largely middle-class organization, reflecting the attitudes and virtues of that demographic, but as fewer and fewer Americans serve in the military, the mutual trust that is necessary for healthy civil-military relations may well erode, raising the specter of praetorianism in the military of the sort that haunted France in the 1950s and 1960s as a result of the French military's experiences in Indochina and Algeria. Some observers detected at least a hint of praetorianism on the part of members of General McChrystal's staff as they took pleasure in calling themselves "Team America" in the infamous *Rolling Stone* article that led to the general's resignation.[45]

Disaffected praetorianism may well arise from the fact that the US military has fought two prolonged conflicts over the last decade and a half, and although civilians have been happy to say to soldiers "thank you for your service," they have largely been unaffected by these wars. The disparity in sacrifice between the uniformed military and civilians has left some veterans bitter. A cohort of disaffected veterans cannot help but contribute to a lack of trust, which will make the maintenance of healthy civil-military relations difficult in the future. Attempts to "buy" veterans with generous entitlements is likely to fail. The best way to gain or retain the trust of veterans is to ensure that they receive "genuine gratitude. Not sympathy or pedestals; but real gratitude. . . . Every civilian should understand that the veteran has done nothing less, and also nothing more, than what is sometimes required to maintain liberty."[46]

Notes

1. Lindsay Cohn, "The Evolution of the Civil-Military 'Gap' Debate," paper prepared for the Triangle Institute for Security Studies Project on the Gap between Military and Civilian Society, 1999.
2. David Margolick, "The Night of the Generals," *Vanity Fair,* March 13, 2007.
3. Scott Wilson and Michael Shear, "Gen. McChrystal Dismissed as Top US Commander in Afghanistan," *Washington Post,* June 24, 2010.

4. Mackubin Thomas Owens, "Obama Dumps a Smart, Independently Minded General," *Weekly Standard,* January 22, 2013, http://www.weeklystandard .com/blogs/obama-dumps-smart-independently-minded-general _697440.html.

5. Greg Miller and Adam Goldman, "Head of Pentagon Intelligence Agency Forced Out, Officials Say," *Washington Post,* April 30, 2014.

6. Robert Scales, "US Military Planners Don't Support War with Syria," *Washington Post,* September 5, 2013. Cf. the reply by David Barno, "US War Decisions Rightfully belong to Elected Civilian Leaders, Not the Military," *Washington Post,* September 12, 2013.

7. References to the YouGov data by question number appear in parentheses throughout this essay with the abbreviations CM1T and CM2T indicating the 2013 and 2014 surveys, respectively. The complete results are available at http://www.hoover.org/warriors-and-citizens-crosstabs-1 (CM1T) and http://www.hoover.org/warriors-and-citizens-crosstabs-2 (CM2T).

8. Richard Kohn, "The Erosion of Civilian Control of the Military in the United States Today," *Naval War College Review,* Summer 2002, p. 9.

9. The others are (1) the influence of the military on society at large, (2) the role of the military, (3) ensuring military effectiveness, and (4) who serves. See Mackubin Thomas Owens, *US Civil-Military Relations after 9/11: Renegotiating the Civil-Military Bargain,* New York: Continuum, 2011, and "What Military Officers Need to Know about Civil-Military Relations," *Naval War College Review,* Spring 2012.

10. Vincent Brooks et al., *Two Hands on the Sword: A Study of Political-Military Relations in National Security Policy,* Carlisle, PA: Army War College, 1999.

11. Samuel Huntington, *The Soldier and the State,* Cambridge: Harvard University Press, 1957.

12. Morris Janowitz, *The Professional Soldier: A Social and Political Portrait,* New York: Free Press, 1960.

13. Owens, *US Civil-Military Relations after 9/11.*

14. Eliot Cohen, *Supreme Command: Soldiers, Statesmen, and Leadership in Wartime,* New York: Anchor, 2002, p. 247.

15. Peter Feaver, "The Right to be Right," *International Security,* Spring 2011.

16. Andrew Bacevich, "Discord Still: Clinton and the Military," *Washington Post,* January 3, 1999, p. C1.

17. Kohn, "Erosion of Civilian Control," pp. 15, 16.

18. Huntington, *Soldier and the State,* pp. 80–85.

19. Cohen, *Supreme Command,* p. 4.

20. Lawrence Delbert Cress, *Citizens in Arms: The Army and Militia in American Society to the War of 1812,* Chapel Hill: University of North Carolina Press, 1982.

21. Letter to Luis d' Onis, July 23, 1818, in Worthington Chauncey Ford, *Writings of John Quincy Adams,* 1914, vol. 6, pp. 386–94; letter to James Monroe, July 8, 1818, ibid., p. 304.

22. John C. Pinheiro, *Manifest Ambition: James K. Polk and Civil Military Relations during the Mexican War,* Westport, CT: Praeger, 2007.

23. Mackubin Thomas Owens, *Abraham Lincoln: Leadership and Democratic Statesmanship in Wartime,* Philadelphia: Foreign Policy Research Institute, 2009, pp. 30–33.

24. Mackubin Thomas Owens, "Force Planning: The Crossroads of Strategy and the Political Process," *Orbis,* Summer 2015.

25. I am indebted to Donald B. Connelly for this observation. See his book *John M. Schofield and the Politics of Generalship,* Chapel Hill: University of North Carolina Press, 2006, p. xii.

26. Mackubin Thomas Owens, "Congress and the Creation of SOCOM," Naval War College faculty paper, May 2013.

27. Owens, *US Civil-Military Relations after 9/11,* pp. 62–70.

28. Albert O. Hirschman, *Exit, Voice, Loyalty: Responses to Decline in Firms, Organizations, and States,* Cambridge: Harvard University Press, 1970.

29. Greg Newbold, "Why Iraq Was a Mistake," *Time,* April 17, 2006.

30. David Cloud and Eric Schmitt, "More Retired Generals Call for Rumsfeld Resignation," *New York Times,* April 14, 2006, and Margolick, "Night of the Generals."

31. H. R. McMaster, *Dereliction of Duty: Lyndon Johnson, Robert McNamara, the Joint Chiefs of Staff, and the Lies that Led to Vietnam,* New York: Harper Collins, 1997.

32. Owens, *US Civil-Military Relations After 9/11,* p. 54.

33. Richard Kohn, "Building Trust: Civil-Military Behaviors for Effective National Security," in Suzanne Nielson and Don Snider, eds., *American Civil-Military Relations: The Soldier and the State in a New Era,* Baltimore: Johns Hopkins University Press, 2009, p. 282.

34. Leonard Wong and Douglas Lovelace, "Knowing When to Salute," *Orbis,* Spring 2008.

35. Don Snider, "Dissent and Strategic Leadership of the Military Profession," *Orbis,* Spring 2008.

36. Huntington, *Soldier and the State,* pp. 143–162.

37. Ibid., pp. 155–57.

38. Richard Kohn and Peter Feaver, eds., *Soldiers and Civilians: The Civil-Military Gap and American Security,* Cambridge: MIT Press, 2001.

39. Ole Holsti, "A Widening Gap between the US Military and Civilian Society? Some Evidence, 1976–1996," *International Security,* Winter 1998/99, pp. 5–42.

40. Colin Powell, "Why Generals Get Nervous," *New York Times,* October 8, 1992; Edward Dorn and Howard Graves, *American Military Culture in the 21st Century: A Report of the CSIS International Security Program,* Washington DC: Center for Strategic and International Studies, February 2000, pp. xvi, xix.

41. Promotions and recognition: black 67.3 percent, Hispanic 54.6 percent, other 77 percent (CM2T 26); opportunity to excel: black 72 percent, Hispanic 58.8 percent, other 83.3 percent (CM2T 27); opportunity for self-improvement: black 73 percent, Hispanic 58.8 percent, other 79 percent (CM2T 28); opportunity for respect: black 69.6 percent, Hispanic 60.9 percent, other 77.9 percent (CM2T 29); living in the middle class: black 63.4 percent, Hispanic 51.4 percent, other 68.6 percent (CM2T 30).

42. Madeline Morris, "By Force of Arms: Rape, War, and Military Culture," *Duke Law Journal,* February 1996.

43. U.S. Dept. of Defense, "Press Briefing by Secretary Panetta and General Dempsey from the Pentagon," transcript, January 24, 2013, http://www.archive.defense.gov/Transcripts/Transcript.aspx?TranscriptID=5183.

44. According to the YouGov data, public estimates for the number of service members serving in the five branches of the military on average were wrong by a count of over five million. Guesses on specific branches of the military, such as the U.S. Army and Marine Corps, were incorrect by hundreds of thousands.

45. Michael Hastings, "The Runaway General," *Rolling Stone,* June 22, 2010.

46. Mackubin Thomas Owens, "Life after Wartime," *Weekly Standard,* June 2, 2014.

CHAPTER 4

Thanks for Your Service

Civilian and Veteran Attitudes after Fifteen Years of War

Jim Golby, Lindsay P. Cohn, and Peter D. Feaver

In 2011, Mark Thompson wrote a piece for *Time* magazine titled "The Other 1%." The title was a direct reference to the then-prominent cry of the Occupy movement about how nearly half of the wealth in the United States was controlled by only one percent of the people. The Occupy movement alleged that "real" or "regular" Americans were estranged from this tiny group of the super-rich, whose lives were utterly different from everyone else's. The one percent to which Thompson was referring, however, was the tiny number of Americans serving in the armed forces. His argument was that, if Americans were unhappy about half of their wealth belonging to only one percent, should they not also feel that it is unfair for the entire defense burden to rest on only one percent of the people?

Thompson's piece was just one more salvo in the long-standing debate about the idea of a civil-military "gap" in American society.[1] The issue is as old as the American republic itself.[2] The Framers of the Constitution wanted to create an army under national control but nevertheless devoted a considerable amount of their efforts to designing a system that would minimize the fledgling republic's dependence on standing military forces to ensure ratification.[3] Along with other institutional checks, the maintenance of the citizen-based militia system would allow for a military that would share "the same spirit as the people" but that would still help meet the country's security needs.

Systematic scholarly attention really took off in the United States in the first decades of the cold war with the publication of two seminal works on civil-military relations: Samuel P. Huntington's *The Soldier and the State* (1957) and Morris Janowitz's *The Professional Soldier* (1960). These works were in part a reaction to the fact that the United States was, for the first time in its history, maintaining a large, standing, conscription-based military to meet an indefinite threat; while perhaps not truly "peacetime," the cold war posture was certainly not the wartime frame of previous conflicts—Civil War, World War I, and World War II—when Americans had tolerated mass mobilization. They set up a debate based not only on differing normative interpretations of military professionalism and civilian control of the military but also about the relationship between civilian and military cultures—the extent to which they do and ought to differ and how to manage whatever differences might arise.

Later, after the war in Vietnam and the return to an all-volunteer military, the literature focused on two issues: first, how the shift to a necessarily smaller and more self-selective volunteer force would change the military and its relations with society; and second, to what extent military officers at the top of the chain should push back against civilian policy decisions, whether coming from the executive branch or the legislature. The end of the cold war ushered in another period in the gap debate, inspired by the changing security environment, the shrinking military establishment, and a spike in friction between civilian and military leaders over controversial policy choices, most visibly the question of whether gays and lesbians should be allowed to serve openly in the armed forces. This era was characterized by various pressures to adapt the military culture to a new, peacetime context.

Now, we are in a new and in some ways unprecedented period. It is an era during which the Afghanistan and Iraq wars required the active duty military to fight prolonged, bloody, and increasingly unpopular engagements with extended and repeated call-ups of the National Guard and the Reserves but without the other resources of a full wartime mobilization of society—something that had never been contemplated for the all-volunteer force (AVF). The strains on the force and the strains on public support for the missions raised anew the traditional themes of alienation, difference, and lack of understanding, despite the apparent popularity and general admiration of military personnel. Many people hope now to move beyond the post-9/11 war on terror and America's long and contentious counterinsurgency wars in Iraq and Afghanistan, yet a new war against the Islamic State of Iraq and al-Sham (ISIS) is accelerating, Russia is actively destabilizing Ukraine, and China is making ever more assertive moves in the South and East China seas. Global uncertainty is increasing. This new period has included public discussion of the apparent partisanship of the military officer corps, the inequity of the defense burden, and the possible policy repercussions of these phenomena.

This new study is thus a timely contribution on a long-standing issue. The YouGov survey is particularly valuable because it provides something that has been comparatively rare over the decades of scholarly analysis: systematic data comparing the responses of civilians and the military across a rich array of questions. The largest study of this kind was the Triangle Institute for Security Studies (TISS) Project on the Gap between the Military and Civilian Society, which marshaled the efforts of some two dozen scholars across a range of disciplines to study the gap from all perspectives. The centerpiece of the TISS study was a one-of-a-kind dataset of survey results comparing the attitudes of "elite civilians" (defined as up-and-coming civilian leaders drawn from *Who's Who* and other similar registries), "elite military officers" (defined as up-and-coming military officers drawn from the professional military education schools—National War College, Army Command and General Staff College, and so on—that prepare such leaders for future promotion), and the general public. The

TISS survey has never been fully replicated, although portions of it have been updated in recent years (which we discuss further, below). The YouGov survey is one of the more extensive updates and sets the stage for a renewed discussion informed by valuable and current public opinion data.

This chapter will summarize the most relevant findings from the TISS survey, discuss the scholarly literature on post-9/11 civil-military relations in the United States, and then compare the YouGov survey results with those from the TISS survey to shed new light on how much the gap has changed over the last fifteen years. We conclude with some thoughts about what may be driving the changes we see, a discussion of the policy relevance of these phenomena, and some suggestions for further research.

Previous Research on the Civil-Military Gap

The TISS Study

In the 1990s, civil-military relations were often on the front pages. President Clinton had a notoriously rocky relationship with the military, and it was not unusual for pundits to voice concerns about the conservative military's loyalty to the liberal president and the American public. Tom Ricks's 1997 book, *Making the Corps,* argued that the virtues and discipline required of military personnel estranged them from what many of them considered the overweight, lazy, pot-smoking, welfare-dependent American people and that this disconnect was a dangerous problem. Debates raged over initiatives to allow homosexuals to serve openly and to allow women to serve in previously closed specialties. In response to this debate, Peter Feaver and Richard Kohn brought together a number of scholars to gather and examine the data. Was there a "gap"? In what sense? What factors were shaping it? Was it different from earlier civil-military relations? Did it matter?

The resulting study was published in 2001 and found the following: there did appear to be several "gaps," only some of which gave reason for concern.[4] There were some differences and disagreements that appeared to threaten military effectiveness and needed to be addressed. There were other gaps that did not seem to have any negative implications. There were yet other areas where no gaps appeared at all. In a number of areas, the views of military officers were more conservative than those of the political elite, but on other subjects they were actually less conservative than those of the American public. It is perhaps interesting to note that almost 70 percent of military leaders agreed (either "strongly" or "somewhat") with the idea of "placing stringent controls on the sale of handguns."[5] Military officers tended to support civil liberties at significantly higher rates than did the general public. On the other hand, military leaders were the least likely of all groups to consider protecting the environment important, and military and Active Reserve leaders were together the least likely to consider growing income inequality to be a problem. Both military and civilian elites were more likely than the general public to feel that most people could be trusted and to have trust specifically in government institutions. The military sample was more "religious" than the civilian elite, but not dramatically so. Veteran status did not appear to have affected Congressional voting patterns, and the gap did not seem to be a major driver of the size of the defense budget or the salience of the military institution in American society. However, the trends were notable, and there was a possibility for a growing gap in the understanding each group had of the others' norms, roles, and nature, which might lead to other negative consequences if nothing was done.

Although the TISS finding most noticed by the media was that military officers were significantly more Republican than the general public, the survey found that this was due largely to a decline in the number of officers who reported themselves as independent or nonpartisan, not to a decline in self-identified Democrats. This was striking because it represented a departure from the tradition of military officers avoiding partisan identification. The TISS study did not pose specific questions to discover whether officers were particularly activist or extreme in their political beliefs or behavior, and thus could not reveal anything about the specific content of the officers' partisan identification.

With respect to attitudes toward military culture and missions, and foreign policy, the opinion gaps between the military and civilian *elite* samples were quite small: about a third of each agreed that a cultural "gap" might hurt military effectiveness; only small percentages thought that a social-engineering role for the military was "important" or "very important" (although the civilians agreed at a slightly higher level than the military officers); and the groups were roughly in agreement about the military's *ability* to perform constabulary missions, although the civilians were more likely than the military to *want* to use the military for such missions. There was a very large opinion gap on the issue of allowing homosexuals to serve openly in the military: 76 percent of the military officers opposed it while more than 50 percent of both the elite and mass civilians supported it. Military and nonveteran civilian respondents were also in some disagreement about providing economic aid to poor countries (with military and veteran respondents less likely to agree to such aid) and about the relative importance of military and economic strength for American security (with civilian nonveterans more likely to rate economic strength as more important).

Another issue the TISS study addressed was that of the "familiarity gap," or the decreasing levels of personal contact and familiarity between civilians and service members. James Davis notes that "elite officers are disproportionately highly educated, middle-aged, and male. They are also somewhat more likely than the general population to be white and Catholic but differ little from it in class or regional origins."[6] James Burk argues that the military remains a highly visible and salient institution in American society, despite its declining numbers and shrinking geographic presence.[7] William Bianco and Jaime Markham find that the trend of veterans' overrepresentation in Congress, which had been evident since at least the late nineteenth century, had begun to fade in the 1970s and disappeared entirely by the mid-1990s. They argue that generational replacement alone could not explain this trend, but their study was unable to produce a clear explanation. However, they also find that veteran status has no significant impact on roll-call votes, so if the dearth of veterans in Congress has an effect on politics, it must be through other means (such as, for example, determining what issues are discussed, setting the tone of debates, or providing information).[8] Feaver and Kohn note, however, that a decline in the number of veterans in Congress could also lead to less knowledgeable oversight of the military and of national security issues.[9] Later research shows that military experience among the policy elite does matter on decisions about the use of force, but that finding includes both appointed and elected members within the "policy elite."[10]

On the very basic issue of personal familiarity with someone who has served in uniform, the TISS survey showed that an average of 63 percent of respondents had an immediate family member who had served in the military at some point. (The group with the lowest level of family connections was the civilian veteran elite, with only 50 percent reporting having a veteran in their immediate family; the military elite had the highest level, with 72 percent.) In the workplace, about 43 percent of both veteran and nonveteran civilian elites reported working with at least some current members of the military; among the military elites and the masses—both veteran and nonveteran—the numbers were closer to 90 percent. As for whether respondents believed the military got more or less respect than it deserved, between 40 percent and 50 percent of civilian elites felt that the military got less respect than it deserved, 56 percent of the military elite thought it got less respect than it deserved, and between 60 percent and 66 percent of the general public felt that Americans gave their military too little respect. In all cases, the vast majority of the remaining respondents felt that the military got about the right amount of respect; in no group did more than 10 percent think the military got more respect than it deserved.

On issues of the civil-military relationship, one problem uncovered by the TISS survey was the apparent willingness of the mass public to give the military far more influence in its dealings with political leaders and in the formation of foreign policy than many elites—including the military themselves—would find appropriate.[11] Another significant gap that emerged between the military and civilian respondents to the TISS survey was over the questions asking what military officers should do if confronted with either unethical (but legal) or unwise orders. Overwhelmingly, the military respondents felt that unethical orders ought to be resisted in various ways while the civilians felt that they ought to be carried out; the officers felt that unwise orders should be met with a smart salute while the civilians thought they should be "appealed" and "resisted." It may be relevant to note, however, that the civilian respondents, both veteran and nonveteran, were also much more likely than the military respondents to *expect* that officers would seek to avoid carrying out orders with which they disagree.

In general, however, there was a lot of agreement. Although military leaders were slightly more likely than civilians to think that media depictions of the military were hostile, the differences were not significant. While the military respondents were more likely than civilians to think that civilians did not understand the sacrifices made by service members, all groups agreed that civilians had a great deal of respect for the military. Military leaders disagreed with civilian leaders about civilian leaders' relative levels of knowledge or ignorance about military matters, but all groups agreed that civilian leaders were neither very knowledgeable nor very ignorant. Both military and civilian elites were almost equally divided on the question of whether civilian political leaders shared values with the American people. Civilian nonveteran leaders were less likely than military elites to believe that military leaders shared the American people's values, but this may be because the civilians felt they did not know what military leaders' values were. On a battery of questions about things that might hurt military effectiveness—such as lack of public trust in military leaders or the military culture becoming less masculine—military and civilian respondents generally agreed that most were not significant threats.

Post-9/11 Studies

THE PARTY GAP The TISS finding that 67 percent of "elite" officers self-identify as Republican generated a great deal of media attention and public commentary. After 9/11, the friction between the administration and high-ranking military officials contributed to scholars' desire to understand the complex relationship between military partisanship and civilian control.[12] The overall tenor of these newer studies is that fears about extreme military partisanship are overblown for several reasons, but the phenomenon still requires attention and management.

Jeremy Teigen finds that veterans' Republican slant appears to have little to do with military service or experience, as such, and more to do with their race, gender, education level, and parents' partisan identification.[13] Similarly, Golby finds that, once you condition for respondents' partisanship, opinion differences between civilian elites and military officers generally disappear on foreign policy issues.[14] In other words, Republican military officers and Republican civilian elites hold roughly the same foreign policy attitudes. Because of the small number of liberals in the senior ranks of the military, however, senior military Democrats tend to be more moderate than Democratic civilian elites. Many of the differences in opinion between military officers and civilian elites appear to be the result of the partisan composition of the force, not time spent or experience in the military.

Heidi Urben's findings support Teigen's argument that military officer partisanship is explained largely by the same demographic factors that explain partisanship among Americans in general. She also finds, as does Jason Dempsey, that military officers appear to be less partisan and activist than civilians in general, though Golby finds that Democrats enter the officer corps at lower rates than Republicans and leave at higher rates after their initial terms of service.[15] Nevertheless,

Dempsey, echoing earlier studies by David Segal, notes that the enlisted ranks are far more politically diverse than the officer corps, and enlisted service members constitute the bulk of military personnel.[16]

A recent Pew Social Trends survey also found some attitudes among post-9/11 veterans that do not seem excessively partisan: "About half of post-9/11 veterans (51 percent) say relying too much on military force creates hatred that leads to more terrorism, while four-in-ten endorse the opposite view: that overwhelming force is the best way to defeat terrorism. The views of the public are nearly identical: 52 percent say too much force leads to more terrorism, while 38 percent say using military force is the best approach." The survey also observed, "About six-in-ten post-9/11 veterans (59 percent) support the non-combat 'nation-building' role the military has taken on in Iraq and Afghanistan. The public and pre-9/11 veterans are less enthused. Just 45 percent of both groups say they think this is an appropriate role for the military."[17]

THE FAMILIARITY GAP Post-9/11 anecdotal commentaries also revived attention to the concerns identified by TISS about the familiarity gap: one, that only a tiny percentage of the population was bearing the brunt of the burden; and, two, that this meant that the general population did not care and was either unwilling or unable to exercise control and oversight over politicians' policies.[18] On the other hand, Mackubin Owens argues that "the nexus of two wars in Iraq and Afghanistan, the explosion of communications, both electronic and otherwise, and the unprecedented reliance of the military services on the reserve component arguably have made the military *more* visible to the American public than it was in the era of the draft and Vietnam" (emphasis added). He argues further that "the idea of a civil-military 'gap' that took hold in the 1990s was probably overstated then and is less salient now."[19]

The 2011 Pew Social Trends survey mentioned above found that 61 percent of Americans had an immediate family member (parent, child, sibling) who served in the military—essentially no change from the TISS study. For Americans under the age of 40, however, about 40 percent had an immediate family member who served in the armed forces, and for Americans under 30 it dropped to 33 percent.[20] One plausible inference is that the pattern of high social familiarity was a legacy of the large World War II and cold-war-era militaries, and as that generation dies off so too do its familial ties to military service. In its stead is a more tightly linked and narrower network, where families with social ties beget new families with social ties. Among veterans under the age of 40, for instance, the percentage with a veteran in their immediate family was 60 percent. Furthermore, veterans were more than twice as likely as the general public to say they had a child who had served in the military (21 percent versus 9 percent), and half of veterans had a parent who served, compared to 41 percent of the general public. However, whites were more likely than African Americans to have such a connection (68 percent versus 59 percent), and Hispanics were much less likely than either (30 percent). Those who live in the South were somewhat more likely than those in the Northeast or West to have a family member who had served (64 percent versus 56 percent versus 57 percent). Finally, Republicans were far more likely to have a family member who had served (73 percent versus 59 percent for Democrats and 56 percent for independents), and it is possible that some of these demographic and partisanship factors explain much of the military family-member effect. Perhaps most importantly, however, a finding that between 30 percent and 60 percent of the American public still report having immediate family members who have served in uniform shows the lingering generational impact of the large mobilization militaries of the mid-twentieth century. It also contrasts markedly with the claim that the US military is isolated from society or that American civilians have no contact with, or familiarity with, the military as an institution—though the demographic trend-line is inexorable and so, barring a massive mobilization, the percentage in coming years will continue to decline.

In determining whether or not this "familiarity gap" matters, the Pew study found that American adults with a veteran in the family were more likely to consider themselves more patriotic than most other Americans, more likely to consider America the "greatest country in the world," and more likely to recommend a career in the military. Interestingly, however, while having a veteran as a close relative did have some negative effect on views of how President Obama is handling his job as commander in chief (41 percent of those with veterans in their families disapprove versus 34 percent disapproval among those with no veteran family member), it had no effect on people's views of whether the wars in Iraq and Afghanistan were worth fighting, nor did it appear to make a difference in their feeling that the wars made little difference in their lives (about half of each sample agreed with that statement). Teigen finds that veteran status did not help candidates for office significantly in elections between 2000 and 2006, and to the small extent that veteran status did make a difference, it benefited Republicans and incumbents more than Democrats and challengers.[21] Donald Inbody argues that the veteran deficit in Congress is temporary: while Bianco and Markham find that veterans in Congress had fallen below their percentage of the general population for the first time, Inbody finds that veterans "remain vastly overrepresented in Congress compared to the population as a whole."[22]

The executive summary of the Pew report states, "Some 83% of all adults say that military personnel and their families have had to make a lot of sacrifices since the Sept. 11, 2001, attacks; 43% say the same about the American people. However, even among those who acknowledge this gap in burden-sharing, only 26% describe it as unfair. Seven in ten (70%) consider it 'just part of being in the military.' "[23]

The New Survey

This much is already known and discussed in the debate. What new insights does the YouGov survey add to the public conversation? While the YouGov data is especially rich and our summaries below only begin to analyze its findings, we argue that a few results are of special importance.

Comparing any two surveys across fifteen years poses challenges, and this effort was no exception. The biggest issue we faced was due to the different techniques that TISS and YouGov used to identify an individual's "military status." Although YouGov did ask all respondents whether they or a family member had served in the military since 1991, YouGov asked only certain respondents whether they were veterans themselves. In order to make apples-to-apples comparisons, we had to go with smaller sample sizes, reducing the YouGov "veteran or family member of a veteran" sample down to just "veterans." Using smaller sample sizes increases our statistical margin of error, but it also ensures that we do not falsely claim that attitudes have changed over the last fifteen years when we are actually just comparing different groups.

Moreover, because the sampling design for identifying elites was different in both surveys, we are cautious about attributing changes among elites to the effects of the last thirteen years of war. The YouGov elite sample differs from the TISS sample across several important demographic categories to a larger extent than we would have expected; for example, the YouGov elite sample, both civilian and veteran, is much more Republican and male than the TISS sample, and the magnitude of these changes is not reflected in similar changes in other polls over the last fifteen years. Consequently, it may be that the changes we note below are due to changes in the underlying attitude profile of the populations (and thus a reflection of deeper societal changes such as the impact of the long wars in Iraq and Afghanistan), but it is also possible that they are due to differences in sampling design, especially among elite respondents.

Several summary findings emerge from the comparison of the two surveys and are depicted in the figures below. First, some of the patterns observed in the TISS survey reappear in the YouGov survey. There is still a significant tendency for veterans and military personnel to identify as Republican at a higher rate than nonveteran and nonmilitary groups (fig. 4.1). Figures 4.2 and 4.3 show that Peter Feaver and Christopher Gelpi's finding about the effects of veteran status on preferences about the use of force appears to remain true, at the very least for the mass public: veterans are more reluctant about the use of force but favor fewer restrictions on its employment, whereas nonveterans support more wide-ranging use but favor greater restrictions on force levels and how they are employed.[24] There is less evidence for this difference among the elite, but that may simply be a result of the fact that the YouGov elite sample is much more Republican and male than was the TISS sample. And, though we do not reproduce every question in a figure, many of the unsurprising results of the earlier civil-military survey show up again.

Second, there are new patterns that emerge that were not evident in earlier data or stand out far more prominently now. There is a significantly higher tendency for nonveterans to respond to questions about the military with "don't know" or "no opinion." Indeed, every time that YouGov asked the nonveteran civilian masses a question about the military, there was a large and significant shift compared to the TISS study in the number of respondents who offered the "no opinion" response (see, for example, figure 4.3). Moreover, as shown in figure 4.4, there appears to be markedly less contact between civilians and military personnel, but this finding should not be taken too literally, as the questions about both work contacts and family members were worded very differently. That being said, the change is so enormous that it is unlikely to be due entirely to question wording.

The later survey indicates that, after the fighting in Afghanistan and Iraq, Americans are less likely to believe that they, as a group, are casualty-phobic, but this appears to be a matter of degree rather than a change in direction (fig. 4.5). The YouGov results also indicate that Americans have even less trust in their civilian leadership than they did at the end of the 1990s. For example, as figure 4.6 shows, respondents in the post-Afghanistan and Iraq YouGov survey were much more likely than their pre-9/11 compatriots to think that civilian

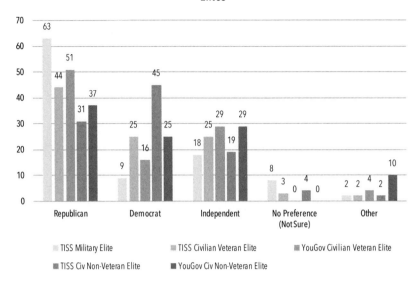

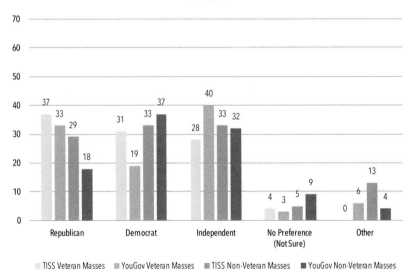

FIGURE 4.1 Party Identification

Results significant at 95 percent CI for all groups except the YouGov Elite, whose Chi-squared (2 d.f.) = 5.48 (p = 0.14).

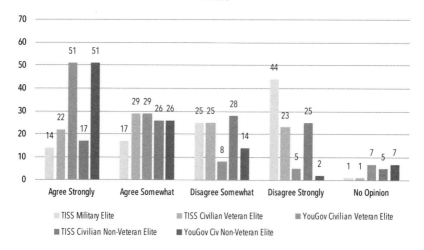

Elites

Legend:
- TISS Military Elite
- TISS Civilian Veteran Elite
- YouGov Civilian Veteran Elite
- TISS Civilian Non-Veteran Elite
- YouGov Civ Non-Veteran Elite

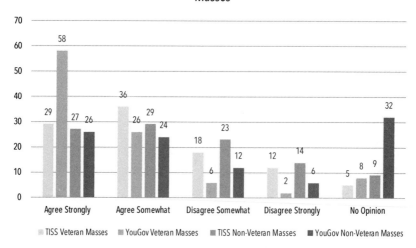

Masses

Legend:
- TISS Veteran Masses
- YouGov Veteran Masses
- TISS Non-Veteran Masses
- YouGov Non-Veteran Masses

FIGURE 4.2 Military vs. Political Goals and the Use of Force

TISS Question Text: This question asks you to indicate your position on certain propositions that are sometimes described as lessons that the United States should have learned from past experiences abroad: When force is used, military rather than political goals should determine its application.

YouGov Question Text: (same as TISS)

Results significant at 95 percent CI for all groups except the YouGov Elite, whose Chi-squared (4 d.f.) = 3.37 (p = 0.50).

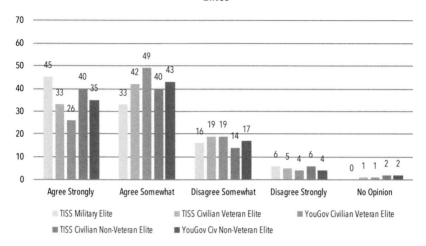

Elites

(Legend:) TISS Military Elite, TISS Civilian Veteran Elite, YouGov Civilian Veteran Elite, TISS Civilian Non-Veteran Elite, YouGov Civ Non-Veteran Elite

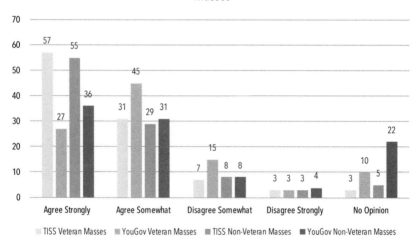

Masses

(Legend:) TISS Veteran Masses, YouGov Veteran Masses, TISS Non-Veteran Masses, YouGov Non-Veteran Masses

FIGURE 4.3 Quick and Massive Interventions vs. Gradual Escalation

TISS Question Text: This question asks you to indicate your position on certain propositions that are sometimes described as lessons that the United States should have learned from past experiences abroad: Use of force in foreign interventions should be applied quickly and massively rather than by gradual escalation.

YouGov Question Text: (same as TISS)

Results significant at 95 precent CI for all groups except the YouGov Elite, whose Chi-squared (4 d.f.) = 4.06 (p = 0.38).

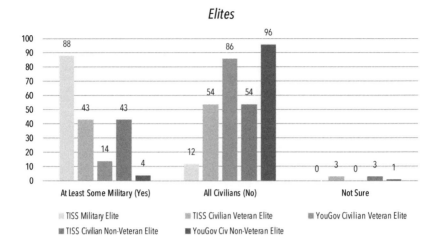

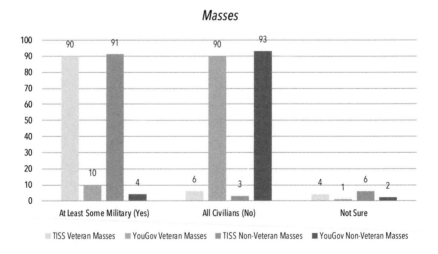

FIGURE 4.4 Workplace Contact with Military Personnel

TISS Question Text: Now consider the people you come in regular contact with at work. Are they all civilians, mostly civilians with some military, about equal civilians and military, mostly military with some civilians, or all military? For the purposes of this question, "civilian" here refers to civilians other than civil servants or contractors working for the military.

YouGov Question Text: Do you work with anyone currently in the military? (Responses in parentheses.)

Results significant at 95 percent CI for all groups except the YouGov Masses, whose Chi-squared (2 d.f.) = 5.53 (p = 0.06).

politicians should essentially let military leaders run the foreign policy show ("when force is used, military rather than political goals should determine its application"). In the TISS survey, the military elite sample sharply disagreed with that sentiment, and sizable portions of both civilian elites and masses also disagreed. For the YouGov survey, supermajorities of both elite and masses supported this claim, with the veterans discernibly more supportive than nonveterans (although again there is a large bump in "no opinion," from 8 percent to 32 percent among nonveteran civilians). Similarly, both groups of masses also are more willing to agree that the president should basically follow the advice of the generals, though the question wording is slightly different. Respondents in the later survey were also more likely than TISS respondents to believe that political leaders did *not* have the same values as the American public (fig. 4.7).

The issue of women in ground-combat units is still controversial, but less so than it was in the TISS era. All groups are likely to support women in combat roles; however, the rise in support among nonveterans has been large, while the rise in support among veterans has been quite modest (fig. 4.8). YouGov still shows strong confidence that the military has addressed racial discrimination within the military more effectively than American society has in general, but the confidence there has ebbed somewhat (fig. 4.9). The gays in the military issue is much less controversial, though there is still a noticeable veteran versus nonveteran gap even today, with nonveterans far more supportive of allowing gays to serve (fig. 4.10).

One of the disturbing findings from the TISS survey was the high numbers of the nonveterans, elite and mass, who seemed to accept improper civil-military norms—in particular, the idea that a military officer ought to resist (actively or passively) direct orders from the civilian political authorities if the officer thinks the orders unwise. It should cause significant concern that the portion of the public that accepts this view is even greater in the YouGov survey (fig. 4.11). Respondents to the YouGov survey were more likely than their earlier

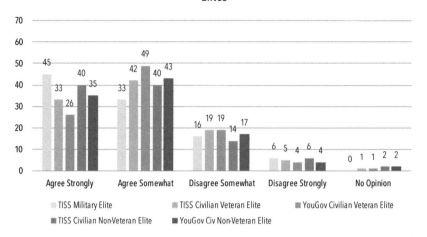

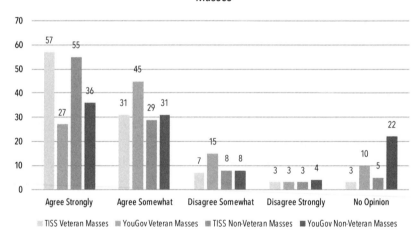

FIGURE 4.5 Perceptions of the Public's Casualty Tolerance

TISS Question Text: This question asks you to indicate your position on certain propositions that are sometimes described as lessons that the United States should have learned from past experiences abroad: The American public will rarely tolerate large numbers of US casualties in military operations.

YouGov Question Text: (same as TISS)

Results significant at 95 percent CI for all groups except the YouGov Elite, whose Chi-squared (4 d.f.) = 1.70 (p = 0.79).

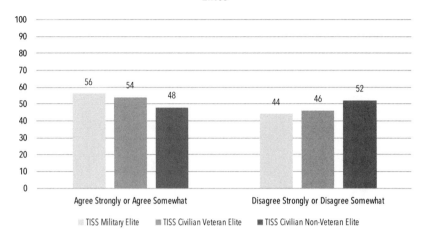

Elites

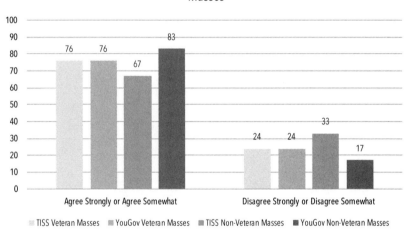

Masses

FIGURE 4.6 The President's and Military's Leadership Roles during War

TISS Question Text: This question asks for your opinion on a number of statements concerning relations between the military and senior civilian leaders: In wartime, civilian government leaders should let the military take over running the war.

YouGov Question Text: When the country is at war, the President should basically follow the advice of the generals.

Results significant at 95 percent CI for all groups except the YouGov Masses, whose Chi-squared (1 d.f.) = 2.06 (p = 0.11).

Elites

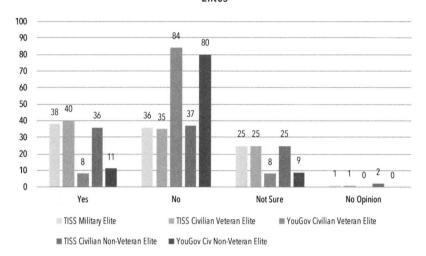

Masses

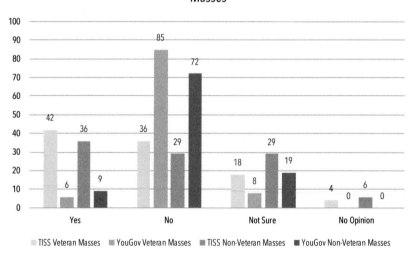

FIGURE 4.7 Political Leaders and the Public's Values

TISS Question Text: Do you think our political leaders, in general, share the same values as the American people?

YouGov Question Text: In general, do you think political leaders share the same values as the American people? (Did not include "No Opinion" response)

Results significant at 95 percent CI for all groups except the YouGov Elite, whose Chi-squared (2 d.f.) = 0.36 (p = 0.83).

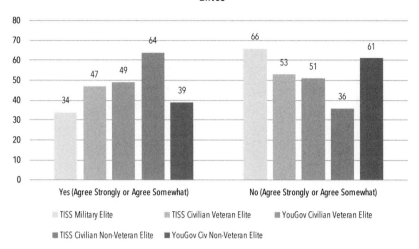

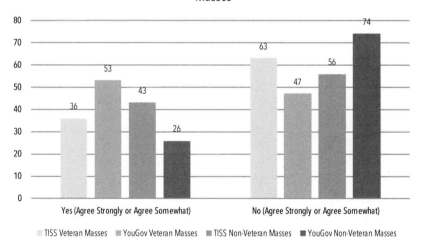

FIGURE 4.8 Allowing Women in Combat Jobs

TISS Question Text: Do you think women should be allowed to serve in all combat jobs?

YouGov Question Text: Do you agree or disagree with excluding women from the infantry? (Responses in parentheses.)

Results significant at 95 percent CI for all groups except the YouGov Elite, whose Chi-squared (1 d.f.) = 1.89 (p = 0.17).

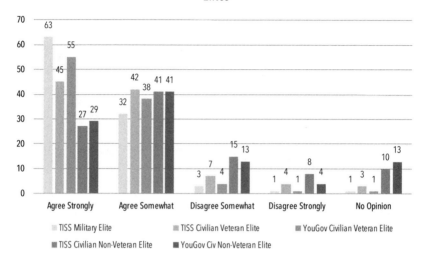

Elites

Masses

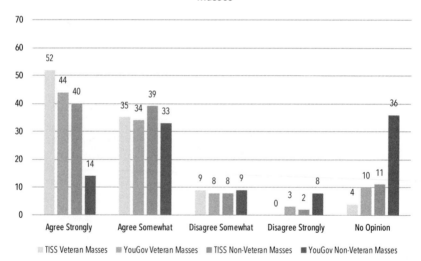

FIGURE 4.9 Racial Discrimination in the Military

TISS Question Text: The US military has done a much better job of eliminating racial discrimination within the military than American society in general.

YouGov Question Text: (same as TISS)

Results significant at 95 percent CI for all groups.

Elites

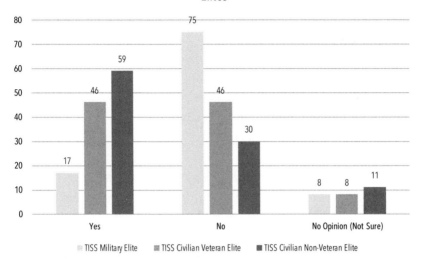

Masses

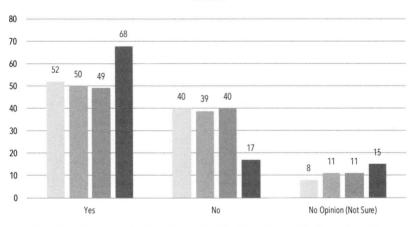

FIGURE 4.10 Allowing Homosexuals in the Military

TISS Question Text: Do you think gay men and lesbians should be allowed to serve openly in the military?

YouGov Question Text: Do you think people who are openly gay or homosexual should be allowed to serve in the US military?

Results significant at 95 percent CI for all groups.

TISS counterparts to support an officer leaking what he or she thinks are unwise decisions to the press, even though that remains the form of resistance considered least legitimate by all respondent groups.

In the TISS surveys, approximately 30 percent of respondents in each group thought it was appropriate for a military officer to retire or leave the service in protest when faced with an unwise order. This was already taken by some scholars of civil-military relations to indicate a dangerous breakdown in what they saw as a critical norm militating against resigning in protest.[25] The YouGov survey shows that this norm has broken down completely among all groups except nonveteran masses. Solid majorities of elite veterans, elite nonveterans, and mass veterans said that an officer could retire or leave the service to protest an unwise order. Additionally, veterans' attitudes regarding civil-military norms shifted on almost every question. Whereas veterans and military respondents in the TISS survey were more likely to give answers consistent with appropriate norms of civil-military relations than were their nonveteran civilian counterparts, the gap has now narrowed, with veterans becoming more likely to give problematic answers with regard to such norms. With the notable exception of resignation, however, the overwhelming majority of veterans still give "correct" answers.[26]

Given its centrality to current debates, it is interesting to compare attitudes on the defense budget. We only have one comparison question, and the wording is not the same. However, the comparison is suggestive. In the TISS survey, 60 percent of both veterans and nonveterans in the mass public disagreed with cutting defense to increase education. By contrast, in the YouGov survey, there is a gap. A 40 percent plurality of veterans is in favor of *increasing* the defense budget, compared with 21 percent of nonveterans (fig. 4.12).

Finally, in both surveys, respondents appear to believe there is a civil-military gap. In the TISS survey, fewer than 10 percent of respondents in every category believed that a "military culture and way of life that is very different from the culture and way of life of those who are

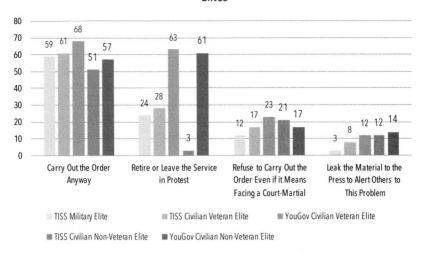

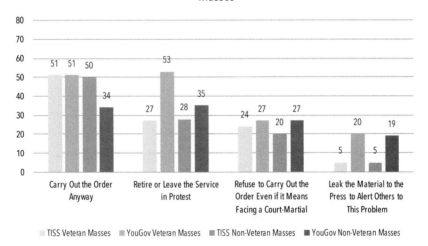

FIGURE 4.11 How Officers Should Respond to Unwise Orders

TISS Question Text: If a senior civilian Department of Defense leader asks a military officer to do something that the military officer believes is unwise, would it be appropriate for the officer to . . .

YouGov Question Text: (same as TISS)

Results significant at 95 percent CI for all groups except the YouGov Elites, which had p > 0.21 for Chi-squared tests for all responses but "Carry out the order."

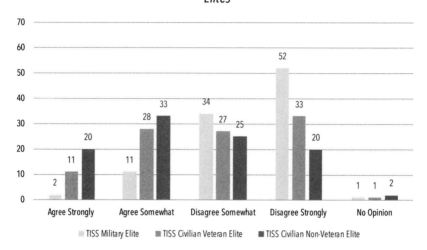

Elites

TISS Military Elite · TISS Civilian Veteran Elite · TISS Civilian Non-Veteran Elite

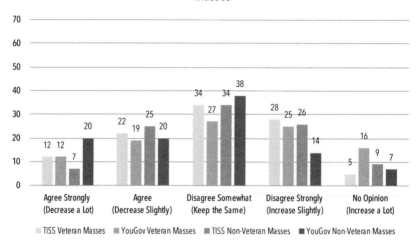

Masses

TISS Veteran Masses · YouGov Veteran Masses · TISS Non-Veteran Masses · YouGov Non-Veteran Masses

FIGURE 4.12 Changing the Federal Defense Budget

TISS Question Text: This question asks you to indicate your position on certain domestic issues: Reducing the defense budget in order to increase the federal education budget.

YouGov Question Text: Do you think the federal government should increase or decrease spending on [National Defense]? (Responses in parentheses.)

Results significant at 95 percent CI for all groups.

not in the military" was "not happening." Similarly, solid majorities in every YouGov category stated that the US military "has different values than the rest of society." The two surveys asked different questions about how to narrow it; but, because the questions were asked in the opposite way, we cannot do a direct comparison. Nevertheless, it is possible that there has been a shift in the "who should change" answer. Neither survey found strong support for the idea that the military should change to be more like society. In the more recent survey, however, the nonveteran mass public became far less likely to venture any opinion at all about whether the military should change its culture.

The perception of the gap should not be overstated, though, since respondents in both surveys believed that civilians respected the military and the military respected civilians in roughly similar proportions. Among the masses, the percentage of veterans who believe the military gets less respect than it deserves has dropped slightly, from 66 percent to 59 percent, while the percentage among nonveterans dropped thirteen points, from 60 percent to 47 percent. The percentage of elite respondents who claim that the military gets less respect than it deserves actually has grown, from 49 percent to 64 percent among veterans and from 40 percent to 50 percent among nonveterans. This fact is striking given the high level of respect afforded to the military in the survey.

Possible Drivers of the Gap

The main variants on the "gap" thesis suggest that any gaps we see are due either to a lack of military experience or a lack of personal familiarity with others who have that experience. The argument is that military training, organization, and experience produce certain attitudes, either through habituation or through a deeper understanding of the issues at stake (for example, with regard to decisions about the use of force). There is some evidence here for both of those claims. There is an enormous drop from the earlier TISS survey to the more recent one in the number of people of all groups reporting a family member in the service, and that drop is significantly greater for nonveteran groups than for veteran groups. It is important to note, however, that part of that drop comes necessarily from the fact that respondents to the TISS survey were reporting all family members who had ever served in uniform, whereas the YouGov respondents were reporting only those family members who had served since 1991.

There is also little evidence in the data to support the popular contention that elites are less likely than the mass public to have a personal connection to a veteran. Among elites, 17 percent of all respondents reported that they or a family member had served in the military since 1991, compared to 20 percent among the masses. However, 47 percent of elites report having "socialized" with someone in the military over the last three months, compared to only 35 percent of the general population. In both cases, veterans were much more likely to socialize with someone in the military than nonveterans were. More than 45 percent of mass veterans and 54 percent of elite veterans reported spending time with someone in the military, compared to 22 percent of nonveterans in the general population and 38 percent of elite nonveterans.

There does seem to be a significant decline in contact with military service members in the workplace: in 1999, about half of both veteran and nonveteran elite groups and close to 90 percent of the mass public reported that they had some workplace contact with someone currently in the military, but by 2014 those numbers had dropped to between 4 percent and 15 percent. This is a striking decline, but we must take care not to overstate its significance. Much of that drop is likely due to differences in the question wording, and it is important to note that both surveys asked about workplace contact with *current* military personnel, not veterans. In all cases, however, veterans were more likely than nonveterans to report workplace contact with military personnel, suggesting that the concentration phenomenon seen in the higher tendency of military families to produce volunteers also extends to postservice workplace selection.[27] So there is some evidence of declining familiarity, but it probably is not as drastic as some critics claim or as this one question at first glance suggests.[28] Nevertheless, all the numbers above are markedly less than the 62 percent of individuals who reported having a veteran in the family in the TISS sample and the 61 percent who did the same in the 2011 Pew survey. Absent a major expansion of the military in the future, demographic trends make the decline in the number of Americans with some kind of military connection inexorable.

Another piece of evidence indicating support for the familiarity gap argument is the surprisingly large increase in the number of "don't know" and "no opinion" responses from nonveterans when asked about issues related to the military. Although Americans typically are willing to venture answers to survey questions even on topics with which they have little familiarity,[29] 25 percent to 30 percent of the nonveteran masses consistently chose not to give an answer when the YouGov survey asked them a question about the military. Table 4.1 shows that this surprising unwillingness to answer questions about the military is strongly related to respondents' social contact with those in uniform. All nonveteran respondents appear to be slightly less willing to offer opinions on military matters than civilians in the TISS study were, but YouGov respondents who had not interacted socially with someone in the military during the last thirty days were more than twice as likely to offer "no opinion" than those who had. A similar pattern holds for social contact with the military over the previous three months.

The YouGov survey does not provide an explanation for why respondents who do not interact with members of the military would be so unwilling to answer questions about the military. One plausible explanation might be that nonveteran citizens know very little about the military and know that they know very little. Americans have less direct contact with service members, but portrayals of the military in movies or on television are common. It might be that these depictions of the military do little to bridge the gap and that they instead only highlight the fact that military service has little to do with the

Have you socialized with someone in the military or their spouse in the past 30 days?	Yes	No
Do you agree or disagree with [or have "no opinion" of] the following statements?	*Percent responding "No Opinion"*	
An effective military depends on a very structured organization with a clear chain of command.	6%	22%
Military symbols—like uniforms and medals and military traditions—like ceremonies and parades are necessary to build morale, loyalty, and comradery in the military.	8%	23%
Even though women can serve in the military, the military should remain basically masculine, dominated by male values and characteristics.	11%	24%
The US military has done a much better job of eliminating racial discrimination within the military than American society in general.	25%	39%
Even though women can serve in the military, the military should remain basically masculine, dominated by male values and characteristics.	11%	24%
The US military has done a much better job of eliminating racial discrimination within the military than American society in general.	25%	39%
Even in a high tech era, people in the military have to have characteristics like strength, toughness, physical courage, and the willingness to make sacrifices.	4%	18%
The bonds and sense of loyalty that keep a military unit together under the stress of combat are fundamentally different than the bonds and loyalty that organizations try to develop in the business world.	11%	26%
Since military life is a young person's profession, the chance to retire with a good pension at a young age is very important in the military.	13%	24%
On most military bases there are company stores, childcare centers, and recreational facilities right on the base. It is very important to keep these things on military bases in order to keep a sense of identity in the military community.	11%	27%
Military leaders care more about the people under their command than leaders in the non-military world care about people under them.	23%	31%
AVERAGE	*12%*	*26%*

TABLE 4.1 Social Contact with the Military and Norms among Non-Veteran Civilians

lives of average Americans. It is interesting to note that, in the YouGov sample, only the nonveteran masses were less likely to think that military leaders shared the same values as the American people. All other groups were more likely to believe that members of the military shared their values, but the nonveteran subsample moved from certainty to "no opinion." Similarly, when asked "Do you think the U.S. military has different values than the rest of American society?" the number of nonveteran masses answering "no opinion" climbed considerably compared to TISS, while the number giving either a yes or a no both dropped significantly. Many nonveteran civilians in the general population appear to think that that they do not understand the military enough to answer, and they are not sure whether members of the military are like them or not. If this is the true explanation and current trends continue, the decreased contact between nonveteran civilians and increasingly smaller numbers of troops will only widen and deepen this lack of understanding.

It is tempting to conclude that any gaps we see between veterans and nonveterans are all due to this familiarity or experience gap, but the data imply that there may be other factors driving the differences. Most prominently, these gaps could be driven largely by partisanship. This was the conclusion one of us reached in earlier analysis,[30] and there are indications that this may be what this data is showing as well. Because our sample sizes were too small to yield a sufficiently high degree of confidence, we offer this as a plausible alternative hypothesis rather than a firm finding. Yet, the evidence is suggestive. For example, in closer analysis of several of the questions, we find that if we control for partisanship, the veteran-nonveteran differences practically disappear—that is, veterans who are Democrats are more like Democrat nonveterans than they are like Republican veterans. Figures 4.13 and 4.14 are illustrative of this pattern, showing civil-military and partisan differences on an additive scale of four questions related to the Powell Doctrine. Figure 4.13 shows that veterans and nonveterans do hold different views about how and when to use

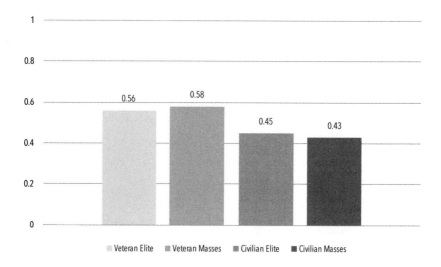

FIGURE 4.13 Mean Support on the Powell Doctrine Scale (by Civil-Military Category)

YouGov Question Text: a) Military force should be used only in pursuit of the goal of total victory; b) Use of force in foreign interventions should be applied quickly and massively; c) When force is used, military rather than political goals should determine its application; d) Public will not tolerate large numbers of US casualties in military operations. (Additive scale runs from 0 to 1, with 1 signifying more support for the Powell Doctrine.)

Results significant at 95 percent CI between both veteran and civilian groups.

military force; both elite and mass veterans score higher on the scale than nonveterans. However, figure 4.14 shows that there are not necessarily monolithic military or civilian positions on issues and that partisan differences are often much larger than civil-military differences.

This general pattern holds for opinions about the appropriate way to use force, and also shows up in opinions about whether people would want a child of theirs to join the military. This finding does not hold for every question—for example, it does not explain the responses to questions about proper norms of civil-military relations (but on

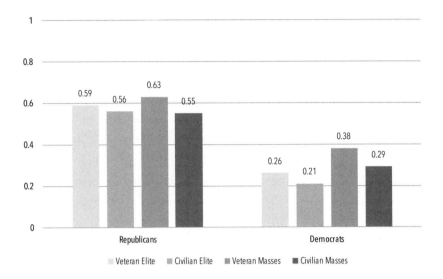

FIGURE 4.14 Mean Support on the Powell Doctrine Scale (by Civil-Military Category within Partisan Groups

YouGov Question Text: a) Military force should be used only in pursuit of the goal of total victory; b) Use of force in foreign interventions should be applied quickly and massively; c) When force is used, military rather than political goals should determine its application; d) Public will not tolerate large numbers of US casualties in military operations. (Additive scale runs from 0 to 1, with 1 signifying more support for the Powell Doctrine.)

Results significant at 95 percent CI between partisan groups, but not within civil-military categories inside partisan groups.

those questions the veteran-nonveteran difference itself shrank significantly). It is, however, a strong contender for explaining a great deal of the apparent divergence of opinions between veterans and nonveterans. Of course, finding that partisanship mediates the civil-military gap does not mean that the civil-military gap is nonexistent or irrelevant. Rather, it underscores the importance of partisan differences even inside the military and, in particular, the propensity of the military to draw and retain more Republicans than Democrats in its ranks.

Moreover, it is highly likely that both of these processes—the declining level of contact and the increasing partisan divide—are happening at the same time. For example, Republican civilians in the general population are almost twice as likely as Democrats to report socializing with someone in the military in the last three months (33 percent versus 16 percent). Among elites, the difference is smaller but still considerable (40 percent versus 29 percent). Much of the partisanship difference may be due to differences in demographics,[31] which is related to the issue of military families being more likely to produce volunteers. The important policy question then becomes, to what extent are any of these trends potential problems for policymaking at the top, for Congressional oversight and lawmaking, for the quality and sustainability of the force, and for the maintenance of the support of the American people for the military establishment?

Policy Implications and Responses

Perhaps one of our most striking overall conclusions from the new study is how many of the results resemble the ones we found fifteen years ago despite the intervening experience of more than a decade of intense combat operations. We cannot say for certain whether this is a sign that the gap was unchanged in the interval or whether the gap did change with 9/11 but then had returned to previous conditions by 2014. Regardless, some of the concerns and the remedies of that earlier study are still relevant today, while others may require a new approach.

FAMILIARITY GAP The main concerns with a familiarity gap are that those who have no experience with, or connection to, the military may not understand the logic or limits of the use of force. Consequently, those with no "skin in the game" might be unable to make knowledgeable cost-benefit calculations about the use of force and might therefore be prone to using force unwisely. Like the TISS study, the YouGov survey cannot answer the normative question about whether the use of force in a given case is appropriate or whether it is likely to succeed; as Feaver and Gelpi made clear, the data could at best only speak to attitude and frequency differences, not the specific wisdom or folly of different attitudes or frequencies. Moreover, although there is still some support in this data for their finding on a veteran-nonveteran gap in preferences over the use of force—and Bryan Groves with Gelpi and Feaver show that this pattern extends well past the 9/11 era—we are mindful of Golby's argument that this effect is heavily mediated by partisanship rather than experience in uniform.[32] Likewise, the YouGov data do not allow us to determine whether those with less personal contact with veterans are more likely to support the use of military force; the only indicator is that a large percentage of the population considers the sacrifices borne by the uniformed services to be "just part of being in the military."[33] That being said, the YouGov data suggest that large numbers of Americans still report having family, work, or social contact with both veterans and active-duty military members. However, the majority of those contacts are almost certainly older veterans from the World War II, Korea, and Vietnam eras, and the trajectory of familiarity is on a steep decline. Given our finding that civilians who report no interaction with the military are less likely to even answer questions about the military, declining contact with the military potentially could become a cause for concern in the future. This indicates a need for both significantly more study on the potential effects of a familiarity gap and initiatives geared toward mitigating the extent to which a small, volunteer military becomes isolated from its host society.

PARTISANSHIP GAP The earlier concern with an officer corps that self-identified as Republican was that a Democratic administration might have more difficulty trusting and being trusted by its top military leadership, and that this could impede policymaking in dangerous ways. The YouGov survey cannot answer the question of whether this dynamic at the top does, in fact, happen, but it does demonstrate that the partisanship gap is persistent and showing no signs of moderation.

DEFERENCE AND ENTITLEMENT We do perceive a troubling level of deference to the military on the side of the civilians and feelings of entitlement on the side of the military. This increased sense of entitlement manifests itself most among veterans and civilians in the general public, with larger gaps on questions about respect for the military, spending on national defense, and deference to the military during war. While some deference to expertise and experience is appropriate, it is unhealthy for civilian policymakers to feel like they cannot question military officers and potentially even more unhealthy for the public to put more trust in the political judgments of its military officers than its elected officials. Moreover, because of the levels of public trust in the military, both parties have an incentive to use military officers as policy salesmen, further undermining the norm of an apolitical military. The United States benefits from a large pool of civilian and academic expertise on defense and security issues, and it is highly problematic for civil-military relations if the public identifies uniformed personnel as uniquely qualified and trustworthy to make policy judgments in those areas.

PROFESSIONALISM We found a significant deterioration in what are considered traditional norms of civil-military relations, including a tendency among officers to feel that they should resist orders they consider unwise and potentially even utilize the separation of powers and the availability of the press as ways to undermine policies with which they disagree. Civilian leaders' desire to obtain the public support of trusted senior military leaders also creates perverse incentives for senior officers to use the threat of public opposition or resignation to extract policy concessions from elected officials. While the authors emphasize that majorities of officers still support the traditional norms, the dissenting minorities are large and appear to be growing. This, added to the above concerns about partisanship and deference, may be grounds for concern about the civil-military relationship at the policymaking levels.

Recommendations

First, institutions of professional military education (PME) need to place renewed emphasis on professional norms of civil-military relations and, in particular, to reestablish the norm that military officers ought not to act as, or even appear to be, partisan figures. We grant that there is a reasonable debate to be had over the extent to which military officers are, should, or must be political actors since they are necessarily involved in the bureaucratic politics of policymaking. We are not recommending that that debate be silenced. However, we submit that there is a crucial distinction between being political and being partisan and that the latter is undesirable, whatever the former may be.

Second, scholars, journalists, and the public must call out both politicians who hide behind military officers and retired officers who use the public's respect of those in uniform to weigh in on partisan debates. While there is no obvious policy solution to this problem, the development and promulgation of norms might help rein it in.

Third, it is important not to exacerbate the otherwise natural tendency for the military to draw heavily from certain regions and demographics. It is an almost universal dynamic that parental work experience familiarizes children with that job and essentially does a significant portion of the recruiter's job for him. But accession into the military is very different from other professions. There is almost no lateral entry, and the military occupies a privileged place in the political discourse and in the competition for societal resources. Moreover, as we have seen in the past decade-plus, the differential burden on the military posed by the high operations tempo of recent wars versus that imposed on civilians can itself become a political problem for the country. The problem can be exacerbated by a temptation in the military to concentrate recruiting efforts on the most promising demographics. One way to address this issue is to ensure that recruiting staff are sent to currently "underserved" areas, such as large cities. At the same time, it would be necessary to change recruiters' incentive structures: quality ought to be emphasized over quantity.

Another solution that has been proposed is to reintroduce some form of universal (or near-universal) military service via a draft in the belief that this will "force" the elites to have more "skin in the game," thus producing more cautious foreign policy. Proponents of compulsory service also claim it will ensure that most Americans either serve in uniform or know someone who has. We view compulsory military service as a cure that is worse then the disease, for the following reasons. First, we note that the current all-volunteer force is actually more representative in many ways than the draft force was at any time in the country's history except during World War II.[34] Second, there is very little evidence in the scholarly literature to indicate that having any form of conscription makes a country less likely to use its military forces.[35] Third, the expense of such a solution—even were it deemed constitutional—would be astronomical. The US military currently accesses a little over 250,000 people per year (including all active, reserve, and National Guard components); the cohort in the United States reaching age 18 every year is more than 4 million.[36] Even assuming that large numbers would be disqualified on grounds of conscience or disability, that is still millions of people who would have to be clothed, fed, housed, trained, and paid some kind of stipend every year. A draft lottery targeting only part of the population obviously would be less costly, but the smaller the drafted force became the less it would address the issue of the civil-military gap. Furthermore, the effects of this on the deployability and capability of the US forces would likely be devastating. As a country, we have come to expect a level of military proficiency that minimizes casualties—among our forces and among innocent civilians—that is only achievable with the highly professionalized force we have today. No draft army could fight to the standards the country and the international community have come to demand of the all-volunteer force. We agree that there are some grounds for concern in the trends identified above, and that some of those trends are due to a declining veteran population, but that veteran bulge was due to large-scale mobilization in the mid-twentieth century, not to a draft as such. The vast majority of the United States' history has been characterized by a military that constituted less than 1 percent of the population, and none of these problems are new.[37]

A peacetime draft is neither politically feasible today nor is it the norm in American history. However, fighting two long ground wars in Iraq and Afghanistan while relying solely on volunteers is also unique in American history. The shift to the Total Force Policy following the Vietnam War was designed in part to make it difficult for political leaders to use the military for a prolonged conflict without also expending the political capital to mobilize the country in support of the war. The designers believed that the draft had shielded the political leadership from the blowback that would have occurred if they had had to mobilize the Reserves (which came from an older cohort with greater political clout). The Total Force Policy succeeded in the sense of reducing the need for a supplemental wartime draft and obliging leaders to mobilize the Guard and Reserves during these conflicts. But in so doing, it required the Guard and Reserves to mobilize on a sustained basis in a way that no one expected. And, as renewed debates about the draft show, the mobilization of the Guard and Reserves did not settle the underlying questions about the degree of political and societal support for the conflicts. Arguably, this reliance made the US military extremely effective tactically and operationally, but it also may have contributed to the growing sense of entitlement among those who served. While the benefits of a supplemental wartime draft may not outweigh its costs in terms of the exceptional competence of the AVF, now is the time to debate how to mobilize the US military and the population to face prolonged conflicts in the future.

Conclusion

This review has just scratched the surface of the YouGov survey, but it suffices to demonstrate the richness of the data and the potential insights they offer into civil-military relations. Far more research is needed into both what factors are causing these trends and what effects the trends may have on policymaking, civil-military relations, and national security as a whole. Here, we have noted that some veteran-nonveteran divisions are growing while others have practically disappeared; some indicate problems for American civil-military relations, and others may be harmless. But, most importantly, we have noted that the issues involved cannot be reduced to the simplistic claim that the all-volunteer force is dangerously isolated from American society. There are some ways in which the all-volunteer force is demographically and culturally similar to society, others in which, for appropriate functional reasons, it is different, and still others where its differences may be due simply to the fact that this profession, like many others, tends to draw people with a certain profile. While it is always appropriate for a society to have lively discussions of the relationship between citizenship and military service, and of the role of the expert in policymaking, it is crucial that those debates recognize the complexity of the forces at work and the trade-offs involved. The YouGov survey has given us the first opportunity since the landmark TISS study to see how more than ten years of war have affected the relationship between the American people and their military, and we find that the subject is just as important to national security and defense policy today as it was fifteen years ago.

Notes

1.   For recent prominent examples in the media, see James Fallows, "The Tragedy of the American Military," *Atlantic,* January/February 2015,

http://www.theatlantic.com/magazine/archive/2015/01/the-tragedy-of-the
-american-military/383516 and Karl W. Eikenberry and David M. Kennedy,
"Americans and Their Military, Drifting Apart," *New York Times,* 26 May
2013, http://www.nytimes.com/2013/05/27/opinion/americans-and-their
-military-drifting-apart.html. For the older literature, see Thomas Ricks,
"The Widening Gap between the Military and Society," *Atlantic,* July 1997,
http://www.theatlantic.com/magazine/archive/1997/07/the-widening-gap
-between-military-and-society/306158/, Lindsay P. Cohn, "The Evolution of
the Civil-Military 'Gap' Debate," paper prepared for the Triangle Institute
Security Studies Project on the Gap between Military and Civilian Society,
1999, available at lpcohn.squarespace.com/storage/Cohn_Evolution%20of
%20Gap%20Debate%201999.pdf, and Peter D. Feaver and Richard H. Kohn,
eds., *Soldiers and Civilians: The Civil-Military Gap and American National
Security,* Cambridge, MA: MIT Press, 2001.

2. Russell F. Weigley, "The American Civil-Military Cultural Gap: A Historical
    Perspective, Colonial Times to the Present," in Feaver and Kohn, Soldiers
    and Civilians, 215–46; Thomas S. Langston, *Uneasy Balance: Civil-Military
    Relations in Peacetime America since 1783,* Baltimore, MD: Johns Hopkins
    University Press, 2003.

3. Richard H. Kohn, *The United States Military under the Constitution of the
    United States, 1789–1989,* New York: New York University Press, 1991.

4. The TISS project resulted in multiple publications, including Feaver and
    Kohn's 2001 edited volume *Soldiers and Civilians,* a special edition of the
    journal *Armed Forces and Society* (27.2, 2001), a special section in the *Journal
    of Strategic Studies* (26.2, 2003), and Peter D. Feaver and Christopher Gelpi's
    Choosing Your Battles: American Civil-Military Relations and the Use of Force,
    Princeton, NJ: Princeton University Press, 2005.

5. Ole Holsti, "Of Chasms and Convergences: Attitudes and Beliefs of Civilians
    and Military Elites at the Start of a New Millennium," p. 49, in Feaver and
    Kohn, *Soldiers and Civilians,* pp. 15–100.

6. James Davis, "Attitudes and Opinions among Senior Military Officers and
    a US Cross-section, 1998–99," p. 122, in Feaver and Kohn, *Soldiers and
    Civilians,* pp. 101–28.

7. James Burk, "The Military's Presence in American Society, 1950–2000," in
    Feaver and Kohn, *Soldiers and Civilians,* pp. 247–74.

8. William T. Bianco and Jaime Markham, "Vanishing Veterans: The Decline of
    Military Experience in the U.S. Congress," in Feaver and Kohn, *Soldiers and
    Civilians,* pp. 275–88.

9. Feaver and Kohn, *Soldiers and Civilians,* p. 464.

10. Feaver and Gelpi, *Choosing Your Battles.*

11. Davis, "Attitudes among Senior Military Officers," p. 121.

12. Jeremy Teigen, "Veterans' Party Identification, Candidate Affect, and Vote Choice in the 2004 U.S. Presidential Election," *Armed Forces and Society* 33.3 (2007), pp. 414–37; Jeremy Teigen, "Invoking Military Credentials in Congressional Elections, 2000–2006," in Derek Reveron and Judith Hicks Stiehm, eds., *Inside Defense: Understanding the U.S. Military in the 21st Century*, New York: Palgrave Macmillan, 2008, pp. 115–25; Jason K. Dempsey, *Our Army: Soldiers, Politics, and American Civil-Military Relations*, Princeton, NJ: Princeton University Press, 2009; Heidi A. Urben, "Civil-Military Relations in a Time of War: Party, Politics, and the Profession of Arms," PhD dissertation, Georgetown University, 2010; James Golby, "Duty, Honor, Party: Ideology, Institutions, and the Use of Force," PhD dissertation, Stanford University, 2011; James Golby, Kyle Dropp, and Peter D. Feaver, "Military Campaigns: Veterans' Endorsements and Presidential Elections," Center for New American Security, 2012, http://www.cnas.org/files/documents /publications/CNAS_MilitaryCampaigns_GolbyDroppFeaver.pdf.

13. Teigen, "Veterans' Party Identification."

14. Golby, "Duty, Honor, Party."

15. Urben, "Civil-Military Relations"; Golby, "Duty, Honor, Party"; Dempsey, *Our Army*.

16. David R. Segal et al., "Attitudes of Entry-Level Enlisted Personnel: Promilitary and Politically Mainstreamed," in Feaver and Kohn, *Soldiers and Civilians*, 163–212.

17. Pew Research Center, "War and Sacrifice in the Post-9/11 Era: The Military-Civilian Gap," October 5, 2011, http://www.pewsocialtrends.org/2011/10/05 /war-and-sacrifice-in-the-post-911-era.

18. Kathy Roth-Douquet and Frank Schaeffer, *AWOL: The Unexcused Absence of America's Upper Classes from the Military—and How It Hurts Our Country*, New York: HarperCollins, 2006; Richard M. Wrona, "A Dangerous Separation: The Schism between the American Society and Its Military," *World Affairs Journal* 169.1 (2006), 25–38; Mark Thompson, "The Other 1%," *Time*, 21 November 2011; Fallows, "Tragedy of the American Military."

19. Mackubin T. Owens, *US Civil-Military Relations after 9/11: Renegotiating the Civil-Military Bargain*, New York: Continuum, 2011, p. 129.

20. Pew Research Center, "The Military-Civilian Gap: Fewer Family Connections," November 23, 2011, http://www.pewsocialtrends.org/2011 /11/23/the-military-civilian-gap-fewer-family-connections.

21. Teigen, "Invoking Military Credentials," p. 122.

22. Donald S. Inbody, "Partisanship and the Military: Voting Patterns of the American Military," p. 141, in Reveron and Stiehm, *Inside Defense*, pp. 139–50; Bianco and Markham, "Vanishing Veterans."

23. Pew Research Center, "War and Sacrifice."

24. Feaver and Gelpi, *Choosing Your Battles.*
25. Richard H. Kohn, "The Danger of Militarization in an Endless 'War' on Terrorism," *Journal of Military History* 73.1 (2009), 177–208.
26. Cf. David S. Cloud and Eric Schmitt, "More Retired Generals Call for Rumsfeld Resignation," *New York Times,* 14 April 2006, A1.
27. David R. Segal and Mady W. Segal, "America's Military Population," *Population Bulletin* 59.4 (2004).
28. For example, Fallows, "Tragedy of the American Military."
29. Philip E. Converse, "The Nature of Belief Systems in Mass Publics," in David Apter, ed., *Ideology and Discontent,* New York: Free Press, 1964.
30. Golby, "Duty, Honor, Party."
31. Urben, "Civil-Military Relations"; Teigen, "Veterans' Party Identification."
32. Feaver and Gelpi, *Choosing Your Battles;* Bryan Groves, Christopher Gelpi, and Peter D. Feaver, "Speak Softly and Carry a Big Stick (Part II)? Veterans in the Political Elite and the American Use of Force," working paper, 2014, building on Christopher Gelpi and Peter D. Feaver, "Speak Softly and Carry a Big Stick? Veterans in the Political Elite and the American Use of Force," *American Political Science Review* 96.4 (2002), 779–93; Golby, "Duty, Honor, Party."
33. Pew Research Center, "War and Sacrifice."
34. Segal and Segal, "America's Military Population," pp. 24, 37.
35. J. Pickering, "Dangerous Drafts? A Time-Series, Cross-national Analysis of Conscription and the Use of Military Force, 1946–2001," *Armed Forces and Society* 37.1 (2011), 119–40.
36. Lawrence Kapp, "Recruiting and Retention: An Overview of FY2011 and FY2012 Results for Active and Reserve Component Enlisted Personnel," Congressional Research Service, May 10, 2013, https://www.fas.org/sgp/crs/natsec/RL32965.pdf; U.S. Dept. of Commerce., U.S. Census Bureau, "Annual Estimates of the Resident Population by Single Year of Age and Sex for the United States and Puerto Rico Commonwealth: April 1, 2010 to July 1, 2013," http://factfinder.census.gov/faces/tableservices/jsf/pages/productview.xhtml?src=bkmk.
37. Segal and Segal, "America's Military Population," fig. 1.

CHAPTER 5

Public Opinion, Military Justice, and the Fight against Terrorism Overseas

Benjamin Wittes and Cody Poplin

Of late, public opinion concerning America's wars—and its confrontation with terrorists overseas—has been volatile and internally conflicted. Americans want to see tough action against our enemies, but we are also suspicious that such action is not doing any good and pessimistic about the prospects for success of military and covert endeavors. The military is by far the most trusted institution in American life, and Americans clearly believe in giving the troops a relatively free hand. But that feeling coexists with real concerns that—across a range of areas—our policies have not made us secure, despite what leaders of the military may say.

The result is solid, sometimes overwhelming, public support for actions such as drone strikes,[1] a new authorization for the use of force against ISIS,[2] detentions at Guantanamo Bay,[3] harsh interrogation methods,[4] surveillance of public spaces,[5] and military trials.[6] But at the same time, even as 63 percent of Americans approve of the campaign against ISIS, 58 percent say the campaign is not going well.[7] More than 60 percent say we are not prepared for a major cyber attack, a problem more than 90 percent of those polled describe as at least somewhat "serious."[8] And while 72 percent of respondents in one poll say the government is doing "well" in reducing the threat of terrorism, 64 percent of Americans are nonetheless at least somewhat worried that another terrorist attack will take place soon inside the United States. What is more, those saying our counterterrorism policies do not go far enough outpoll those saying they go too far by double digits.[9]

Public opinion on these matters also fluctuates enormously in response to events, the most recent of which tends to play an outsized role in conditioning attitudes. For example, while today people worry that government counterterrorism policies are not aggressive enough, before ISIS began beheading people, when the media were more focused on the Edward Snowden revelations, the public believed by an even wider margin that they went too far.[10] And this wavering of confidence, in turn, followed a long period in which the public was enthusiastic about even relatively intrusive surveillance policies. More generally, public hawkishness increased substantially after ISIS began its campaign of wanton violence; whereas people were previously war weary and disinclined to favor renewed involvement in the Middle East, ISIS's barbarism left Americans angry and favoring military action.[11]

A number of factors contribute to both the volatility and the conflicting feelings evident in public opinion data about military and intelligence activities. One is that there is a causal relationship between people's worry about terrorism and their support for strong measures against it; that is, the pessimism people feel about policy outcomes is causing the support for strong action. People are worried about terrorist attacks, so they want to see action to reduce the likelihood of their taking place.

At the same time, the vacillation and contradictions also reflect a competing tension in public attitudes, as the perceived need to do something about threats clashes with a certain fatalism and war weariness born of years of conflict that has not ended with decisive victory and whose results have fallen well short of the promises made by war proponents.

Another related factor is the genuine intractability of the long-term, difficult problems we employ military and covert tools to address. It just is not clear with respect to these problems what the appropriate or optimal use of these tools looks like, so mixed feelings are often a sign of good thinking.

Finally, there is the issue of what, at any given moment, is the most salient threat in the public's mind. The Snowden revelations came long after the fear associated with 9/11 had faded, so people looked at aggressive government surveillance programs and saw them as a threat. By contrast, after ISIS reared its head, people's sense of the threat from government receded as they looked to the military to conduct operations against a force of particular barbarity.

All of these factors contribute to the apparently split personality of Americans with respect to their attitudes about confronting overseas terrorists. Yet the data collected for this project suggests another factor: one that is less discussed but may lie beneath the inconstant and inconsistent attitudes towards military tools for counterterrorism. Specifically, the data suggest both that Americans think they know a great deal more than they actually do about the military and that the public expects wildly inconsistent things from it in general. More particularly, the public has a weak understanding of matters related to justice, crime, and law as these things pertain to the military's chain of command and unique institutional structures. The result, we suggest in the discussion that follows, is that the public is ill positioned to develop solid, stable, or even internally consistent views of how the military and the intelligence community might reasonably be used in a complex conflict that integrates elements of traditional warfare with elements we traditionally associate more with law enforcement and justice.

A Trusted but Isolated Military

Americans express a high degree of confidence in the military. It is the only government institution with a consistently positive approval rating; a full 78 percent of Americans expressed confidence in the military in a June 2011 Gallup poll, for example.[12] Americans also believe (64 percent) that members of the military have a "great deal of respect for civilian society" (CM2T 50).[13]

But this high regard translates only oddly into trust as most people would understand the term. A majority (54 percent) of poll respondents, for example, also believe that the picture this very trusted organization is giving the American public about the war in Afghanistan is inaccurate (CM1T 37). Americans also believe (61 percent), somewhat paradoxically, that our "lack of trust in uniformed leaders of the military hurts effectiveness" (CM2T 56). In other words, more Americans than not seem to think that their own attitudes hurt military effectiveness. Perhaps most dramatically, only 8 percent of Americans believe that modern wars are winnable and that the military is winning them (CM1T 45). So while people trust the military and 85 percent "have confidence in the ability of our military to perform well in wartime" (CM2T 50), people also think the military is inflating its successes and that its fundamental project is not accomplishable. It's a strange kind of trust.

And perhaps oddly, even as they express it, American civilians are also more isolated from the military than ever before. No longer do America's wars consume society in general. The majority of Americans will never spend a great deal of time with a US active duty soldier or a combat veteran of a foreign war. Rather, relatively small segments of society, which increasingly stand apart from the general population, do the lion's share of fighting America's wars.

How separate is the military culture? Consider that during the past decade of warfare only about one half of one percent of the US population has been on active military duty at any given time. According to a 2011 Pew poll, some 84 percent of post-9/11 veterans say the public does not understand the problems faced by those in the military or their families. The public agrees, though by a less lopsided majority: 71 percent. In that same poll, only a quarter of Americans said they were following the news of the wars closely; half of the public says the wars made little difference in their lives. However, even among those who acknowledge the gap in who has carried the burden of war, only

26 percent describe it as unfair. Seven in ten consider it "just part of being in the military."[14]

Meanwhile, only 19 percent of Americans say that they themselves or a member of their immediate families have served in the military since 1991 (CM2T 1). When the same question was asked about military service after September 11, 2001, only 16 percent of Americans said that either they or a close member of their family had served. Of those with college degrees, the number was even smaller, a mere 12 percent (CM2T 2).

A 2011 Pew poll found that "veterans are more than twice as likely as members of the general public to say they have a son or daughter who has served (21 percent versus 9 percent),[15] leading Amy Schafer of the Council on Foreign Relations to wonder whether America is currently creating its own "warrior caste."[16] As a nation, America is at war. As a people, Americans are not.

Elsewhere, we find even more evidence of the marginalization of America's military forces from its civilian life. When asked if they currently worked with anyone who was in the active-duty military, only 8 percent of Americans say yes (CM2T 3). A mere 36 percent work with a veteran (CM2T 4). In fact, American society is so estranged from its warfighters that in the last year, only half of Americans have even socialized with a service member or their spouse on a single occasion (CM2T 8).

Author Rebecca Frankel told James Fallows of the *Atlantic* that part of the reason she based her book *War Dogs* on the dog-and-handler teams in the US armed forces is that dogs are one of the few commonalities left between America's troops and the public.[17] In the introduction of her book, she writes, "When we cannot make that human connection over war, when we cannot empathize or imagine the far-off world of a combat zone . . . these military working dogs are a bridge over the divide."[18] "You don't have to walk a mile down a bomb-laden road in Kandahar to know the pull of devotion of a dog, or the sadness you feel when it becomes clear that the four-legged member of your family is fading and it is time to say goodbye," she concludes.[19]

That may be true, but it is a remarkable statement that our closest affiliation with modern combat—with its arcane missions in mysterious places—is found in our relationship with our pets. It should be troubling that someone who spent years covering America's modern wars on the front lines believes that soldier and civilian are most closely aligned in their devotion, not necessarily to one another, but to their four-legged friends.

Americans express concern about the effects of an isolated military, even if they do not clearly recognize that we have one. When asked whether the military is isolated from American society, respondents are split, with 33 percent answering yes, and a plurality of 46 percent saying no (21 percent were unsure) (CM2T 23). When asked whether a "military that is isolated from American society [is] a good thing or a bad thing," 60 percent say that it is bad (CM2T 24).

Note that civilian-military isolation is largely a one-way street. Members of the military interact all the time with civilian society, after all. Most grew up in it and will return to civilian life after a spell in the military. Members of the armed services are not unfamiliar with the larger society's institutions of justice, education, and law. Rather, the estrangement is an *alienation of civilians from military life*—one that creates an asymmetric mutual understanding between the military and civilian spheres.

But what does this estrangement mean for the ability of the citizenry to form opinions about military policy? And what does it mean, in particular, for those situations in which the public has to assess military institutions against the norms of civilian justice systems?

What Americans Think They Know and What They Do Know

One important factor here is that Americans do not appreciate the degree of their isolation from the military. When asked how familiar they are with the country's armed forces, 70 percent say they are either very familiar or somewhat familiar (CM1T 39). This perceived familiarity makes a certain amount of sense, even if it is—as the data below suggest—something of a delusion. The military is a pervasive presence in our culture. We see it represented daily on the news and in movies, even on racecar decals. We see "support the troops" banners on minivans. Every politician pays homage. The military is also a giant instrument of American foreign policy, always present in our political consciousness.

In fact, however, American civilian ignorance about the armed forces is far more striking than is the public's knowledge. Americans do not know how big the services are or how much they cost; they do not know whether troops are well paid; they are unsure about who can serve and why. And the problem goes beyond mere facts. Americans demand divergent, at times mutually inconsistent, things of the armed forces, asking it to be all things, at all times, to all people. Here are a few examples. When asked how many people are currently serving in all five branches of the US military, the public overestimates the size by a factor of five: the average answer was 6.5 million (CM1T 58), whereas the United States has only 1.4 million active duty soldiers.[20] When asked how many people were currently serving in the U.S. Army, in particular, the mean answer was 1.9 million (CM1T 56), whereas the actual number of soldiers in the army, according to the Pentagon, is just under 550,000.[21] When the same question was asked about the number of people currently serving in the U.S. Marine Corps, Americans misjudged again by a factor of six, estimating the force of under 200,000 active duty Marines to be 1.2 million (CM1T 57).[22] Things only get worse when it comes to the defense budget, where one can see the public's wildly mixed messages concerning the military. Roughly 75 percent of respondents want to keep funding at current levels or see cuts (CM1T 4). At the same time, however, 91 percent of respondents want to either keep military pay the same or see it raised (CM1T 10).

The public also believes service members are underpaid: only 26 percent believe that an officer's military pay is higher than what he or she would make as a civilian (CM1T 49). And 45 percent believe that civilian pay is higher than military pay for enlisted members. Perhaps, as a result of this perceived imbalance, 51 percent of Americans think that enlisted service members are paid too little (CM1T 26). Only 11 percent think that military pay is higher than comparable civilian pay (CM1T 50). Overall, 42 percent believe that civilian pay is higher than military pay for similar jobs, while only 13 percent said the opposite (CM1T 51).

Yet the public, as things turn out, has all this backwards. The Pentagon's last quadrennial review of military compensation, released in 2012, found that the average regular military compensation for enlisted personnel in 2009 was \$50,747 and for officers it was \$94,735. According to the review's findings, those amounts correspond to about the 90th percentile of wages for enlisted equivalent civilians and to about the 83rd percentile of wages for officer equivalent civilians' wages,[23] suggesting that enlisting in the military means you will make more than four-fifths of your peers. The Center for Strategic and Budgetary Assessments found that from 2001 to 2011, the cost of military pay and benefits per person increased by 46 percent, excluding war funding and adjusting for inflation.[24] In the last decade, regular pay and compensation has been the fastest growing part of the military budget.

And while Americans say they want to see a smaller defense budget while wanting to increase service member compensation, they do not seem to actually want to cut anywhere else either. Only 18 percent want cuts in the operations and training budget (CM1T 11); only 34 percent would like the military construction budget to shrink (CM1T 12); a mere 32 percent want less spent on weapons procurement (CM1T 13); and fewer than 40 percent want to see a reduction in the war operations budget (CM1T 14).

The problem is even more acute with respect to the intelligence community, which is even more isolated—intentionally so—than is the military from the country's normal life. One recent poll found that 71 percent of respondents either think the National Security Agency, which does signals intelligence, conducts operations to capture or kill foreign terrorists or are not sure whether it does. A whopping 77 percent of people believe or are not sure whether the NSA interrogates detainees.[25]

It is surely unfair to expect the public to have any kind of detailed understanding of the defense budget or the size of the military, much less of signals intelligence programs. The public, after all, famously believes that foreign aid is a big part of US budget expenditures. But it is not too much, we believe, to expect that a public that relies on the military as a major instrument of foreign policy might be able to guess its size within the right order of magnitude. And it is not too much to expect that people might sense a tension between cutting military spending and raising military salaries or might have some even vague sense of what the NSA does and does not do.

Contradictory Attitudes and Expectations

The problem is not limited to basic ignorance. Americans seem to hold at times contradictory views on the most basic questions of military policy. For example, 56 percent of those polled agree that "military force should be used only in pursuit of the goal of total victory" (only 24 percent disagreed) (CM2T 79). Similarly, 59 percent say they think the use of force "should be applied quickly and massively" rather than through a gradual escalation (only 15 percent disagreed) (CM2T 79). At the same, however, nearly 70 percent of Americans view increasing the use of drones as a good thing, though drone strikes are the ultimate pinprick use of force.[26] More generally, Americans have not favored the use of overwhelming force in our re-engagement in Iraq, nor have Americans opposed the gradual drawdown of US forces in Afghanistan.

The inconsistent attitudes are particularly stark when the public is asked about matters related to the military's unique institutional arrangements that have no analogues in civilian life. For example, 86 percent agree that "an effective military depends on a very structured organization and a clear chain of command" (CM2T 67). But, when we dig deeper, a majority (52 percent) says that it would be appropriate for an officer to appeal an order he or she disagrees with to a higher authority, "even if it means leaping the chain of command and/or going over the head of the leader making the request" (CM2T 86). And while people want gay soldiers to be able to serve openly in the military (66 percent) (CM1T 30), a majority also wants servicemen to be able to object to their service even if it means bringing discredit on the military (57 percent) (CM2T 43). That is a hard circle to square.

It is particularly hard to square in the justice arena, where civilian norms are extremely strong and normally do not have to be reconciled with a legal culture that mandates taking orders from other people. By contrast, in the military, not showing up to work can be a crime,[27] as can just about anything that constitutes conduct unbecoming an officer and a gentleman or erodes military discipline.[28] To a certain degree, Americans are comfortable with the military's difference in this respect, with 52 percent of respondents saying that for the military to do its job, it must have different standards from the rest of society (CM1T 43). The trouble is that if you ask about any specific differential standard, Americans turn out to be pretty libertarian in their views of how service members ought to be treated when they defy their superiors.

For example, as we noted above, only 23 percent believe service members should go to jail for opposing women or homosexuals serving with them (CM2T 43). Only 12 percent believe they should go to jail for expressing upsetting ideas in public, even if those ideas bring discredit upon the country (CM2T 42). Fewer than half of respondents (40 percent) think it inappropriate for an officer to refuse a lawful order, even if that refusal would mean facing a court-martial (CM2T 85). A similar number believe that a military person should be imprisoned for "anything that causes an international incident" (CM2T 41). And around half of Americans say that a service member should not go to jail for acts "offending the sensibilities of other cultures" such as burning the Koran (CM2T 40). Our point is not that a soldier should, in fact, go to jail for any of these things—the merits of which may differ a lot depending on what precisely the service member did and on the context in which he did it. Our point, rather, is that poll respondents are reflexively privileging First Amendment values over military discipline and assuming that service members should receive the same rights as civilians.

And, in fact, that is more or less what people believe: 75 percent of respondents say they believe that an American service member should go to jail for "anything that they would be punished for as civilians." (CM2T 44). In other words, while acknowledging in response to direct questions that the military needs rules of its own that might not fly in civilian life—rules that limit free speech and individual autonomy—Americans are not that comfortable with such rules in practice and want soldiers, sailors, airmen, and Marines to be accountable to rules similar to those that govern the larger society.

You can see this tension clearly in the recent controversies over sexual assault in the military. The public takes this problem seriously. Eighty-one percent of Americans view sexual assault in the military as an extremely or very important issue, according to a June 2013 Pew poll.[29] About four in ten (38 percent) respondents say the issue is so serious that it is a sufficient reason by itself to dissuade a friend or daughter from joining the military at all. Despite widespread admiration for the American military, in other words, 40 percent of Americans would tell their daughters to stay away from it.

At the same time, the poll finds that the public is evenly divided over whether the better way to handle the problem is for Congress to make changes in military laws (45 percent) or for military leaders to address the problem internally (44 percent).

This tension is not new. The military justice system has migrated towards the civilian justice system in a lot of ways since World War II in response to exactly this instinct on the part of the public. But there is a limit to how far this trend can go without impairing military performance. Military life is profoundly different from civilian life, after all, and the apparent public expectation that members of the military should be punished only for activities forbidden to civilians ignores the fact that members of the military have lawful powers that civilians do not have (up to and including the use of offensive lethal force) and, on account of those powers, live under restraints it would be grossly improper to impose on members of the public.

What Does It All Mean and What Is to Be Done?

How much do public ignorance and mixed messages about the military really matter? The public, after all, has all kinds of crazy ideas about how its government works, and it weighs a great many factors in public policy differently from the way elites or experts in those areas do. Just as it demands greater salaries for military members while also wanting to see defense cuts, for example, it also wants to cut the larger federal budget without touching entitlement programs. Public ignorance and mutually inconsistent policy demands are more rule than exception.

That said, they have consequences in this area, as they certainly do in others, too. For one thing, the deep trust in the military and attraction to tough-minded, military-oriented solutions, when combined with a pessimism about outcomes, may make the public quick to support wars that it is then almost as quick to sour upon.

A public-opinion environment in which Americans know little about the military generally while thinking of themselves as knowing a lot, in which they offer conflicting attitudes concerning what they expect of it, and in which they offer confused attitudes regarding how distinct its justice system and norms should be does not offer a fertile ground on which to grow a solid, stable understanding of the military's role in bringing terrorists to justice. It is not much of a surprise that public attitudes are fickle in the face of policy disappointments given this background. A public that knows so little about the military while putting great faith in it will tend to be overambitious about what it can accomplish and then overly disappointed at outcomes that fall short of the ideal. A public that wants to see geopolitical problems obliterated with lightning uses of overwhelming force will tend to have little patience for the sort of long slog of nation building and counterinsurgency that characterizes a great deal of modern, asymmetric warfare.

This has obvious national security implications. The combination of ignorance and admiration sustains a public willingness to rush into conflicts and then pressure politicians to end them quickly. This involves many risks, chief among them is the threat that our great confidence will lead the United States unquestioningly into unwinnable wars. In recent years, we have also seen the flip side of this coin—drawdowns and withdrawals before local forces[30] are able to consolidate gains in the theater of battle.[31] This can ultimately mean that much of what we accomplish in counterterrorism or counterinsurgency is wasted effort.

More subtly, a public attracted to military solutions to problems of a hybrid nature—problems with military, intelligence, and criminal justice elements—yet profoundly ignorant of the military's justice system and capabilities as an instrument of justice will tend to be unusually susceptible to symbolism.

Despite their underperformance relative to institutions of civilian justice for trying terrorists, for example, the public prefers military commissions to terrorism trials in civilian courts.[32] The public favors maintaining Guantanamo Bay. The public loves drone strikes. Multiple polls show that the public favors the use of torture.[33] What these seemingly disparate findings have in common is that they all reveal an attraction to perceived wartime toughness, to the symbolic language of warfare, in abstraction from the question of how effective the measures really are. These tactics are, in fact, of very different actual value. The public attraction to measures framed as instrumentalities of warfare will sometimes—as in the case of drone strikes—coincide with measures of enormous strategic and tactical value. In some instances, however, they will not. And the political pressures public ignorance will generate will take discipline on the part of policymakers to resist.

The problem of public ignorance of the military and its culture is a tough one to address, because it stems directly from positive developments. Unless we are going to reinstitute a draft, we have to accept that the American people as a whole will be more removed from their defenders. Fewer members of the population are going to war; our military is generally successful; automation and technological developments have separated civilians and warfighters from the battlefield; these are good things that most Americans are not willing to give back in order to have deeper civilian-military ties.

Yet the degree of public ignorance has an important process message for policymakers, who often spend very little time explaining military and defense-policy issues to the public: America needs more messy debates about national security policy. How many elections in 2014 were about war and peace or surveillance and privacy? Policymakers cannot expect the public to "get it" intuitively. Issues of complex military policy require sustained conversations with the public, sustained education and messaging and debate, and, critically, this messaging cannot assume a real public grounding in the underlying institutional frameworks for defense and security policy. These have to be taught and retaught and retaught again. To fail to do so is to invite failure elsewhere—when it really counts.

Notes

1. Associated Press-GFK, "AP-GFK Poll: A Survey of the American General Population," April 2015, http://ap-gfkpoll.com/main/wp-content/uploads /2015/04/AP-GfK_Poll_April_2015_Topline_drones.pdf; New York Times/ CBS News, "Americans' Views on the Issues," Poll, May 31–June 4, 2013, http://www.nytimes.com/interactive/2013/06/06/us/new-york-times-cbs -news-poll-june-2013.html?_r=0; NBC News/Wall Street Journal, Survey, May 30–June 2, 2013, http://online.wsj.com/public/resources/documents

/poll06052013.pdf; Alyssa Brown and Frank Newport, "In U.S., 65% Support Drone Attacks on Terrorists Abroad," Poll, March 20–21, 2013, Gallup, http://www.gallup.com/poll/161474/support-drone-attacks-terrorists -abroad.aspx.

2. Alexandra Jaffe, "Poll: Most Disapprove of Obama Handling of ISIS," February 17, 2015, http://www.cnn.com/2015/02/16/politics/cnn-poll-isis -obama-approval/; CNN/ORC International, Poll, February 12–15, 2015, http://i2.cdn.turner.com/cnn/2015/images/02/16/isis.poll.pdf; Marist Poll, "Obama's Request for Military Action against ISIS Receives Majority Support . . . Many Americans Say Boots on the Ground Are Needed," February 12, 2015, http://maristpoll.marist.edu/212-obamas-request-for -military-action-against-isis-receives-majority-supportmany-americans -say-boots-on-the-ground-are-needed.

3. Hart Research Associates/Public Opinion Strategies, "NBC News/Wall Street Journal Survey," June 11–15, 2014, http://online.wsj.com/public/resources /documents/wsjnbc06182014.pdf; Sarah Dutton et al., "Americans' View of the Economy Most Positive in Eight Years," CBS News, January 14, 2015, http://www.cbsnews.com/news/americans-view-of-the-economy-most -positive-in-eight-years.

4. Sarah Dutton et al., "Most Americans Consider Waterboarding to Be Torture: Poll," CBS News, December 15, 2014, http://www.cbsnews.com/news/torture -and-reaction-to-the-senate-intelligence-report/; Pew Research Center, "Terrorism Worries Little Changed; Most Give Government Good Marks for Reducing Threat," January 12, 2015, http://www.people-press.org /2015/01/12/terrorism-worries-little-changed-most-give-government-good -marks-for-reducing-threat/; Washington Post-ABC News, Poll, December 11–14, 2014, https://www.washingtonpost.com/apps/g/page /politics/washington-post-abc-news-poll-december-11-14-2014/1516.

5. CNN, "CNN/Time Poll: Cut Back Civil Liberties to Fight Terror?" May 1, 2013, http://politicalticker.blogs.cnn.com/2013/05/01/cnntime-poll-cutback -civil-liberties-to-fight-terror; CNN/ Time/ ORC, Poll, April 30, 2013, http://i2.cdn.turner.com/cnn/2013/images/05/01/top5.pdf.

6. Quinnipiac University, "Hillary Clinton Owns 2016 Dem Nomination, Quinnipiac University National Poll Finds; Support for Immigration Reform Drops," May 2, 2013, http://www.quinnipiac.edu/news-and-events /quinnipiac-university-poll/national/release-detail?ReleaseID=1891.

7. Pew Research Center, "Growing Support for Campaign against ISIS—and Possible Use of U.S. Ground Troops," February 24, 2015, http://www.people -press.org/2015/02/24/growing-support-for-campaign-against-isis-and -possible-use-of-u-s-ground-troops.

8. Dutton, "Americans' View of the Economy."

9. Pew Research Center, "Terrorism Worries Little Changed."

10. Quinnipiac University, "New Jersey Gov. Christie Is Hottest Politician in U.S., Quinnipiac University National Thermometer Finds; Pope Has Biggest Impact on Our Lives," January 4–7, 2014, http://www.quinnipiac.edu/news-and-events/quinnipiac-university-poll/national/release-detail?ReleaseID=1994.

11. A Quinnipiac University poll in June 2014 that asked "Do you think it is in the national interest of the United States to be involved in the conflict in Iraq?" found that 39 percent said yes while only 29 percent supported sending ground troops to Iraq. Following the beheading of James Foley and other Americans, a February 2015 CBS poll found that 65 percent of Americans thought ISIS was a "major threat" to US security and 57 percent favored sending ground troops to Iraq. Quinnipiac University, "Iraq—Getting In Was Wrong; Getting Out Was Right, U.S. Voters Tell Quinnipiac University National Poll; 92 Percent Back Background Checks for All Gun Buys," June 24–30, 2014, http://www.quinnipiac.edu/news-and-events/quinnipiac-university-poll/national/release-detail?ReleaseID=2057; Sarah Dutton et al., "Do Americans Want to Send Ground Troops to Fight ISIS," CBS News, Feb. 19, 2015, http://www.cbsnews.com/news/do-americans-want-to-send-ground-troops-to-fight-isis.

12. Jeffrey M. Jones, "Americans Most Confident in Military, Least in Congress," Poll, June 23, 2011, Gallup, http://www.gallup.com/poll/148163/Americans-Confident-Military-Least-Congress.aspx?utm_source=military&utm_medium=search&utm_campaign=tiles.

13. References to the YouGov data by question number appear in parentheses throughout this essay with the abbreviations CM1T and CM2T indicating the 2013 and 2014 surveys, respectively. The complete results are available at http://www.hoover.org/warriors-and-citizens-crosstabs-1 (CM1T) and http://www.hoover.org/warriors-and-citizens-crosstabs-2 (CM2T).

14. Pew Research Center, "The Military-Civilian Gap: War and Sacrifice in the Post-9/11 Era," October 5, 2011, http://www.pewsocialtrends.org/files/2011/10/veterans-report.pdf.

15. Ibid.

16. Amy Schafer, "Does America Have a Warrior Caste?" Defense in Depth, Council on Foreign Relations, January 22, 2015, http://blogs.cfr.org/davidson/2015/01/22/does-america-have-a-warrior-caste.

17. James Fallows, "The Tragedy of the American Military," *Atlantic,* January/February 2015, http://www.theatlantic.com/features/archive/2014/12/the-tragedy-of-the-american-military/383516.

18. Rebecca Frankel, *War Dogs: Tales of Canine Heroism, History, and Love,* New York: Palgrave Macmillan, 2014, p. 5.

19. Ibid.
20. U.S. Dept. of Defense, "2012 Demographics Profile of the Military Community," p. iii, http://www.militaryonesource.mil/12038/MOS/Reports/2012 _Demographics_Report.pdf.
21. Ibid.
22. Ibid.
23. James E. Grefer, David Gregory, and Erin M. Rebhan, "Military and Civilian Compensation: How Do They Compare," *The Eleventh Quadrennial Review of Military Compensation,* 2011, p. 4, http://militarypay.defense.gov/Portals/107 /Documents/Reports/SR04_Chapter_1.pdf.
24. Todd Harrison, "Rebalancing Military Compensation: An Evidence-based Approach," Center for Strategic and Budgetary Assessments, 2012, p. 2, http://www.csbaonline.org/publications/2012/07/rebalancing-military -compensation-an-evidence-based-approach.
25. Amy Zegart, "Real Spies, Fake Spies, NSA, and More: What My 2012 and 2013 National Polls Reveal," *Lawfare,* November 7, 2013, http://www.lawfareblog .com/2013/11/real-spies-fake-spies-nsa-and-more-what-my-2012-and-2013 -national-polls-reveal.
26. Pew Research Center, "Military-Civilian Gap."
27. U.S. Code, title 10, sec. 886, art. 86, https://www.law.cornell.edu/uscode/text /10/886.
28. U.S. Code, title 10, sec. 933, art. 133, https://www.law.cornell.edu/uscode/text /10/933; U.S. Code, title 10, sec. 933, art. 134, https://www.law.cornell.edu /uscode/text/10/934.
29. Pew Research Center, "Sexual Assault in the Military Widely Seen as Important Issue, but No Agreement on Solution," June 12, 2013, http://www.people-press.org/2013/06/12/sexual-assault-in-the-military -widely-seen-as-important-issue-but-no-agreement-on-solution.
30. Janine Davidson and Emerson Brooking, "In Afghanistan, Path to Lasting Success Will Also Be the Hardest," Defense in Depth, Council on Foreign Relations, April 7, 2014, http://blogs.cfr.org/davidson/2014/04/07/in -afghanistan-path-to-lasting-success-will-also-be-the-hardest.
31. Karen DeYoung Ernesto and Greg Miller, "Afghanistan Gains Will Be Lost Quickly after Drawdown, U.S. Intelligence Estimate Warns," *Washington Post,* December 28, 2013.
32. Quinnipiac University, "Hillary Clinton."
33. Dutton, "Most Americans Consider Waterboarding Torture"; Pew Research Center, "Terrorism Worries Little Changed"; Washington Post-ABC News Poll.

CHAPTER 6

Public Opinion and the Making of Wartime Strategies

Nadia Schadlow

The symbols of public opinion, in times of moderate security, are subject to check and comparison and argument. They come and go, coalesce and are forgotten, never organizing perfectly the emotion of the whole group. There is, after all, just one human activity left in which whole populations accomplish the union sacrée. It occurs in those middle phases of a war when fear, pugnacity, and hatred have secured complete dominion of the spirit, either to crush every other instinct or to enlist it, and before weariness is felt.

—Walter Lippman, *Public Opinion*

American public opinion is at once impassioned and changeable. It is much less of a constraint on the making of wartime strategies than political leaders might think. The relationship between inconstant public opinion and the shaping of wartime strategies is an uneasy one, complicated by differences in knowledge, interpretation, and historical appreciation as well as competing interests. There is no straightforward empirical answer to the question of the degree to which the American public influences political leaders in the development of wartime strategies. But the data suggest that it is an interactive relationship, open to the influence of compelling leaders and shaped by convincing explanations and the course of events. The making of strategy in wartime requires of leaders clear thinking, detailed and historical knowledge of the situation, clear objectives, and a willingness to commit and sustain the military, political, and economic resources required to overcome enemies and achieve successful outcomes. As Carl von Clausewitz observed, "Everything in strategy is very simple, but that does not mean that everything is very easy. Once it has been determined from the political considerations what a war is meant to achieve and what it can achieve it is easy to chart its course. But great strength of character, as well as great lucidity and firmness of mind, is required in order to follow through steadily, to carry out the plan, and not be thrown off course by thousands of diversions. . . . It takes more strength of will to make an important decision in strategy than in tactics."[1]

The purpose of this paper is to offer three considerations when thinking about this issue. First, America's "strategic culture" matters. In a democracy, the culture, history, and experiences of a nation inform and shape public opinion in wartime. Second, the public's view of what constitutes war influences its support for, or opposition to, wartime strategy. Is war regarded simply as the dropping of bombs and the conduct of raids, or does it adhere to the Clausewitzian view that war is a continuation of politics by other means, whereby a strategy should focus upon prospects for achieving sustainable goals? Does the public expect the war to end quickly, perhaps after key enemy leaders are killed, or does it anticipate that political consolidation will be required? Differences among the public—as well as among civil and military leaders—over the nature of war and anticipated costs and consequences influence public support for strategic goals. Third, and perhaps most important of all, is the factor of civilian and military leadership. Leaders' ability to demonstrate what Clausewitz described as "great lucidity and firmness of mind" is essential to reconciling public opinion and the steadfastness required to make and sustain wartime strategy. It is leadership that "captures" and articulates a nation's strategic culture, explains to citizens the true nature and character of war, inspires support required to pursue victory, and sustains the scale and duration of the national commitment necessary to consolidate military gains and, ultimately, achieve political goals.

These three factors may not satisfy pollsters or political scientists who track the course of public opinion in wartime. Nor will they necessarily satisfy historians who focus on discrete periods in history and attempt to explain the complex causality of events in war. Nonetheless, a discussion of these factors can help interpret polling data while shedding light on how the American public influences wartime strategies and the degree to which leadership may shape the public's views. Polls on the subject of national security and war suggest that while public opinion may be considered a constraint on security policy and strategy, it not immutable: it is responsive to evolving strategic culture, to shifts in the public's perception of war, and to the ability of leaders to galvanize its citizens in support of war efforts.

Strategic Culture

Walter Russell Meade's *Special Providence* described four traditions in American society which have shaped the way that the public and political leaders have thought about foreign policy, the use of force. In a reaction to what Meade called "simplistic" poles of isolationism and moralism that often define American opinion on foreign policy, he developed four schools of thought that correct the tendency to assume that citizens "proceed out of a single, unified word view . . . [rather than] a balance of contrasting, competing voices and values . . . a symphony."[2] Meade decried the tendency among top diplomatic and political leaders to dismiss, "wholesale" the country's foreign policy traditions and the tendency to reduce this tradition to a "legacy of moralism and isolationism."[3] Meade's four schools of thought capture the range of popular reactions to past and recent wars, contribute to an understanding of American strategic culture, and may offer a useful framework for interpreting the survey data that is a basis for this volume.

First, the Hamiltonian school put economics first and foremost. It sought the promotion of the American enterprise at home and abroad and supported the rights of American merchants and investors. Today, this tradition sees free trade and the preservation of free trade as critical. Indeed, as the YouGov poll demonstrates, the public believes that the economy should be the president's top priority by a substantial margin (29 percent more than the next priority, which is the budget deficit) (CM1T 2).[4] In extrapolating from this tradition, there are many examples in American history where leaders invoked freedom of the seas as part of a rationale for war. One is after the Revolutionary War, as American commercial shipping (no longer under Britain's protection) came under attack in the Mediterranean from the Barbary pirates of North Africa. In response, Congress passed the Naval Act of 1794, which reestablished the U.S. Navy and authorized the construction of six frigates to defend American interests. Another is when, in his weekly fireside chats during World War II, President Roosevelt eloquently explained to the American public that the United States "must fight at these vast distances to protect our supply lines and our lines of communication with our allies—protect these lines from the enemies who are bending every ounce of their strength, striving against time, to cut them." He deliberately challenged those who thought that we could "pull our warships and our planes and our merchant ships into our own home waters and concentrate solely on last ditch defense," and believed that perceptions of geographic separation from security problems overseas was likely to remain important in sustaining public support for wartime strategies.[5]

Second, the Wilsonian tradition (which, Meade points out, was shaped even before World War I by American missionaries) maintained that the United States had a practical and moral duty to spread its values throughout the world. For Wilsonians, American interests required other countries to accept basic American values and conduct their foreign and domestic affairs accordingly. During World War II, Franklin Delano Roosevelt consistently explained that "freedom of person and security of property anywhere in the world depend upon the security of the rights and obligations of liberty and justice everywhere in the world."[6] Third, the Jeffersonian school sought to protect American democracy but to avoid imposing American values on other countries. Meade argued that George Kennan was a Jeffersonian and that containment was designed to preserve the American system but avoid a direct confrontation with the Soviet Union. Most recently, seeking to explain America's more limited involvement in the Middle East, President Obama has emphasized that America would "defend this nation and uphold the values" that we stand for but that the role of American forces would be markedly limited.[7] The YouGov poll reflects this impulse in American politics: 69 percent of respondents want to decrease slightly, or decrease a lot, spending on foreign aid; 68 percent want to decrease assistance to foreign militaries; and 67 percent oppose returning to a draft (CM1T 6, 15, 36). The fourth, Jacksonian, tradition represented a populist culture of "honor, independence, courage, and military pride," that later translated into "unwavering popular support for the bloody and dangerous Cold War."[8] Today, the American public's support for the pursuit of "total victory" (55.8 percent of those polled) and the use of quick and massive force (58.5 percent), as opposed to gradual escalation, evokes this Jacksonian tradition (CM1T 79). So too does the overwhelming public support for increasing or maintaining spending levels on military pay, operations and training, construction, weapons procurement, and the war operations budget (CM1T 10–14).

These traditions shape American strategic culture and how Americans think about war and the necessary steps required in war. They are not, however, mutually exclusive. Rather, views about decisions to deploy forces derive from dynamic combinations of these traditions. One example is America's deployment of troops to Somalia in 1992. At that time, as thousands of Somalis were starving, President George H. W. Bush emphasized the limitations of the United States, explaining that he understood that the "the United States alone cannot right the world's wrongs," but that humanitarian requirements often required US involvement. At the same time, conscious of long-term commitments, he rejected the idea that the politics of Somalia would need to be changed and maintained that American troops would not seek to influence Somalia's political crisis and would not allow themselves to become targets in that country's tribal wars. At the time, his approach was supported by the American public, with some polls reporting that over 70 percent of the public supported the humanitarian intervention.[9] This separation of the use of force from political outcomes was not new and appears to be reflected in the American public's view that force, when used, should be determined by military rather than political goals (in the current data set, 61.5 percent of respondents stated that nonmilitary people getting too involved in purely military affairs hurts military effectiveness) (CM2T 79). Such a distinction, however, proved to be shortsighted and impossible to maintain. Politics, in war, tend to be insistent. Ten months after the initial intervention, following the death of eighteen American soldiers, the new Clinton administration announced its decision to withdraw American soldiers from Somalia. Interestingly, polling results at the time were mixed. Two polls, conducted by ABC News and CNN/*USA Today* in the hours just after the deaths were reported, found that between 37 percent and 43 percent supported immediate withdrawal of the troops, though most respondents wanted more involvement in Somalia, at least over the short term.[10] An ABC poll at the time showed 75 percent favored going after Somali warlord Aideed with a "major military attack" if the American prisoners were not released through negotiations[11]—suggesting that Meade's tough Jacksonian tradition was at play.

More recently, on the eve of the US intervention in Afghanistan, the Wilsonian and Jeffersonian traditions seemed to be at play. President George W. Bush later recounted that he was "sensitive to the [accusations] that this was a religious war and that somehow the United

States would be the conqueror" but explained that there was a "human condition we must worry about in times of war."[12] The debate over the subsequent US intervention in Iraq also reflected, fundamentally, several strategic cultural traditions at play: the Wilsonian tradition of exporting American values and the Jacksonian tradition of containing our enemies abroad. Overall, Meade's description of these four traditions succeed in covering the range of explanations leaders use to justify interventions abroad and illuminate the role of strategic culture in determining whether publics will support and sustain a wartime strategy over time in light of the costs and sacrifices associated with that strategy.

The Nature and Character of War

The people are discontented, but it is with the feeble and oppressive mode of conducting the war, not with the war itself.

—George Washington, letter to John Laurens, 1781

In October 2000, presidential candidate George W. Bush rejected the concept of nation building as well as the suggestion that the United States military should take the lead in reconstructing failed states. A year later, against the backdrop of early US combat successes in Afghanistan, President Bush reaffirmed that US forces would not stay, since they "did not do police work."[13] Years later, reflecting on the war and his experiences, Bush wrote in his memoir that Afghanistan was "the ultimate nation building mission" and that the United States, having liberated the country from a "primitive dictatorship, had the moral obligation to leave behind something better."

Indeed, some five years after the US intervention, with the support of the Bush administration, tens of thousands of American and allied troops as well as US interagency "provincial reconstruction teams" were working in Iraq and Afghanistan to rebuild the economies and governments of both countries—efforts that were seen, often reluctantly, as essential to the consolidation of military gains. In 2008, the much heralded counterinsurgency manual described how U.S. Army and Marine Corps forces would conduct operations to defeat insurgencies and achieve sustainable political outcomes. And in 2009, a Department of Defense directive put postconflict "stability operations" on par with combat operations. Experiences in Afghanistan and Iraq had revealed that in most conflicts, stability tasks such as support to governance and the development of indigenous security forces were not optional—rather they were integral parts of war.[14] Policy officials then had to explain this to the American people.

Civilian and military views about what constitutes war shapes the public's understanding of the character of war. That understanding, in turn, influences the degree to which the public will support particular courses of action or underwrite the levels of risk and resources associated with those courses of action. The degree to which the public understands what strategy entails—the ways and means needed to achieve a set of objectives—is essential to generating and sustaining public support. Knowledge and agreement on "ways and means" is inconsistent and variable among civilian leaders and military officials—and thus changeable among the public as well. For instance, respondents asked to guess the number of people serving in all five branches of the military on average were wrong by a count of over five million people (CM1T 58). Estimates of numbers in specific branches of the military, such as the U.S. Army and Marine Corps, were incorrect by hundreds of thousands of people (CM1T 56–57).[15]

Public confusion over strategy often stems, in part, from disagreements between civilian policymakers and military leaders concerning the character of war—what constitutes war and what kind of military forces may be necessary at a given time. To what degree then are leaders treating as a constraint something that is in their power to effect? It is up to leaders to explain the character of war, drawing upon history and experience. Does war require the commitment of ground forces? Can strategic objectives be accomplished through airpower alone? What does it take to win a war and to achieve goals that are consistent with US interests? If the military is involved in nonmilitary tasks, during a war, what does this mean? What is part of the military profession and what is not? The prevailing views of the character of war affect the public's willingness to support a particular course of action. Polls suggest that the public does think about what constitutes war and how wars should be fought, but the degree to which such views have been drawn out remain unclear. Over 55 percent (55.8 percent) believed that military forces should be used only in pursuit of the goal of total victory—but total victory was not defined. What would that have meant in Desert Storm in 1991 or in April of 2003 in Iraq? Over 58 percent (58.5 percent) believed that the use of force in foreign interventions should be applied "quickly and massively" as opposed to gradually escalating forces—perhaps a lessons-learned effect from Vietnam? And while, as noted earlier, close to 63 percent of those polled said that "military rather than political goals" should determine the use of the military (CM2T 79, 80), during the Gulf War in 1991, when George H. W. Bush made the decision to deploy American ground troops to force Saddam Hussein out of Iraq, around 80 percent of the American public supported this step—and about this percentage also supported "see[ing] to it that Saddam Hussein is forced from power."[16]

During the wars in Iraq and Afghanistan, there was consistent disagreement among military and civilian leaders over the kinds of wars being fought—which complicated messages to the public. Some two years into the war in Iraq, top civilian leaders—such as Secretary of Defense Donald Rumsfeld—were still reluctant to call the unfolding conflict an insurgency, which in turn affected explanations of what the war would require of the nation. When Rumsfeld's view did change, he believed that the insurgency would be put down by the Iraqi people and not by coalition forces. Although in 2005 civilian leaders still argued that hat the insurgency was in its "last throes," top military commanders were actively fighting insurgents throughout the country.[17] Such differences had implications for the resources and troops devoted to supporting a particular strategy—and for how civil and military leaders would explain the strategy to the American people.

Similarly, during the 2009 time period, there was consistent disagreement between military and political leaders over the nature of the war in Afghanistan. Top civilian advisors in the Obama White House argued against the resources required to undertake a long-term counterinsurgency strategy to defeat the Taliban and argued against military leaders, such as "Petraeus and his ilk," who were advancing the view that 40,000 additional troops would be needed in Afghanistan.[18] Moreover, the Obama administration's stance was that they would need "the support of the American people."[19] With this mindset, the White House appeared to be led *by* the American public. An alternative approach could have been to explain to the American people the risks of a smaller Afghan surge. As explained by General Petraeus at the time, with a smaller surge "you would see spots on the map that we control—and that the Afghan government controls—slowly recede."[20] The civilian explanation of the strategy was that the bulk of the war effort would require the United States to "target, train and transfer," which was a different set of requirements than one based on a fully resourced counterinsurgency strategy.

It is hard to say which explanations would have resonated more among the American public since the data suggests that the public's confidence in the accuracy of the military's picture of how the war in Afghanistan was unfolding was not high: around 54 percent believed that the military's information was "somewhat inaccurate" (31 percent) or "very inaccurate" (23 percent), while some 26 percent believed that it was accurate—with 20 percent undecided (CM1T 37). To further complicate matters, the public also lacks confidence in the knowledge that political leaders have of the modern military, with over 51 percent believing that political leaders were "not very knowledgeable" or "not knowledgeable at all" about the military (CM2T 15). This reinforces the changeable nature of public opinion.

One example of the problems that stem from a different baseline of knowledge of military matters occurred during the summer of 2009, when President Obama and Secretary of Defense Robert Gates debated and disagreed on key numbers for the Afghan surge. This was a disagreement driven in part by a lack of understanding of what the range of numbers included. When Secretary Gates explained that the military had assumed that the 5,000 "enablers" would be *in addition to* combat troops and were not part of the additional 21,000 troops that the military had requested, President Obama angrily asserted that this was "mission creep" and that the public and Congress would not differentiate among types of troops and only look at final numbers deployed.[21]

Inconsistency in civilian and military leaders' views about the character of war and the strategy necessary to accomplish wartime objectives ultimately play out in the public domain and affect the public's views about and support for the war effort. Who defines the character of war may matter. The polling data indicates that in the making of policy the public (52 percent) believes that the military shares its values but that the political leadership does not, suggesting that the discussions of the character of war by the military may have more resonance among the public (CM2T 16). The data suggests that the public trusts the military when it explains what a strategy requires in order to achieve a particular end state.

The problem of explaining the character of wars—especially what is required to defeat particular enemies or threats—has been complicated in recent years due to a lack of clarity and consensus concerning the nature of those threats. As part of the first Triangle Study over fifteen years ago, the military historian Russell Weigley explained that at the end of the cold war there was essentially a consensus on the external threat posed by the USSR, which in turn helped to unify civil-military relations. He wrote that the Civil War and the world wars created pressures for "civil-military harmony in defense of common national interests" and helped the "civilian government [bestow] on the military resources sufficient to win overwhelming victories."[22] There is simply no comparison today to the 1950 National Security Council's paper "United States Objectives and Programs for National Security" (sometimes known as NSC-68) and today's National Security Strategy.[23] NSC-68 referred to the "hostile design" of the Soviet Union and to Moscow's "fanatic faith" which was antithetical to that of the United States and drove the USSR "to impose its absolute authority over the rest of the world."[24] The current strategy document uses the word "threats" in much more diffuse terms, to include everything from climate change to general "terrorism," and it barely mentions, in any depth, the nature of specific regional threats or countries. Perhaps this reflects the public's disinterest—more believe in the need to increase or maintain spending on space travel (54 percent) than foreign aid (31 percent) (CM1T 6, 7). Indeed, today there are significant disagreements over defining the character of one specific enemy—violent radical Islamists such as the Islamic State and al Qaeda—who are responsible for disorder and violence throughout the Middle East as well as attacks in the West. A lack of clarity over who these enemies are and what goals they are pursuing complicates the development of strategy and leaders' ability to explain wartime strategy to the public.

The ambiguity surrounding the "kind of war" necessary to defeat radical insurgents in Iraq, the Taliban groups in Afghanistan, and the violent radical Islamists represented by groups such as ISIS today, has been a consistent feature of the post-9/11 landscape. Instead of discussions to clarify who US forces were fighting and how the United States intended to apply national power to defeat those enemies and achieve sustainable outcomes, public debate focused on the means—such as the numbers of troops committed. For example, during the war in Iraq there was continuous debate over means and resources but little discussion of the elements of the strategy, such as, how to move

Iraq's increasingly polarized communities toward political accommodation; how to build capable and legitimate Iraqi security forces; how to reduce insurgent freedom of movement; and how to restore security and order in key areas to create a patchwork of safe zones until the Iraq government and security forces were strong enough to maintain order. Absent an understanding of strategy and clear evidence that the situation in Iraq in 2006 was deteriorating rapidly, American public support for the war waned. The data suggests that the experiences in Iraq and Afghanistan incurred doubts among the public that modern wars are winnable (only 19 percent think so). On the other hand, the public was willing to consider that modern wars were winnable if the right type of decisions were taken, with 45 percent believing that it was either military or civilian decision making that created obstacles to winning (CM1T 45).[25] This is important because, again, it reinforces the point that the quality of the explanations given by leaders matter.

Even if the public has doubts about strategy and manifests a lack of support for military operations, that support is not static and can change based on events and how threats are perceived over time. For example, polls from early 2014 show that attitudes toward the use of military force in Syria changed significantly over the course of the conflict. In September 2013, when a deal to disarm Syria's chemical weapons was struck, 62 percent of Americans opposed the use of military force while only 20 percent supported it. Today, when asked whether they support the use of military force against ISIS militants in Syria, the situation is reversed. Some 63 percent of Americans now support the use of military force in Syria, compared to only 16 percent who oppose it.[26]

In early 2014, similar debates concerning the appropriate types of operations against ISIS focused primarily on means employed rather than the character of the conflict and the strategy necessary to achieve the objective of defeating that organization and its associated radical Islamist movement. For example, President Obama has made it clear that US forces will not be required on the ground, thus rejecting means that may prove essential to an effective strategy. Means are eclipsing ends even in presidential requests to Congress for the authorization to use military force (AUMF).[27] President Obama's February 2014 AUMF placed restrictions on the use of ground forces as well as the duration of military operations against ISIS. The focus on the means employed in war in the 2014 authorization contrasts with broad authorities contained in the 2001 authorization, which allowed for "all necessary and appropriate force against those nations, organizations, or persons" he [the president] determines planned, authorized, committed, or aided the terrorist attacks that occurred on September 11, 2001." Today's more narrow focus on means such as air strikes; support for the training of local forces; "assistance" to various opposition groups; humanitarian assistance to groups displaced by ISIS and other groups; and efforts to cut off funding to radical groups may prevent the public from understanding the stakes associated with war as well as how the means employed will achieve wartime objectives.[28] As the Golby, Cohn, and Feaver chapter in this volume notes, nonveterans "are supportive of more wide-ranging use [of force], but favor greater restrictions on force levels and how they are employed." However, some of the YouGov data may contradict this finding, as 58.5 percent of respondents agreed that the use of force in foreign interventions should be applied quickly and massively rather than by gradual escalation (CM2T 79). By explicitly rejecting the use of ground forces the president is advancing a specific view of the nature of war—a form of war that can be conducted from afar, primarily through targeting with the use of technology. This view of war does not encompass the problem of how to consolidate political gains or how to reestablish the basic security and order necessary to advance progress in other political and economic domains. The military actions contemplated, therefore, are likely to prove inconsistent with the stated objective—the defeat of ISIS. That inconsistency, over time, will likely lead the American public to lose faith in the effort as it becomes impossible to see how military operations are contributing to outcomes worthy of the investment in blood and treasure.

Leadership: The Persuasion Pulpit

[Lincoln] made efforts at all times to modify and change public opinion and to climb to the Presidential heights; he toiled and struggled in this line as scarcely any man ever did.

—William H. Herndon, letter to Jesse W. Weik, 1891

Foreign policy does not rank high on the list of the American public's priorities. The YouGov poll shows that when asked about their top priorities, only 1 percent named terrorism or Afghanistan (CM1T 2). Indeed, as noted previously, more Americans valued the importance of the space program. Having said that, the YouGov poll does not include all foreign policy issues. A 2014 Gallup poll found that 4 percent of Americans list foreign aid/focus overseas as the most important problem the United States faces. This is significant in comparison to the 20 percent who rate unemployment as the top problem.[29] Yet polls also suggest that the public, if convinced both of the threat and the effectiveness of the strategies to remove the threat, has shown a willingness to support significant change and investments overtime. Walter Lippmann's 1922 book *Public Opinion* emphasized leaders' roles in shaping public opinion and his observation from that book remains relevant: American public opinion is changeable and is receptive to strong and clearly articulated statements by political and military leaders. Although the term "bully pulpit" has been at times used to refer to the power of the presidency,[30] a more accurate phrase might be "persuasion pulpit," whereby a president and his team explains its strategy to the American public and thus persuade the public of a necessary course of action.

Given the public's relative lack of knowledge when it comes to foreign affairs or the details of a conflict (how many Americans could name the main Taliban groups fighting in Afghanistan or describe the nature of Pakistan's support for these groups?), it is necessary for leaders to explain and persuade. During World War II, FDR played a central role in shaping public opinion about what the war would entail. He used his fireside chats to explain his strategy in detail, encouraging the listening public to get out their maps as he summarized the course of military campaigns, highlighted progress, and provided his rationale for ongoing actions and next steps in those campaigns. Although the Japanese attack on Pearl Harbor brought the United States fully into the war, the president had already, over the course of the previous year, implemented a series of actions to strengthen the United Kingdom and had convinced the American public to support a strategy that prioritized the European over the Pacific theater.

In August 2009, President Obama sought to bolster American support for additional troops in Afghanistan. He explained that the "insurgency in Afghanistan didn't just happen overnight" and that we would not defeat it overnight. He explained that this would not be "quick, nor easy. But we must never forget: This is not a war of choice. This is a war of necessity. Those who attacked America on 9/11 are plotting to do so again. If left unchecked, the Taliban insurgency will mean an even larger safe haven from which al Qaeda would plot to kill more Americans. So this is not only a war worth fighting. This is fundamental to the defense of our people."[31]

It is difficult to determine linkages—with certainty or clear causality—between the public's view of a conflict and a leader's decision to pursue particular strategies in wartime. Different leaders will respond to public opinion in different ways. Consider, for instance, the dramatic shifts in policy during World War I and World War II. Consider also the consistency with which America pursued a grand strategy toward the Soviet Union during the cold war. To prevail during that long war, America had to overcome its fear of entangling alliances, sustain a military presence in Europe, and maintain a large peacetime army—all of which represented significant breaks with American traditions. Different leaders respond to different pressures. Some scholars have called Abraham Lincoln a man who was "never above the fray of political conflicts" and a "prodigious political manipulator."[32] Winston Churchill famously said, "there is no public opinion, just published opinion," and many maintain that Churchill put party politics behind his determination to pursue victory during the war. In contrast to *leading* the public in a certain direction, during the Vietnam War President Lyndon Johnson was very conscious of missteps in the war that could cost him an election win. In January 1964, President Johnson was thinking of the November election. He wanted to be seen as a moderate candidate and this affected his support for particular wartime strategy—supporting Defense Secretary Robert McNamara's concept of "graduated pressure."[33] And President Obama's presumption of war weariness among the American public seemed to underpin his decision to "end the war" in Iraq by the complete withdrawal of US troops there, as well as his preference for "limited engagements," such as the bombings in Libya.[34] The president seemed cognizant that 51.3 percent of YouGov respondents strongly or somewhat opposed continued military involvement in Afghanistan beyond 2014 while only 34.4 percent strongly or somewhat supported it (CM2T 72).

Other variables are likely to influence public thinking about the course of a war and its views about appropriate responses. These might include the state of the economy at a particular time; memories and interpretations of previous wars; recent events that depict Americans as victims or as perpetrators of crimes; the tenor of media coverage; and more. Recent polls regarding the public's views about the threat posed by ISIS reveal how quickly public support can spike (or drop). Recent surveys have shown that some 86 percent of the public believe that ISIS poses an "immediate and serious threat," a "somewhat serious threat," or a "minor threat" to the United States and that most support military action against the terrorist group.[35] In September 2010, only 3 percent of Americans named terrorism as the most important problem facing the country.[36] And of course, public opinion changes as events unfold. A March 2003 Pew Research Center poll indicated that 72 percent of US adults supported the decision to attack Iraq; by February 2008, another Pew poll had found that 58 percent believed it was the wrong decision.[37]

The evidence suggests that Americans seek strong civilian leadership but that they are also open to alternative arguments or viewpoints. Shortly after President Obama's statement that he did not have a strategy for dealing with ISIS, support for his administration dropped. A Rasmussen poll reported in early September 2014 that voters were "very worried that President Obama doesn't have a strategy for dealing with the problem." At the same time, the same poll showed that just 33 percent of likely US voters thought the current level of US involvement around the globe was "about right." How many of those polled could articulate the nature of this involvement or the level of troops around the world? Would these voters likely make the connection between their desire to deploy airpower or drones with the need to actually have individuals on the ground to direct targets? Despite such concerns, the American public supports a president's final decisions on matters of strategy. The polling data suggests that if a president makes a policy decision on wars, over 72 percent of the public believes that the military has a responsibility to support that policy (CM1T 74). In this vein, some 64 percent said their decisions were affected only a "little" or "not at all" if the military supported continued involvement in Afghanistan beyond 2014 (CM1T 73). Around the same number (63 percent) said that if the president decided to withdraw completely from Afghanistan the military had a responsibility to support the policy, even if the military had concerns to the contrary.

But this data is tempered too by the fact that public and elites think civilian leaders are not knowledgeable about the military. As noted previously, more than half of the public believes that civilian leaders are "not very" or "not knowledgeable" about the military, with elites sharing that general proportion (CM1T 15). Furthermore, while 51.9 percent of YouGov respondents believe that the military leaders share the same values as the American people, only 10.9 percent believe the same of political leaders (CM2T 16, 17). This suggests that the public is likely to have greater skepticism of civilian leaders who make decisions about war. At a much more micro level the various levels of trust the public has in military or civilian officials may affect the kind of behavior the public will accept—or not—during wartime. For instance, the survey results suggest that while the American public is considerate of cultural sensitivities (for example, offending other cultures) they were uncertain about the degree to which transgressions in this area should be punished: some 50 percent did not agree that a military person should go to jail for doing something like burning the Koran; while 23 percent were unsure and 26.1 percent agreed that jail was warranted. By the same token, some 40 percent agreed with jail if an "international incident" were caused, while more than a majority— some 68 percent—believed that a "military person" should be allowed to express "upsetting ideas in public." Clearly, in any specific situation the degree to which incidents on the ground—at the tactical level— may or may not have broader strategic effects in a war would need to be explained and assessed by civilian and military leaders. In addition, the public wants to hear different viewpoints and to ensure that actors are permitted to express such considerations. Over 61 percent believed that even if the president decides to withdraw from Afghanistan, for instance, the military would have a responsibility to make its views heard before Congress; similarly, about half of the public (50.4 percent) believed that the military has a responsibility to educate the public about its concerns (with 33 percent saying no and some 16 percent undecided) (CM1T 76, 78).

Public opinion can be inconsistent or shift based on different types of information. For instance, regarding Iran's nuclear program, over 68 percent of those polled believed that Iran's nuclear program posed an "immediate and serious" or a "somewhat serious" threat to the

United States (CM1T 69). Over 46 percent believed that the United States was "very likely" or "somewhat likely" to succeed at eliminating Iraq's nuclear weapons, but only 33.7 percent believed that military strikes on Iran's nuclear sites would reduce the threat from Iran and 28 percent were unsure (CM1T 71). It is reasonable to assume, however, that these views would shift depending upon leaders' assessments of Iran's nuclear program as well as other sources of knowledge about the program. As the public considered American strikes against Iran, was it aware that some critical components of Iran's nuclear program are located deep underground, in a facility called Fordow, which most experts doubt could be penetrated by the most accurate and powerful of America's conventional "bunker busting" weapons? Moreover, regarding the seriousness of the threat, few are likely to realize that, once Iranians are able to enrich uranium to a level of 20 percent (which is what is needed for so-called "peaceful" nuclear programs), it only takes about three to twelve months to enrich uranium to 90 percent— which is what is necessary for use in nuclear warheads.[38] This kind of detailed information is likely to change public opinion and influence public support for a particular course of action.

Similarly, events can impact the views of the public. As the intensity of fighting in eastern Ukraine between government forces and Russian-backed rebels grew, the public became more supportive of sending arms to the Ukrainian government and increasing sanctions on Russia. While as of early February 2015 more still opposed (53 percent) than favored (41 percent) the United States sending arms and military supplies to the Ukrainian government, support for arming Ukraine had gone up eleven points since April 2014.[39]

Given that there is low support for sustained involvement around the world—around 69 percent believe that the United States should decrease slightly (25 percent) or a lot (44 percent) its foreign aid budget—civil and military leaders must persuade the public of the links between American foreign aid and US interests. In addition, they need to provide information as well. How many of those polled know that the US foreign aid budget is about 1 percent of its Federal spending?

According to a 2013 Kaiser Family Foundation survey, misperceptions persist about the size of US foreign aid and how aid is directed. On average, Americans think 28 percent of the federal budget is spent on foreign aid, when it is actually about 1 percent.[40]

Conclusions

The relationship between public opinion and the making of strategy during wartime encompasses many of the specific issues explored in the Triangle Institute Study's previous examination of civil-military relations as well as in the current volume. The public responds to and has opinions about the military as a domestic entity as well as an instrument of American power abroad, as a representative of the American people (themselves), and as an embodiment of American history and values. The public response to its elected civilian leaders is more diffuse and dependent on a range of specific domestic issues, including how civilian actors are perceived, their qualities of leadership, and their domestic and international policies. In wartime, the public's view of both entities becomes intertwined and specific civil-military relationships are taken apart and scrutinized as decisions to use force are made. The data from the current survey suggests that public views change based on specific incidents, explanations, levels of trust in leaders, as well as a broader view of America's role in the world. All of these factors are very much amenable to shaping by US civil and military leaders and this shaping and explaining are all required to execute a specific strategy. Strategy is the overarching glue that brings the public together with civil and military leaders to make sense of the disorder and violence that is war. As Richard Betts has observed, "Strategy is the essential ingredient for making war either politically effective or morally tenable. It is the link between military means and political ends, the scheme for how to make one produce the other. Without strategy, there is no rationale for how force will achieve purposes worth the price in blood and treasure."[41]

The making and articulation of strategy has, for a range of reasons that are beyond the scope of this paper, become dissatisfying and disappointing. The British military historian Hew Strachan observed that throughout the cold war the idea of "total war" required active public participation and underpinned the stability of the international order. With the end of the cold war, and with America's so-called "wars of choice," Strachan writes that the United States has "recast limited war" and distanced itself from "lessons of the past."[42] Smaller, seemingly *ad hoc* wars may make it more difficult for the public to understand the rationale for the use of force and to sustain their commitment to seeing wars through to a favorable conclusion. In addition, as Weigley pointed out in his chapter for the Triangle Study volume, the "harmonious conditions" which characterized World War II (even if there was dissension behind the scenes) meant there was no "public military disagreement with the civilian leadership" during the course of that war.[43] The implication is that a unified front on strategy made is much easier for a public to support that strategy.

Today the situation is markedly different, with much dissention among civilian and military leaders over the nature of the threats to US interests. With different threats emanating from Russia and China to the Middle East, the disputed lessons of the wars in Iraq and Afghanistan, and budgetary pressures, more is required of civil and military leaders to bring the public on board—to understand the complexity of the disorder, to establish linkages between events in one part of the world to another in order to steer away from the isolationism that Meade said was exaggerated but is still a present theme in America's strategic culture. Strategy implies an attempt to exert agency over a problem. Leaders who are effective at crafting and executing strategy will, therefore, be more likely to overcome the self-limiting tendency to be bound by public resistance that does not exist. If their strategy is sound and the stakes are clear to the American public, they will also be more effective at generating and sustaining public support for military efforts despite the costs in blood and treasure.

The degree to which the public is informed could in turn influence the *degree or nature* of the public's influence over the making of wartime strategy. Information changes public opinion and while it is incumbent upon the public to stay informed, it is incumbent upon political and military leaders to provide full information. Both sides are involved. The survey information revealed that the public had more trust in the knowledge of military leaders on military matters (half of those surveyed believed that political leaders were not very knowledgeable or not "knowledgeable at all" about the modern military) (CM2T 15). This then suggests that the public might be less willing to believe arguments made by civilian leaders about the requirements of holding territory or beating back enemy threats (for example, ISIS today). On the other hand, the survey makes clear that the public believes that the military needs to carry out orders and policies, even when considered unwise.

Future surveys might consider the question of how the public gets its information about wars and about the individuals most likely to be trusted. In addition, they might provide more granularity to explore, for instance, whether economic pressures or particular events impact public attitudes. A reasonable assumption would be that they do. Questions to determine the level of the public's knowledge about an ongoing war are important in determining how informed the public is about the war that they are seeking to influence. For example, is the public able to name particular enemies? Surely during World War II the majority of Americans—even children, perhaps—could name the Japanese and the Germans as primary enemies. It is much less likely that the public could do so today (or at least not in more than general terms). Could the public, during World War II, articulate the beliefs held by the Nazis? Could they do so today, vis-à-vis the various Taliban or ISIS groups? Do political leaders speak to the public with a sense that the public understands the contours of a particular war, or do they assume little knowledge?

Perhaps the one generalization that can be made from the often inconsistent views illustrated in the current data is that civil-military relationships and strong civil-military leadership seem to effect both the development of strategy and the public's support for it. Overall, we are not that far from the Triangle study's findings over fifteen years ago that the American public will support military operations if it understands the approach and thinks that a particular approach is working. The public is willing to show faith in America's leaders, but the White House and the Pentagon must communicate clearly and consistently about the strategy—and its requirements—necessary to uphold the strategic interests of the United States in wartime.

Notes

1. Carl von Clausewitz, *On War,* edited and translated by Peter Paret and Michael Howard, Princeton: Princeton University Press, 1976, reprint 1989, p. 178.
2. Walter Russell Meade, *Special Providence: American Foreign Policy and How It Changed the World,* New York: Routledge, 2002, p. 54.
3. Ibid., pp. 6–7.
4. References to the YouGov data by question number appear in parentheses throughout this essay with the abbreviations CM1T and CM2T indicating the 2013 and 2014 surveys, respectively. The complete results are available at http://www.hoover.org/warriors-and-citizens-crosstabs-1 (CM1T) and http://www.hoover.org/warriors-and-citizens-crosstabs-2 (CM2T).
5. Franklin D. Roosevelt, "Fireside Chat 20: On the Progress of the War," transcript, February 23, 1942, http://millercenter.org/president/fdroosevelt/speeches/speech-3326.
6. Ibid.
7. Barack Obama, "Statement by the President on ISIL," September 10, 2014, http://www.whitehouse.gov/the-press-office/2014/09/10/statement-president-isil-1.
8. Meade, *Special Providence,* p. 87.

9. Matt Lait, "The Times Poll: O.C. Residents Strongly Back US Role in Somalia," December 10, 1992, *Los Angeles Times,* http://articles.latimes.com/1992-12 -10/news/mn-2495_1_times-poll.

10. Cited in Steven Kull, "Misreading the Public Mood," *Bulletin of Atomic Scientists,* available at http://www.policyattitudes.org/misreadoped.html.

11. Robert Young Pelton, "Black Hawk Down Redux? Another Famine, Another War: What Did America Learn from 1993?" *Somalia Report,* July 21, 2011, http://www.somaliareport.com/index.php/post/1196/Black_Hawk_Down _Redux.

12. George W. Bush quoted in Robert Woodward, *Bush at War,* New York: Simon & Schuster, 2002, p. 131.

13. Ibid., p. 310.

14. U.S. Dept. of Defense, *Instruction Number 3000.05: Stability Operations,* September 16, 2009, http://www.dtic.mil/whs/directives/corres/pdf /300005p.pdf. U.S. Army and Marine Corps, *The U.S. Army/Marine Corps Counterinsurgency Field Manual,* foreword by David H. Petraeus, James F. Amos, and John A. Nagl, Chicago: University of Chicago Press, 2007. See also Nadia Schadlow, "War and the Art of Governance," *Parameters,* vol. 33, no. 3, Autumn 2003, pp. 85–94.

15. U.S. Dept. of Defense, "Personnel," https://www.dmdc.osd.mil/appj/dwp/dwp _reports.jsp.

16. Reported in Adam Clymer, "War in the Gulf: Public Opinion; Poll Finds Deep Backing While Optimism Fades," *New York Times,* January 22, 1991, http://www.nytimes.com/1991/01/22/us/war-in-the-gulf-public-opinion-poll -finds-deep-backing-while-optimism-fades.html.

17. For Vice President Richard Cheney's comments during this period, see "Iraq Insurgency in 'Last Throes,' Cheney Says," CNN.com, June 20, 2005, http://www.cnn.com/2005/US/05/30/cheney.iraq. On the emerging counterinsurgency battles, see Jonathan Finer, "Among Insurgents in Iraq, Few Foreigners Are Found," *Washington Post,* November 17, 2005, http://www.washingtonpost.com/wp-dyn/content/article/2005/11/16 /AR2005111602519.html.

18. Tom Donilon quoted in Bob Woodward, *Obama's Wars,* New York: Simon & Schuster, 2010, p. 297.

19. Woodward, *Obama's Wars,* p. 298.

20. Woodward, *Obama's Wars,* p. 299.

21. Robert M. Gates, *Duty: Memoirs of a Secretary at War,* New York: Alfred A. Knopf, p. 362.

22. Russell F. Weigley, "The American Civil-Military Culture Gap: A Historical Perspective, Colonial Times to the Present," in Peter D. Feaver and Richard

H. Kohn, eds., *Soldiers and Civilians: The Civil-Military Gap and American National Security,* Cambridge: MIT Press, 2001, pp. 216–217.

23. National Security Strategy, May 2010, http://www.whitehouse.gov/sites /default/files/rss_viewer/national_security_strategy.pdf.

24. "A Report to the National Security Council - NSC 68," April 12, 1950, President's Secretary's File, Truman Papers, available at https://www .trumanlibrary.org/whistlestop/study_collections/coldwar/documents /pdf/10-1.pdf.

25. Eleven percent polled said modern wars were winnable but the military had not figured out how to win them; 34 percent said the problem was due to civilian decision making.

26. Peter Moore, "One Year Later Americans Back Military Action in Syria," YouGov, August 29, 2014, https://today.yougov.com/news/2014/08/29 /military-action-syria.

27. The 2014/2015 text of the Authority for the Use of Military Force against the Islamic State of Iraq and the Levant Act was introduced on June 16, 2015 and is available at https://www.govtrack.us/congress/bills/114/s1587/text. The 2001 "Text of Authorization for Use of Military Force" is available at https://www.govtrack.us/congress/bills/107/sjres23/text/enr. In addition, see testimony of General Jim Mattis (Ret.) to the House Intelligence Committee on September 18, 2014, available at http://www.businessinsider.com/mattis -testimony-isis-2014.

28. Barack Obama, "Statement by the President on ISIL," September 10, 2014, http://www.whitehouse.gov/the-press-office/2014/09/10/statement -president-isil-1.

29. Rebecca Riffkin, "Jobs, Government, and Economy Remain Top U.S. Problems," May 19, 2014, Gallup, http://www.gallup.com/poll/169289/jobs -government-economy-remain-top-problems.aspx.

30. President Theodore Roosevelt reportedly coined the phrase to describe the power of the presidential office to shape public sentiment and mobilize actions. Doris Kearns Goodwin, *The Bully Pulpit,* New York: Simon & Schuster, 2013, p. xi.

31. Barack Obama, "Remarks by the President at the Veterans of Foreign Wars Convention," August 17, 2009, http://www.whitehouse.gov/the_press_office /Remarks-by-the-President-at-the-veterans-of-foreign-wars-convention.

32. Quoted in Kenneth L. Deutsch and Joseph R. Fornieri, http://abrahamlincolnsclassroom.org/abraham-lincoln-in-depth /abraham-lincoln-and-public-opinion.

33. See discussion in H. R. McMaster, *Dereliction of Duty,* New York: HarperCollins, 1997, pp. 62–63, 70.

34. See, for example, Office of the Press Secretary, "Remarks by President Obama and the Presidents of Estonia, Lithuania, and Latvia," August 30, 2013, http://www.whitehouse.gov/the-press-office/2013/08/30/remarks -president-obama-and-presidents-estonia-lithuania-and-latvia.

35. "YouGov/*Economist* Poll," September 20–22, 2014, http://d25d2506sfb94s .cloudfront.net/cumulus_uploads/document/0pgcgrpbx9/econToplines.pdf. See also Rasmussen Reports, "73% Worry about Obama's Lack of Strategy for ISIS," September 2, 2014, http://www.rasmussenreports.com/public_content /politics/general_politics/september_2014/73_worry_about_obama_s_lack _of_strategy_for_isis. This shift occurred in other countries as well, such as the United Kingdom, where British support for confronting ISIS went from over 36 percent to over 57 percent after the second beheading by ISIS. See also Alexandra Jaffe, "Poll: Most Disapprove of Obama Handling of ISIS," CNN, February 17, 2015, http://www.cnn.com/2015/02/16/politics/cnn-poll -isis-obama-approval.

36. Mark Preston, "CNN Poll Finds Majority of Americans Alarmed by ISIS," September 8, 2014, http://www.cnn.com/2014/09/08/politics/cnn-poll-isis.

37. Pew Research Center, "Public Confidence in War Effort Falters but Support for War Holds Steady," March 25, 2003, http://www.people-press.org/2003/03/25 /public-confidence-in-war-effort-falters.

38. Valerie Lincy and Gary Milhollin, "Iran's Nuclear Timetable," August 31, 2015, Iran Watch, http://www.iranwatch.org/our-publications/articles-reports /irans-nuclear-timetable.

39. Pew Research Center, "Increased Public Support for the U.S. Arming Ukraine," February 23, 2015, http://www.people-press.org/2015/02/23 /increased-public-support-for-the-u-s-arming-ukraine.

40. Henry J. Kaiser Family Foundation, *2013 Survey of Americans on the US Role in Global Health,* November 7, 2013, http://kff.org/global-health-policy /poll-finding/2013-survey-of-americans-on-the-u-s-role-in-global-health.

41. Richard K. Betts, "Is Strategy an Illusion?" *International Security,* vol. 25, no. 2, Fall 2000, p. 5.

42. Hew Strachan, "The Strategic Consequences of the World War," *American Interest,* vol. 9, July/August 2014, p. 51.

43. Weigley, p. 237.

CHAPTER 7

Testing the "Flournoy Hypothesis"

Civil-Military Relations in the Post-9/11 Era

Thomas Donnelly

"It's an Eliot Cohen world." Thus spake Michele Flournoy, former under-secretary of defense for policy, possibly a future secretary of defense, and certainly a leading-edge indicator of attitudes among the Washington smart set on matters of military affairs, at a recent conference on the future of war.[1] While her precise meaning was cryptic, the context was the topic of civil-military relations. What Flournoy meant was that she had accepted the argument advanced in Cohen's *Supreme Command*,[2] the most widely read if not necessarily the most widely understood book on the subject in the last generation, that soldiers and statesmen in wartime engage in an "unequal dialogue" wherein civilians must strive to give due consideration to commanders' best military judgments but retain the power and responsibility of decision making. Let's call this, for the purposes of this essay, the Flournoy Hypothesis.

But is it, indeed, an "Eliot Cohen world"? Do American presidents and their advisers in fact attempt to engage in this kind of unequal dialogue or otherwise emulate the models of wartime leadership—Abraham Lincoln, Winston Churchill, Georges Clemenceau, and David Ben-Gurion—sketched in *Supreme Command*? And, perhaps even more critically given the United States' role as guarantor of a system of international security, does this unequal dialogue continue in peacetime or in the formulation of broader defense policy? Finally, can one see a reflection of the Flournoy Hypothesis at work in public opinion polls or when the US Congress performs a subordinate but critical role in the raising and regulating of the American military?

This essay will argue that, although advanced thinkers such as Flournoy have sworn *bay'ah* to the need for energetic civilian oversight of military affairs, in behavior the US defense establishment is a creature in a Samuel Huntington world, meaning that it endorses a rigid distinction between military and civilian spheres of competence and, frequently, a *de facto* embrace of "objective control"—Huntington's model for achieving civilian supremacy while granting a special status to military "professionals." The argument will begin by placing Cohen within the context of the civil-military debate of the post-cold-war era, a debate shaped largely by critiques of Huntington. A second section will present a brief summary of the wartime actions of the Bush and Obama administrations, suggesting that, with the exception of the last two years of the Bush administration and the attempt to implement the Iraq "surge," the pattern of behavior has been more Huntingtonian than Cohenian. A third section will consider the actions of Congress and attitudes of the public to claim that the world of American civil-military relations is actually becoming increasingly Huntingtonian. This is particularly so when the broader range of defense issues is taken into account and most especially when one looks closely at the issue of post-traumatic stress disorder (PTSD); the oft-observed civil-military gap may not merely be "professionalized" but increasingly medicalized. Lastly, the essay will conclude with a reflection on the work of Morris Janowitz, the sociologist whose observations about the "constabulary" nature of many forms of military operations—though driven by the advent of "limited war" in the shadow of nuclear arms rather than the kind of long-running irregular wars of today—would enrich the discussion about American civil-military relations in the post-9/11 period, even if it does not provide an alternative theory.

It's a Kohn-Feaver-Cohen World

The Flournoy Hypothesis is certainly true in one respect: it captures in shorthand the trend of post-cold-war scholarship on civil-military relations. A comprehensive survey of the field is well beyond the scope of this paper, but sketching the academic trends will suggest how the most perceptive policymakers approach their dealings with military leaders; Cohen and like-minded observers have profoundly shaped what intelligent civilian leaders think a healthy civil-military relationship looks like, as the Flournoy quip indicates.

The point of departure for any survey of recent and influential literature on civil-military issues must be Richard H. Kohn's article "Out of Control: The Crisis in Civil-Military Relations," published in the spring 1994 issue of the *National Interest*.[3] The piece was written during Bill Clinton's first year as president, a year that had seen a deepening divide between the White House and the Pentagon. Les Aspin, a longtime defense intellectual and formerly chairman of the House Armed Services Committee, had been fired as Clinton's defense secretary in the wake of the "Black Hawk Down" mission in Mogadishu, Somalia, but his replacement had yet to be named or confirmed; indeed, the first choice to replace Aspin, Admiral Bobby Ray Inman (Ret.), had withdrawn from consideration amid controversy. The first line of Kohn's article, "The US military is now more alienated from its civilian leadership than at any time in American history, and more vocal about it," very much captured the zeitgeist.

Kohn's article received a further boost because it dealt with the topic of permitting homosexuals to serve openly in the military, a proposal made by candidate Clinton in the 1992 campaign and a key issue for gay-rights activists in their efforts to achieve greater acceptance in the social mainstream and thus for an increasingly important component of the Democratic Party's political base. While Kohn did not take a position on the underlying issue, he—quite correctly—stigmatized the tactics of the very popular chairman of the Joint Chiefs of

Staff, General Colin Powell. The general, wrote Kohn, "virtually defied the President-elect, never denying rumors in November-December 1992 that he might resign over the issue, doing nothing to scotch rumors that his fellow chiefs might do the same, doing nothing to discourage retired generals from lobbying on Capitol Hill to form an alliance against lifting the ban [on open homosexual service]. General Powell and the Joint Chiefs then appeared to negotiate publicly with the President at a meeting in late January 1993—and privately through the Secretary of Defense, the press, and Congress—for the compromise finally forced on Bill Clinton last summer. On this issue, the military took advantage of a young, incoming president with extraordinarily weak authority in military affairs."[4]

Alas, the topicality and political saliency of Kohn's piece probably served to obscure its structural and scholarly critique; the article was widely read for the wrong reasons and reinforced a predisposition by liberal Democrats to see the military as irredeemably conservative and prone to insubordination. Lost in the hubbub were two historical and structural observations that bore on the changing nature of modern American civil-military relations. First, Kohn gave a brief but powerful account of the "consequences of growth" in the size and permanence of the professional US military from World War II to the creation of the all-volunteer force of the post-Vietnam era, resulting in a kind of military "clientism." The Pentagon, he wrote, had become an entrenched bureaucratic interest group that had "refined into art the pitting of Congress and President against each other in pursuit of its own ends."[5] Second, Kohn pointed to a problem not well understood— or much considered—even now: the "reforms" of the 1985 Goldwater-Nichols Act, and particularly the centralization of power around the Joint Chiefs of Staff (JCS) chairman had created additional civil-military obstacles; if Powell was the criminal, his Goldwater-Nichols powers provided many of his weapons.

Finally, Kohn's article was an unstated but incisive critique of Huntington's model of separate civilian and military spheres of competence and his theory of "objective" control by promoting an ethos of military "professionalism." Proper "civilian control is not a fact but a process," argued Kohn. Moreover, "the system does not work smoothly much of the time. . . . [E]ven when there appears to be harmony, there is ongoing negotiation, compromise, conflict, and maneuvering, the reality of which makes 'civilian control' a far more complicated and less certain business." He observed that, beyond wartime decision making, the weight of military influence in "foreign, defense, economic and social policy" was also an important measure of civil-military relations. Ultimately, "just where the line defining civilian control and proper civil-military relationships lies has never been, and cannot be, determined with clarity and finality; [the] demarcation [is] situational."[6]

Peter Feaver's Armed Servants: *Agency, Oversight, and Civil-Military Relations* advanced a model of the interactions between soldiers and statesmen that was very much a critique of Huntington, notwithstanding that Huntington had served as one of Feaver's dissertation mentors. Feaver has been a peripatetic influence on the discussion of civil-military affairs for the past generation; beyond his academic career and stature as a political scientist, he served on the National Security Council staff in both the Clinton and George W. Bush administrations. He also, along with Kohn, directed the Triangle Institute for Security Studies (TISS) Project on the Gap between Military and Civilian Society, conducting a comprehensive survey of both civilian and military attitudes; the prominence of the TISS project has made the idea of the "gap" the understood framework for civil-military discussions for the past two decades.

Feaver's *Armed Servants* begins with an acknowledgement of the durability of Huntington's work: "Huntington's theory, outlined in *The Soldier and the State* [1957], remains the dominant theoretical paradigm in civil-military relations, especially the study of American civil-military relations." The durability of the theory has had consequences: Huntington's "institutional approach"—that is, the granting of an autonomous, "professional" sphere of competence to the military—"continues to frame analyses of democratic control over the military." And lastly, Feaver makes an observation central to the arguments in this essay: "Huntington's prescriptions for how best to structure civil-military relations continue to find a very receptive ear within one very important audience, the American officer corps itself."[7]

But if *Armed Servants* takes the Huntingtonian model as a point of departure, Feaver's principal purpose is to advance an alternative, adapting an economic "principal-agent" framework to his analysis of recent American civil-military relations. From this, Feaver builds a cause-and-effect theory of how soldiers and statesmen participate in "strategic interactions" within a "hierarchy."[8] In other words, Feaver wishes to preserve the Huntingtonian distinction between civilian and military spheres—as he rightly observes, the whole concept of civil-military relations is dependent upon this distinction—but introduce a more dynamic understanding of the relationship, in a way similar to Kohn's concept of a situationally defined process.

This essay can do no more than summarize Feaver's painstaking explication and argumentation. A few passages will have to suffice: "The civilian principal establishes a military agent to provide the security function for the state, but then must take pains to ensure that the military agent continues to do the civilian's bidding. Given the adverse selection and moral hazard problems endemic in any agency relationship, but particularly acute in the civil-military context, civilian oversight of the military is crucial."[9] Feaver further adapts two concepts from principal-agency theory to explain the "strategic interaction" he posits. In the military context, "working" means, essentially, following civilian direction as intended, while "shirking" is to manipulate the implementation of civilian direction in a way that shapes decision making. Finally, Feaver extracts from this model a normative theory of civil-military relations, whereby, in short, civilians have a "right to be wrong" and the military is obligated to follow their direction even if unwise.[10]

The latter chapters of *Armed Servants* apply Feaver's agency theory to case studies of the early post-cold-war years up through the Balkans wars of the 1990s. These echo many of the themes in Kohn's work: "[T]he collective picture that emerges is of a much messier civil-military relationship than traditional theory admits, although perhaps not the full-blown crisis that is prominent in the conventional wisdom on the post-cold war era."[11] In fact, says Feaver, the mess is so great that, in a substantial number of examples, it is unclear that military professionalism—the rock upon which Huntington stands—has an uncontestable claim on operational competence. "History shows," he writes, "that the military is not as 'right' in civil-military disputes as the military triumphalists might suppose. . . . But even when the military is right, democratic theory intervenes and insists that it submit to the civilian leadership that the polity has chosen. . . . The republic would be better served even by foolish working than by enlightened shirking."[12]

To read Eliot Cohen's *Supreme Command* is to wonder whether soldiers ever are right in their arguments with statesmen. Cohen paints vivid portraits of energetic and intrusive civilian leadership in wartime. Contrary to much historiography, Abraham Lincoln did not so much "find a general" from among his officers as force his army and the country into giving him the war he wanted, even while he changed his war aims.[13] Georges Clemenceau loved France enough to mistrust Frenchmen, especially French generals bent on restoring a glory that had passed.[14] Winston Churchill demanded that he see, touch, hear, and smell every detail of World War II and employed verbally enhanced interrogation techniques on his generals, especially those who attended him most personally.[15] David Ben-Gurion agreed; in war, he believed, "there are no great issues, only details," and thus did he convert the underground Haganah into the Israel Defense Forces.[16] None of these great leaders was willing to grant much autonomy to his military men, and indeed much of their greatness came from their willingness to intrude into the sphere of military affairs.

Cohen is, like Feaver, a student of Huntington's committed to a view of civil-military relations that originates in a critique of *The Solder and the Statesman*, what Cohen characterizes as the "normal" theory of civil-military relations. A short passage in the book's opening chapter shows, however, how radical Cohen's intent is. He begins with one of Clausewitz's most quoted but least considered aphorisms: "[W]ar is not merely an act of policy but a true political instrument, a continuation of political intercourse, carried on with other means."[17] As Cohen then rightly argues, the Clausewitzian definition of the nature of war— now such a commonplace in both American military and civilian elite understandings—is directly at odds with the Huntingtonian assertion of military "professionalism" and the acknowledgement of a separate sphere of military competence. And thus the very structure that defines "civil-military relations" begins to shake:

> If every facet of military life may have political consequences, if one cannot find a refuge from politics in the levels of war (saying, for example, that "grand strategy" is properly subject to civilian influence, but "military strategy" is not), civil-military relations are problematic. The Clausewitzian formula for civil-military relations has it that the statesman may legitimately interject himself in any aspect of war-making, although it is often imprudent for him to do so. On most occasions political leaders will have neither the knowledge nor the judgment to intervene in a tactical decision, and most episodes in war have little or no political impact. But there can be in Clausewitz's view no arbitrary line dividing civilian and military responsibility, no neat way of carving off a distinct sphere of military action.[18]

In the concluding chapter of *Supreme Command,* Cohen elaborates on this point, not only with a more detailed critique of Huntington but also of revisionists and dissenters from the ideal of military professionalism. In advancing an alternative framework for civilian control—the "unequal dialogue" whereby the discussion is open but the decision making rests, finally, with the civilian power—Cohen proceeds from the Clausewitzian premise that soldiers and statesmen are embarked upon a common endeavor, one inevitably defined by politics.[19]

In sum, the larger meaning of the Flournoy Hypothesis might be taken as "it's no longer a Sam Huntington world." The most influential scholars of the past generation—those who have both retained an academic gravitas while achieving a familiarity with, and a reputation among, policy practitioners—have been, to use Peter Feaver's term, Huntington-slayers.[20] Kohn, Feaver, and Cohen alike attack the idea of separate and fixed spheres of civilian and military competence, see the actual practice of civil-military interaction as a messy process fraught with uncertainty even while retaining a hierarchical structure, and reject the notion of civilian control through professional autonomy. But how deeply has the Kohn-Feaver-Cohen paradigm penetrated the recent practice of strategy making and statecraft?

Civil-Military Relations since 9/11

President George W. Bush famously included *Supreme Command* in his summer 2002 vacation reading list, and both Cohen and Feaver served at very high levels in his administration.[21] But how much their ideas influenced the conduct of Bush military policy—or how widely shared the Flournoy Hypothesis really has been in the Obama years—is not apparent. The following, somewhat potted, history of the recent past will necessarily highlight anecdotes in lieu of a more complete and nuanced account that could only emerge over time. This section will highlight two cases of close and energetic civilian scrutiny—two moments that appear to support the Flournoy Hypothesis—and contrast them with the larger and longer trends that would seem to suggest the durability of the Huntington view of fundamentally separate civilian and military realms of competence. Moreover, there may be in this larger pattern a dangerous proclivity on the part of civilians to opt for a form of "subjective control" by means of appointing politically pliable senior generals, while the military itself clings ever more tightly to the ideal of "objective control" and military autonomy.

To say that the terrorist attacks of September 11, 2001, were a strategic surprise to the US military is a very large understatement. Yet that surprise gave then defense secretary Donald Rumsfeld the opportunity to force the armed services to respond in a manner of his choosing, and the two very rapid and hugely successful invasions of Afghanistan and Iraq that followed stand as exemplars of energetic, intrusive, and productive civilian oversight. That Rumsfeld made himself personally obnoxious—on a near-Churchillian scale—to his generals or that he failed disastrously to anticipate or to adapt to the consequences of his victories may cloud or even obscure but does not erase his accomplishments. Subtract Rummy from the equation and both wars would have been very different.[22]

Rumsfeld received his first briefing on potential plans for invading Afghanistan from General Tommy Franks, then head of U.S. Central Command, on September 20, 2001. He summarized it for President Bush thus: "You will find it disappointing. I did."[23] Bob Woodward describes the situation thus: "Rumsfeld also made his disappointment clear in National Security Council meetings, and Bush also felt the military had to be pushed to move more rapidly. Franks had said, 'it would take months to get forces in the area and plans drawn up for a major military assault in Afghanistan.' 'You don't have months,' Rumsfeld had said. He wanted Franks to think days or weeks. Franks wanted bases and this and that. . . . Rumsfeld said he wanted creative ideas, something between launching cruise missiles and an all-out military operation. 'Try again,' Rumsfeld hammered."[24]

Rumsfeld did indeed force Franks and the military to develop and support a creative plan combining small special operations and Special Forces units with air power in support of Uzbek and Tajik militias to oust the Taliban quickly and at low cost; an operation that sage Washington observers warned would immediately become a Vietnam-like "quagmire" was largely complete by March 2002.[25] Rumsfeld intruded into every aspect of military planning, including minute details of deployment lists. Thus encouraged by success, the secretary redoubled his efforts as planning for an invasion of Iraq began. In *Cobra II: The Inside Story of the Invasion and Occupation of Iraq,* Michael R. Gordon and Marine General Bernard E. Trainor (Ret.) reported on the initial briefing for Rumsfeld on Iraq planning in late 2001:

> As [the operations director for the Joint Chiefs of Staff Marine Lieutenant General Gregory] Newbold outlined the plan, which called for as many as 500,000 troops, it was clear that Rumsfeld was growing increasingly irritated. For Rumsfeld, the plan required too many troops and supplies and took too long to execute. It was, Rumsfeld declared, the product of old thinking and the embodiment of everything that was wrong with the military.
>
> [JCS chairman Air Force General Richard] Myers asked Rumsfeld how many troops he thought might be needed. The defense secretary said in exasperation that he did not see why more than 125,000 troops would be required and even that was probably too many. . . .
>
> General Tommy Franks, the [US Central Command] commander, would draw up the new plan, but Rumsfeld would poke, prod, and question the military at every turn. Defense Department civilians would move into Franks's planning cells to monitor his work, and the general would be summoned to Washington repeatedly to present his evolving plan and receive new guidance from his civilian master. The JCS chairman and his staff would be little more than onlookers. Two momentous signals had been sent at Newbold's briefing. Iraq would be the next phase in the Bush administration's self-declared "global war on terror" and the defense secretary would insist on an entirely new kind of Iraq war plan.[26]

In retrospect it might be quipped that Rumsfeld was auditioning to be the subject of a case study in *Supreme Command,* and he came to the post of defense secretary with an aggressive view of proper civil-military relations shaped by the debates of the 1990s and a wariness about the power of forceful JCS chairmen like Powell.[27] But Rumsfeld's energy and indeed his interest seemed to wane as invasion turned, much against his wishes, to occupation and reconstruction in both Afghanistan and Iraq. The defense secretary began to delegate authority to lieutenants he trusted politically such as Ambassador L. Paul Bremer and generals John Abizaid and George Casey. But there was no greater measure of Rumsfeld's disengagement than the hapless Lieutenant General Ricardo Sanchez, a man of little political experience or clout, unprepared to, and, as his forces were drained away, unable to respond, as Iraq demanded not reconstruction but counterinsurgency. On a visit to troops in Kuwait in December 2004, Rumsfeld was challenged by a soldier about the shortages of body armor and other protection. His unfortunate reply was indicative of his emerging attitude: "You go to war with the army you have, not the army you might want or wish to have at a later time."[28]

In short, late-vintage Rumsfeld began to resemble Huntington's model of "subjective control," ceding to, but minimizing, military "professionalism" while selecting generals for their political reliability. Officers like Sanchez might protest that, in their professional opinion, they lacked the resources to do the mission; Rumsfeld's response was less to contest that judgment than to ignore it. In Abizaid and Casey, and in JCS chairmen such as Myers and his successor Marine General Peter Pace, he found subordinates whom he knew would not protest. A sizeable majority of the public disapproves of Rumsfeld's style of interaction with the military; 61.5 percent of YouGov respondents think that nonmilitary people getting overly involved in purely military affairs hurts military effectiveness (CM2T 61).[29]

By contrast, Rumsfeld's behavior reinforced the military's belief in Huntington's separate-sphere model and ideals of objective control and autonomy. Ironically, in retirement, Lieutenant General Gregory Newbold became a symbol of the officer-class critique of Rumsfeld. In April 2006, he was one of a handful of generals to call on Rumsfeld to resign. Americans have mixed views of officers resigning in protest of an order (that they perceive as unwise) from a senior civilian in the Defense Department. Some 43.9 percent think resignation is appropriate, 26.9 percent think it is inappropriate, and 29.2 percent are not sure (CM2T 84). Writing in *Time* magazine, Newbold charged that Rumsfeld's Iraq planning "was done with a casualness and swagger that are the special province of those who have never had to execute these missions—or bury the results."[30] Although Newbold was speaking after the fact, the public in general roundly disapproves of military officers airing their grievances to the press. Some 60.4 percent of Americans think it is inappropriate for officers to leak their thoughts about orders that they believe to be unwise to the press while only 17.2 percent think it is appropriate (CM2T 88). Newbold later told Gordon and Trainor, "My regret is that at the time [of the initial Franks briefing] I did not say, 'Mr. Secretary, if you try to put a number [of troops] on a mission like this you may cause enormous mistakes. Give the military the task, give the military what you would like to see them do, and then let them come up with it.'"[31]

By the end of 2006, and in the wake of the Democrats' sweeping victories in the midterm elections, the once-invincible Rumsfeld became a casualty of the failures in Iraq. But so did, in large measure, the Bush administration's confidence in military "professionalism" or "autonomy," which had become associated with Abizaid and Casey's willingness to cut America's losses and withdraw from Iraq. George W. Bush had styled himself as a delegator and "decider," but to accomplish a "surge" that might revive his Iraq policy, the commander in chief had to become at least a temporary intruder and override his senior generals to change the course of the war. In the period between winter 2006 and the end of his presidency, Bush's behavior bears out the Flournoy Hypothesis but, paradoxically, can also be viewed as an example of subjective control. The president engaged in military affairs to ensure that Iraq strategy mirrored his policy, while at the same time passively delegating the execution to personalities and generals he could trust politically. Bush was "given" a pair of generals in David

Petraeus and Raymond Odierno but did not "find" them to the degree that Lincoln, for example, found—and made—Ulysses S. Grant or William Tecumseh Sherman. But arguably the most important "general" in shaping the Iraq surge was a retired one: former army vice chief of staff Jack Keane.

In his well-researched telling of the surge tale, *The Gamble*, Thomas Ricks introduces Keane in a chapter entitled "Keane Takes Command": "In the fall of 2006, Jack Keane effectively became the chairman of the Joint Chiefs of Staff, stepping in to direct US strategy in a war, to coordinate the thinking of the White House and the Pentagon, and even to pick the commander who would lead the change in the fight. . . . Keane was given his opening by the failure of the chairman of the Joint Chiefs, Gen. Peter Pace, who was proving unable to deal with the Iraq war. With no official backing, and nothing but his credibility and persuasive abilities to go on, Keane helped . . . formulate 'the surge' as a new strategy for Iraq, pitched it to the president, and then, with a green light from [President] Bush, told top officials at the Pentagon about how to proceed."[32]

In his push for a troop surge and a switch to a counterinsurgency approach in Iraq, Keane had two important allies in uniform in Odierno, then corps commander in Baghdad, and Petraeus, then head of the army's Command and General Staff College and supervising a very public rewrite of the services counterinsurgency manual that also served as a debate about Iraq strategy. But most of the rest of the senior military establishment was against him, including Rumsfeld and his generals, Abizaid and Casey, along with new JCS chairman Pace. Even Rumsfeld's replacement as defense secretary, Robert Gates, initially recommended a kind of split-the-baby option with a smaller troop surge but retained the existing strategy he outlined to Bush. "The 'big idea' here is the 'pivot point,' " Gates emphasized, "to transfer leadership and primary responsibility for security in Iraq to Iraqis, with the United States in a support role. As they gain confidence and show success, we can begin to stand down."[33]

When it bought the idea of the surge, the Bush White House wanted Keane to return to active duty to run the war. Though Keane demurred, his recommendation of Petraeus to take the job ensured that both his approach and his influence would endure, to the continuing irritation of the Joint Chiefs. The full story of Keane's role has yet to be told, but his prominence makes it difficult to fully assess the Iraq surge as a case of civil-military relations. Yes, President Bush (and Vice President Dick Cheney) intervened to remove commanders and change the direction of Iraq strategy. The White House was also energetic in engaging with the Iraqi government and with Prime Minister Nouri al-Maliki to ensure that the Shi'a majority exercised some restraint toward other factions, particularly the Sunni tribe leaders of Anbar Province. But, having at last aligned the military strategy with his overall strategy of building a representative government in Baghdad and found a winning team in Keane, Petraeus, and Odierno, Bush again seemed content to delegate the conduct of the war to one group of "professionals"—professionals including Ambassador Ryan Crocker, a career foreign service officer in place of the politically connected Bremer—while bypassing or ignoring others such as Abizaid or Casey, whom Bush made army chief of staff upon his relief from Iraq command. To his credit, Bush did back Defense Secretary Gates's efforts to browbeat the Pentagon into supporting the war effort more fully, but Gates's moves were driven by immediate necessity and have proved evanescent, not lasting reforms.

If this assessment of civil-military relations in the late Bush years is incomplete and ambiguous, coming to grips with the behavior of the Obama administration is probably a larger fool's errand. But the broad outlines of the story are clear: the relationship was a tense one from the start. It was framed at one end by a new president who had won election in large measure due to his critique of Bush policy and promises to "end" the conflicts in Iraq and Afghanistan and an underlying desire to "demilitarize" US foreign policy and reduce the "military-industrial complex." At the other end stood Secretary Gates, a cadre of generals who had earned distinction for leading what now appeared to be a successful counterinsurgency campaign in Iraq, and a larger officer corps and dissenting defense bureaucracy opposed to the surge strategy, in part because such irregular wars posed a threat to the larger-scale conventional conflicts they believed to be the core competency of military professionals. The public perceives the military to be biased towards Republicans. Some 42 percent of the public believe that members of the military are somewhat or much more likely to vote for Republicans than for Democrats in elections (versus the 11 percent who believe the opposite) (CM1T 40). In other words, this was an accident waiting to happen both in the realms of the conduct of war and larger defense policy.

Barack Obama's approach to the use of US military power may be better suited to the powers of the psychoanalyst than the historian, and no case has been more painful to the president than that of the war in Afghanistan. Candidate Obama first differentiated himself from George Bush by describing Afghanistan as the "right" and "good" war by contrast to the "dumb" war in Iraq. Yet from beginning to end, Obama has struggled to find or to sustain a successful Afghanistan strategy or even to define a strong role as commander in chief. This shortcoming likely has affected the public's views of the war. Some 51.3 percent (versus 34.4 percent) of Americans somewhat or strongly opposed continued military involvement in Afghanistan after 2014 (CM2T 72).

In his memoir *Duty,* former secretary of defense Robert Gates recalls a January 20, 2011, Oval Office meeting to review Afghanistan strategy and set targets for troop reductions that would lead to a withdrawal by the end of 2014. As in nearly every previous Afghanistan review, the administration had engaged in a prolonged debate about the issue, leading almost inevitably to leaked press reports from all sides in the debate. A further pattern played itself out: the president and his counselors complained that the military was "jamming" or "boxing them in" by leaking proposals of higher levels of American commitment, while a group centered around Vice President Joe Biden, which wanted to limit the effort, not only spun stories of military insubordination but strategic failure. "It was as if we had never stopped arguing since 2009," writes Gates.[34]

As the review continued, temperatures rose. Obama opened a March 3, 2011, session, as Gates reports, "with a blast," saying, "I am troubled by people popping off in the press that [the beginning of troop reductions in] 2011 doesn't mean anything. . . . My intention is to begin the security transition in July 2011 and complete it by the end of 2014. We will think through the glidepath [of troop drawdowns], but I will push back very hard if anyone proposes [delaying] the drawdowns. I prefer [accelerating them]. I don't want any recommendations trying to finesse the orders I laid out. If I believe I am being gamed. . . ."[35] Gates concluded that "the president doesn't trust his [on-scene military] commander . . . doesn't believe in his own strategy, and doesn't consider the war to be his" and that "Biden was subjecting Obama to Chinese water torture, every day saying, 'the military can't be trusted.'"[36]

A remarkably similar picture is drawn in Bob Woodward's account of the administration's initial Afghanistan strategy reviews. These reviews consumed most of Obama's first year in office and established the pattern of mistrust described by Gates; as one review followed another, press leaks mounted, including the bleak assessment and troop-increase recommendations of General Stanley McChrystal, newly promoted to lead the effort in Afghanistan. Woodward describes the mood in the White House: "Facing an unexpected and stunning strategic request was not where Obama had planned to be in the fall of the first year of his presidency. On top of that, the military was out campaigning, closing off his choices, and the White House was losing control of the public narrative. Obama vented to [his closest political advisers, Rahm] Emanuel, [David] Axelrod, and [Tom] Donilon, the national security staffer with whom he spent the most time. . . . Donilon unloaded on many people at the Pentagon, invoking the president's name and insisting Obama wanted this fixed immediately. He was a lawyer with one client—the president. But instead of absorbing Obama's frustration, he was a pure transmission belt for it."[37] Civil-military mistrust also framed subsequent administration decisions both when the president chose to use force, as in Libya,[38] and when he chose not to, as in Syria.[39]

But as Peter Feaver has pointed out, in the late Obama years the larger driver of civil-military tensions are the deepened, accelerated, and across-the-board budget and forces cuts mandated in the 2011 Budget Control Act, and in particular its "sequestration" provision. What Feaver writes about the administration—that, in search of other, domestic political advantages, the "president's refusal to negotiate with Republicans has raised fears that he is willing to prolong sequestration, at least insofar as it applies to the Defense Department"[40]—could equally be said about the Republican congressional majority.[41] Indeed, while journalistic and scholarly interest in civil-military matters most often centers on use-of-force issues, there are underlying institutional and social divisions that undercut the Flournoy Hypothesis and suggest that the separation of the Huntingtonian civil and professional-military spheres is growing.

The YouGov Survey and the Civil-Military Meaning of the PTSD "Crisis"

One of the now standard measures of the civil-military gap is the "familiarity gap"; indeed, this phenomenon is discussed at length in the essay in this volume by Jim Golby, Lindsay Cohn, and Peter Feaver. In many cases, the quality of familiarity is taken as personal familiarity and associated with having a family member in uniform, working with a veteran, and so forth. For instance, only 8.3 percent of Americans currently work with someone actively serving in the military (CM2T 3). But there is another kind of familiarity, call it "knowledge familiarity," that is increasingly likely to be an important measure of the ability of

American politicians to exercise the kind of vigorous civilian control captured in *Supreme Command* or stipulated in the Flournoy Hypothesis. The inability of Americans to guess the number of people serving in the U.S. Army and in the Marine Corps is an example of Americans' lack of "knowledge familiarity."[42] This is especially so given the continued desire—despite laments about the "other 1 percent" of Americans in uniform—to retain a very small, "all-volunteer," professional force.[43]

The YouGov survey confirms that military service is an increasingly unfamiliar pursuit for most Americans, and somewhat more so for American "elites," despite the experience of the 9/11 attacks. Asked whether "you or a member of your immediate family served in the military after 1991"—the end of the cold war—77 percent of the general population and 82 percent of elites said no (CM2T 1). The equivalent post-9/11 numbers were 80 percent for the general population and more than 86 percent of elites (CM2T 15). (I take the survey's "elite" designation and, in the context of other questions, high-income levels to be more or less indicative of attitudes among the political establishment; admittedly these are imprecise terms of art.)

The survey also asked whether US politicians were "knowledgeable" about the US military, and about half of both the general population and elites believed either that they were "not very knowledgeable" or "not knowledgeable at all." The results also revealed a consistent distinction in party attitudes: while about 37 percent of self-described Democrats reached a similarly negative conclusion, fully 67 percent of Republicans did (CM2T 15). A substantial number of Americans— about a third of both the general and elite respondents—felt the military was "isolated from American society." Forty-nine percent of self-described "very liberal" survey takers agreed, and there was a 13 percent partisan gap in responses, with Republicans less likely to see an isolated military (CM2T 23). A second set of "agree-disagree" survey questions addressed similar concerns and revealed similar partisan divides. Asked whether "the military is out of step with the rest of society and needs to adapt," 46 percent of Democrats agreed but only

17 percent of Republicans. Fifty-nine percent of Democrats believed there is a "crisis of ethics in our military," compared to 36 percent of Republicans. An even larger partisan gap opens over the "military's treatment of women and homosexuals"; 66 percent of Democrats thought it was unfair, versus 22 percent of Republicans (CM2T 43).

Further, the survey revealed a serious misunderstanding of some of the most basic facts about the US military, beginning with its size. When asked to estimate the number of people "currently serving in all five branches of the US military combined," the mean answer was about 6.5 million (CM2T 58). In fact, the total active-duty force is less than 1.4 million, and even when one includes the reserve components, the force still only totals 2.2 million. If the full cuts inflicted by the 2011 Budget Control Act come to pass, the active-duty army could fall below 400,000. According to the survey, Americans think there are 1.9 million soldiers currently serving; Democrats put it at 2.2 million, while Republicans say 430,000 (CM2T 56).

Finally, the YouGov survey charts attitudes that not only reflect the overall civil-military gap but comprise two of the salient military-social matters recently before Congress: first, the nexus of issues related to sexual harassment and assault, spousal abuse, and domestic violence; second, that of post-traumatic stress. These two sets of issues, also reflected in enacted and proposed legislation, reflect not only the extent of the gap but its character.

It is only a little hyperbolic to conclude that some Americans— those who feel most removed from military life—see the service as an experience leading to pathological behavior. About a third of the survey respondents believed "the military has more sexual harassment and assault than the rest of society." Almost 58 percent of Democrats agree; fewer than 20 percent of Republicans do (CM2T 48). A similar pattern occurs in regard to spousal abuse. Thirty percent of the general population and 34 percent of elites think spousal abuse is a bigger problem in the military than in civilian life. And again, Democrats are more prone to see problems: 45 percent, versus 18 percent of

Republicans (CM2T 45). Additionally, 50.3 percent of Democrats (compared to 15.8 percent of Republicans) believe that the military treats women less fairly than the rest of society (CM2T 25). When the issue is generalized to a propensity to "anti-social behavior," a quarter of the general population thinks the military is a bigger problem, 39 percent of Democrats and just 15 percent of Republicans (CM2T 47).

These survey results could be the product of increased media attention to reports of harassment, assault, and abuse in the military and a concomitant interest in Congress, including proposed legislation. In the spring of 2013, the Pentagon published a study, the Workplace and Gender Relations Survey of Active Duty Members, declaring 3,374 reported cases of sexual assault in the military for 2012.[44] Despite the survey capturing a 35 percent drop from the rate of unwanted sexual contact reported in 2006,[45] the new study excited a bevy of press reports and sparked congressional activity. Typical of the media play was a September 5, 2013, *National Journal* story headlined "How the Military's 'Bro' Culture Turns Women into Targets." The piece was built around a number of vivid anecdotes and a few statistics, but perhaps most revealing were assertions of supposed fact. The article declared that "the military's sexual-assault epidemic is well-known," that it follows from "the military's culture of abuse" that itself reflects the "fundamental . . . values" of the "military's closed society."[46] The *Washington Post* agreed there was an "epidemic" of sexual abuse in the military and the *New York Times* that there was an "entrenched culture of sexual violence."[47] On Capitol Hill, liberal New York senator Kirsten Gillibrand teamed with conservative senators Rand Paul and Ted Cruz to offer legislation that would dramatically overhaul the way in which the military justice system deals with these cases, particularly by taking authority out of the chain of command.

A charge of media and congressional confirmation bias would be difficult to prove—especially since good statistical measures of comparison, both over time and in comparing the military to the civilian world, are hard to come by. But it is difficult, at the same time, not to recognize a pattern of civilian attitudes that sees the world of military professionals as an increasingly distant and dangerous subculture. While 59.6 percent of Americans believe that an isolated military is a bad thing, only 32.5 percent believe that the military is isolated at the moment (CM2T 24, 23). In this regard, the sexual-abuse debate is just the tip of a much larger iceberg of opinion that has formed around the issue of post-traumatic stress and the much-diagnosed "disorder" that is said to result from prolonged military service.

Perhaps the most striking single statistic in the YouGov survey was that 80 percent of the respondents agreed with the statement "Many veterans have difficulty adjusting to civilian life because of the stresses they have experienced in the military" (CM2T 47). The image of the stressed-out veteran, a trope in Hollywood and across popular culture since Vietnam and given renewed life in the wake of the Iraq and Afghanistan wars, has become deeply embedded in Americans' minds and politics. In his memoir, Gates gave voice to an increasingly common view: "I came to believe that no one who had actually been in combat could walk away without scars, some measure of post-traumatic stress." This haunted his sleep: "I would wake in the night, think back to a wounded soldier or Marine I had seen in Landstuhl, Bethesda or Walter Reed [military hospitals], and in my imagination I would put myself in his hospital room and I would hold him to my chest, to comfort him. Silently, in the night at home, I would weep for him."[48]

Compared with other countries, the United States diagnoses PTSD in its military at very high rates. Estimates run between 20 percent and 30 percent; by way of contrast, the Danish military in Afghanistan—which saw as much combat *per capita* as any contingent—has a PTSD diagnosis rate of 2 percent.[49] While there are no doubt many factors contributing to this statistic, one is surely that, as former Marine David J. Morris wrote in his elegant *Evil Hours: A Biography of Post-Traumatic Stress Disorder,* "PTSD is now . . . the *lingua franca* of suffering." He goes on to explain that "it seems that PTSD spoke to something in us at the end of the twentieth century, as if the diagnostic concept held up a fractured mirror to ourselves. . . . In time, PTSD would break out of the VA clinics and begin to insinuate itself into the dream life of the culture in a distinctly civilian fashion. Every age finds its disease. By the 1990s, PTSD as a concept had outgrown its close association with Vietnam and become a cultural meme."[50]

If so, it is one that does not resonate with many in uniform, who react viscerally against being described in this language of suffering. This reaction may also resonate on some level with the public. A majority (51.6 percent) of Americans believe that the military gets less respect than it deserves. Only 10.9 percent believe that it receives more respect than it deserves (CM2T 14). This language of suffering is particularly anathema to those who embrace the idea of Huntingtonian professionalism. "We who are serving, and have served, demand not to be categorized as victims," declared Marine General John Kelly, chief of U.S. Southern Command, in a 2013 Memorial Day address. Kelly, whose son was killed in Afghanistan, contended, "What the experts and commentators are missing, what they will also never understand, is the sense of commitment, joy, and honor, of serving the nation in its uniform."[51] This is the rebuttal of someone who wants honor rather than therapy, expressing his estrangement from those he means to serve.

Is it a Janowitz World?

The persistence of the civil-military gap, wherein a recognition of distinct spheres of competence hardens into something like a view that soldiers and civilians dwell in separate moral universes, presents a continuing challenge in American politics. The challenge comes not only from the expanse of the gap but also from its changing quality: if statesmen begin to treat soldiers as doctors do patients, it will be difficult to restore a healthy civil-military relationship.

The current divide also reflects a second, underlying problem: a failure to come to grips with the Clausewitzian nature of war as a continuation of politics by violent means. One of the Prussian's most apt aphorisms was that "War has its own grammar, but not its own logic."[52] In other words, the logic is political and fundamentally the responsibility of civilians, while the military supplies the grammar by the articulation of violence or the threat of violence. These are two aspects of a single enterprise, not distinct and separate enterprises. Americans especially struggle with this reality. We prefer to divide events into "wartime" and "peacetime," with the presumption that peace is the normal condition. This sentiment manifests itself in American's beliefs about what the president should prioritize. Some 45 percent of Americans believe that the president's top priority should be the economy. By comparison, only 2 percent and 1 percent, respectively, believe that terrorism and the war in Afghanistan should be the president's top priority (CM1T 2). While this predilection may be morally admirable, it is debilitating to a nation that finds itself—still—the guarantor of global security, a position that forces the United States now to fight what Max Boot describes as "savage wars of peace" while maintaining a favorable balance of great powers across Eurasia.[53] These are quite different conflicts from the standoff of the late cold war, the time when the current all-volunteer force was created, the current compact between soldier and state forged, and the Huntington model of civil-military relations enshrined. If American civil-military relations are to retain—or regain—their vigor, they must encompass the ambiguities, both the opportunities and constraints, that the times present and acknowledge the traditional habits of American geopolitical leadership.

Reconsidering the work of sociologist Morris Janowitz would enrich today's civil-military debate. Though he wrote in a very different period and preferred to describe rather than prescribe, his 1960 work *The Professional Soldier* paints a portrait that very much resembles today's civil-military landscape. Although the book was primarily concerned with describing the limits that the proliferation of nuclear weapons in the early cold war had imposed upon the no-substitute-for-victory ethos of World War II, he introduced a more complex notion of military professionalism. "No longer is it feasible for the officer corps, if it is to be organized effectively for strategic deterrence and for limited war, to operate on a double standard of 'peacetime' and 'wartime' premises," he wrote, claiming also that "the use of force in international relations has been so altered that it seems appropriate to speak of constabulary forces rather than military forces."[54]

Janowitz accepted that the US military inhabited a "special environment" reflecting the fact that "it alone has the organizational responsibility for preparing and managing war and combat,"[55] but he did not think that was its sole purpose. Janowitz's "constabulary" force had a wide variety of "lower end" duties that resonate with the tasks taken on in the post-9/11 wars: "military aid programs . . . paramilitary operations . . . guerilla and counter-guerilla warfare."[56] "The officer in the constabulary force," Janowitz claimed, "is particularly attuned to withstand the pressures of constant alerts and tension. He is sensitive to the political and social impact of the military establishment on international security affairs. He is subject to civilian control, not only because of the 'rule of law' and tradition, but also because of self-imposed professional standards and meaningful integration into civilian values."[57] In other words, Janowitz did not expect to extract the political dimension from warfare or the use of armed force or relegate the statesman and the soldier to entirely separate spheres; in Clausewitzian terms, Janowitz's military professional was not a mere grammarian but someone who had been educated in the logic of war from the start: "Under the constabulary concept, even the most junior officer, depending upon his assignment, may be acting as a political agent. Political-military education cannot be delayed until the middle of the officer's career, when he enters the war college. Officer education in politico-military affairs should start in the academy where tactical training must be related to the requirements of international relations, and continue at higher levels of education and professional experience."[58]

Janowitz, whose work on the ideological indoctrination of the World War II Wehrmacht and the importance of a "Nazi nucleus" or "hard core" in sustaining combat effectiveness even as the regime collapsed added a controversial element to the standard "band of brothers" account of small-unit cohesion,[59] believed it was important to inculcate nationally shared but essentially civilian social values into his constabulary force. Although he proposed an "all-volunteer" US military, he questioned "whether a political democracy should have a constabulary force motivated purely by monetary incentives."[60] The goal of political education, Janowitz imagined, was "to develop a commitment to the democratic system and understanding of how it works,"[61] that is, to minimize the civil-military gap by trying to break down the social isolation of the military, acclimating the force to the norms of the larger society. Even absent this education, Americans on balance believe that military leaders share the same values as the American people.[62]

Janowitz did not write systematically about the mechanism of civilian control, but he thought that his model would allow for developing "new devices" to accomplish that end. Indeed, his observation that the health of the civil-military relationship "rests on the vitality of civilian political leadership" seems to anticipate the Kohn-Feaver-Cohen school.[63] Janowitz certainly rejected the Huntington model of objective control, dismissing the idea that "professional ethics alone" would do the job. Janowitz urged that civilian society should permit the military professional to "maintain his code of honor" and develop distinct skills, and thus the constabulary professional would be "amenable to civilian political control because he recognizes that civilians appreciate and understand the tasks and responsibilities of the constabulary force."[64]

Alas, the current generation of American politicians appears to lack the vitality of leadership—either in wartime or in the many tasks that go into managing today's "savage peace"—or an appreciation or understanding of the tasks that befall their military in its constabulary duties. The public concurs. Only 10.9 percent believe that political leaders share society's values while 70.9 percent believe that they do not (CM2T 17). Indeed, in the case of PTSD, it would appear that American society at large is intent upon inculcating an ideology of victimhood rather than one of democratic citizenship; there is an extraordinary range of PTSD therapies, but few that focus on sustaining a code of honor or morality. I will make one last nod to Morris Janowitz, who concluded *The Professional Soldier* with a warning that sounds a very current note: "To deny or destroy the difference between the military and the civilian cannot produce genuine similarity, but runs the risk of creating new forms of tension and unanticipated militarism."[65]

Put it this way: if it's not "an Eliot Cohen world" yet, it needs to become one, and quickly; both soldiers and statesmen seem to be having increasing difficulty either resolving or accommodating the inherent paradoxes of civil-military relations. Perhaps a new edition of *Supreme Command* is needed, one which portrays vitality in leadership in small wars rather than big ones. In any case, neither the soldier's wish for autonomy nor the statesman's desire for political reliability seem to suffice to command a small force with a large task: the preservation of the American peace and the prosperity and political liberty that—for now—the world enjoys.

Notes

1. "Future of War: First Annual Conference," symposium, Washington DC, New America Foundation, February 24-25, 2015, http://www.newamerica.org /international-security/future-of-war.
2. Eliot A. Cohen, *Supreme Command: Soldiers, Statesmen, and Leadership in Wartime,* Free Press, New York, 2002.
3. Richard H. Kohn, "Out of Control: The Crisis in Civil-Military Relations," *National Interest,* Spring 1994, http://nationalinterest.org/article/out-of -control-the-crisis-in-civil-military-relations-343.
4. Ibid.
5. Ibid.
6. Ibid.

7. Peter D. Feaver, *Armed Servants: Agency, Oversight, and Civil-Military Relations,* Cambridge, Massachusetts: Harvard University Press, 2003, p. 7.

8. Ibid., p. 55.

9. Ibid., p. 93.

10. Ibid., pp. 55–95.

11. Ibid., p. 282.

12. Ibid., pp. 300, 302.

13. Cohen, *Supreme Command,* pp. 15–51.

14. Ibid., pp. 52–94.

15. Ibid., pp. 95–132.

16. Ibid., pp. 133–72.

17. Quoted in Cohen, *Supreme Command,* pp. 7–8.

18. Cohen, *Supreme Command,* p. 8.

19. Ibid., pp. 208–48.

20. Feaver, *Armed Servants,* p. 8.

21. See Eliot Cohen, interview by Margaret Warner, *PBS Newshour,* PBS, October 22, 2002, http://www.pbs.org/newshour/bb/entertainment-july -dec02-cohen_10-22.

22. Among the many books already written describing the decision making regarding the Afghanistan and Iraq invasions, several Rumsfeld-centric, nearly sycophantic accounts are illustrative of how the defense secretary saw his role. See Rowan Scarborough, *Rumsfeld's War: The Untold Story of America's Anti-Terrorist Commander,* Washington DC: Regnery Publishing, 2004, esp. pp. 29–63. See also Douglas J. Feith, *War and Decision: Inside the Pentagon at the Dawn of the War on Terrorism,* New York: HarperCollins, 2008.

23. Quoted in Feith, *War and Decision,* p. 63.

24. Bob Woodward, *Bush at War,* New York: Simon & Schuster, 2002, pp. 43–44.

25. See, for example, R. W. Apple, "Afghanistan as Vietnam," *New York Times,* October 31, 2001, http://www.nytimes.com/2001/10/31/international/asia /31ASSE.html.

26. Michel R. Gordon and Bernard E. Trainor, *Cobra II: The Inside Story of the Invasion and Occupation of Iraq,* New York: Pantheon Books, 2006, pp. 4–5.

27. Ibid., pp. 5–10.

28. Quoted in Larry Diamond, *Squandered Victory: The American Occupation and the Bungled Effort to Bring Democracy to Iraq,* New York: Times Books, 2005, p. 289.

29. References to the YouGov data by question number appear in parentheses throughout this essay with the abbreviations CM1T and CM2T indicating the 2013 and 2014 surveys, respectively. The complete results are available

at http://www.hoover.org/warriors-and-citizens-crosstabs-1 (CM1T) and http://www.hoover.org/warriors-and-citizens-crosstabs-2 (CM2T).

30. Gregory Newbold, "Why Iraq Was a Mistake: A Military Insider Sounds Off against the War and the Zealots Who Pushed It," *Time,* April 9, 2006, http://content.time.com/time/magazine/article/0,9171,1181629,00.html.

31. Gordon and Trainor, *Cobra II,* p. 4.

32. Thomas E. Ricks, *The Gamble: General David Petraeus and the American Military Adventure in Iraq, 2006–2008,* New York: Penguin Press, 2009, pp. 79–80.

33. Michael R. Gordon and Bernard E. Trainor, *The Endgame: The Inside Story of the Struggle for Iraq, from George W. Bush to Barack Obama,* New York: Pantheon Books, 2012, p. 307.

34. Robert M. Gates, *Duty: Memoirs of a Secretary at War,* New York: Alfred A. Knopf, 2014, p. 556.

35. Obama quoted in Gates, *Duty,* pp. 556–57.

36. Gates, *Duty,* p. 557.

37. Bob Woodward, *Obama's Wars,* Simon & Schuster, New York, 2010, p. 195.

38. See Gates, *Duty,* pp. 518–23.

39. See, for example, Micah Zenko, "The Soldier and the State Go Public: Civil-Military Relations Haven't Been This Bad in Decades," *Foreign Policy,* September 26, 2013, http://foreignpolicy.com/2013/09/26/the-soldier-and -the-state-go-public/ and Robert H. Scales, "US Military Planners Don't Support War with Syria," *Washington Post,* September 5, 2013, http://www .washingtonpost.com/opinions/us-military-planners-dont-support-war-with -syria/2013/09/05/10a07114-15bb-11e3-be6e-dc6ae8a5b3a8_story.html.

40. Peter Feaver, "How to Better Navigate the Coming Civil-Military Challenges," *Foreign Policy,* October 14, 2013, http://foreignpolicy.com/2013/10/14/how-to -better-navigate-the-coming-civil-military-challenges.

41. Thomas Donnelly and Gary Schmitt, "AWOL on the Defense Budget," *Weekly Standard,* March 30, 2015, http://www.weeklystandard.com/author/thomas -donnelly-and-gary-schmitt.

42. Public estimates in the YouGov poll for number of people serving in the U.S. Army and Marine Corps were incorrect by hundreds of thousands (CM1T 57). Cf. Defense Manpower Data Center, "Total Military Personnel and Dependent End Strength by Service, Regional Area, and Country." March 1, 2015.

43. Mark Thompson, "The Other 1%," *Time,* November 11, 2011, http://content .time.com/time/magazine/article/0,9171,2099152,00.html.

44. Defense Manpower Data Center, "2012 Workplace and Gender Relations Survey of Active Duty Members," March 15, 2013, http://www.sapr.mil/public /docs/research/2012_workplace_and_gender_relations_survey_of_active _duty_members-survey_note_and_briefing.pdf.

45. See Gail Heriot, "Harassing the Military: There Is No Sexual Assault Crisis," *Weekly Standard,* vol. 8, no. 41, http://www.weeklystandard.com/print /articles/harassing-military_738058.html.

46. Sara Sorcher, "How the Military's 'Bro' Culture Turns Women into Targets: The Sexual-assault Epidemic Plaguing the Armed Forces Is Rooted in a Hypermascualine Ethos that Fosters Predation," *National Journal,* September 5, 2013, http://www.nationaljournal.com/magazine/how-the -military-s-bro-culture-turns-women-into-targets-20130905.

47. Heriot, "Harassing the Military."

48. Gates, *Duty,* p. 593.

49. For a fuller explication, see Thomas Donnelly, "The Military Epidemics That Aren't," *Wall Street Journal,* August 15, 2013, http://www.wsj.com/articles /SB10001424127887324769704579008950507165032.

50. David. J, Morris, *The Evil Hours: A Biography of Post-Traumatic Stress Disorder,* Boston: Houghton Mifflin Harcourt, 2015, pp. 163–64.

51. John Kelly, "Memorial Day Speech in San Antonio Texas," May 23, 2013, https://www.arsouth.army.mil/news/southcomnews/5391-transcript-gen -kelly-memorial-day-speech.html.

52. Carl von Clausewitz, *On War,* trans. Michael Howard and Peter Paret, Berlin: Ulstein, 1980, p. 683.

53. Max Boot, *The Savage Wars of Peace: Small Wars and the Rise of American Power,* New York: Basic Books, 2002.

54. Morris Janowitz, *The Professional Soldier: A Social and Political Portrait,* New York: Free Press, 1971, p. 418–19.

55. Ibid., p. 423.

56. Ibid., p. 418.

57. Ibid., p. 420.

58. Ibid., p. 426.

59. Edward A. Shils and Morris Janowitz, "Cohesion and Disintegration in the Wehrmacht in World War II," *Public Opinion Quarterly,* vol. 12, no. 2, Summer 1948, pp. 280–315.

60. Janowitz, *Professional Soldier,* p. 422.

61. Ibid., p. 439.

62. Some 51.9 percent said that military leaders did share society's values, 23.6 percent said they did not, and 24.5 percent were unsure in the YouGov poll (CM2T 16).

63. Janowitz, *Professional Soldier,* p. 435.

64. Ibid., p. 440.

65. Janowitz, *Professional Soldier,* p. 440.

CHAPTER 8

The "Very Liberal" View of the US Military

Tod Lindberg

Public opinion is hardly monolithic. Although some views are a matter of almost perfect consensus—for example, that firefighters running into burning buildings to save people's lives are heroes—most questions divide Americans in some way. Sometimes it is old versus young, or rich versus poor, or men versus women, or Democrats versus Republicans. In the case of the US military, the divide appears to be ideological, but not quite between liberal and conservative. On many questions, liberals appear only modestly more skeptical of the US military than are moderates or conservatives, or even those calling themselves "very conservative." More precisely, the group whose skepticism distinguishes itself as a category apart consists of those Americans who identify themselves as "very liberal." They constitute a small but influential segment of American public opinion.

The United States military has long been the American institution in which the public expresses the most confidence. A 2014 Gallup poll found 39 percent of Americans saying they had a "great deal" of confidence in the military and an additional 35 percent saying "quite a lot" (the other choices being "some" confidence and "not very much").[1] The Supreme Court was next closest among government institutions, at a distant 12 and 18 percent, respectively. The confidence figures for the presidency were 14 percent and 15 percent, and for Congress 4 percent and 3 percent. Confidence in the military among Americans outpolls that in "small business," "the police," "the church or organized religion," and "the medical system," the next highest four in Gallup's list. However, the American people are fully capable of carrying seemingly conflicting notions in their heads. In the YouGov data, only 12 percent of respondents stated that a lack of trust in the uniformed leaders of the military "is not happening" (CM2T 56).[2] Perhaps the message here is "I trust the military but am concerned that others do not." An interesting avenue for investigation, then, would be where this notion of others' distrust for the military is coming from.

This high level of trust would seem to be a bedrock component of the American social compact. Throughout its annual surveys during the 1990s, the Gallup poll never registered a combined total of those expressing "a great deal" of confidence and "quite a lot" of confidence below 60 percent—1997 being an outlier, with all other scores in that decade at 64 percent or higher. In the period since 9/11, the *lowest* combined figure was 69 percent, observed in the June 2007 survey, which surely reflected the deteriorating security conditions in Iraq of the previous several years. By 2009, the combined confidence figure once again reached its previous all-time high of 2003, 82 percent. In the decade-plus since, the Gallup survey has recorded figures in the mid to upper 70 percent range.

Harvard University's Institute of Politics, meanwhile, has done annual surveys of young Americans for the past quarter century. The most recent found, once again, that the military was the institution most trusted "to do the right thing . . . all or most of the time," at 47 percent, leading the Supreme Court (36 percent), the United Nations (34 percent) and the presidency (32 percent).[3] To the extent that there is a "generation gap" in attitudes—as some have found in views of gay marriage, for example—it is hardly a crisis in which the younger generation has turned antimilitary, as youth arguably were in the 1960s and 1970s when the draft loomed large in the lives of young men. The generation gap now, such as it is, appears to arise most significantly over the question of whether others regard the military highly enough. Respondents aged 18 to 29 and 65 plus in the YouGov poll had significantly different views on the military in response to questions such as: Does the military get the respect it deserves? (less respect: 35 percent versus 60.9 percent); Does Americans' lack of trust in the uniformed leaders of the military hurt effectiveness? (yes: 48.8 percent versus 72.6 percent); and Does the military have a responsibility to support the war policy of the president (yes: 55.1 percent versus 82.1 percent) (CM2T 14, 56, 74). There is little generational divide on a number of questions asking respondents to assess the characteristics of the military: Does the military have different values from the rest of society? (yes: 46.9 percent versus 41.8 percent); Is the military more or less religious than the rest of society? (more: 24.3 percent versus 28.8 percent); and Is the military isolated? (yes: 30 percent versus 33.8 percent) (CM2T 18, 22, 23).

While 32.5 percent of respondents viewed the military as "isolated from American society," and 59.6 percent agreed that a military isolated from society would be a "bad thing," 46.2 percent did not perceive such isolation, while 21.3 percent were not sure. Clearly, if there is a crisis in civil-military relations, a very large majority of the public seems to be unaware of it or unconcerned about it. Nevertheless, opinion on the subject of the military is hardly unanimous. For an illustration of the contentiousness, one need look no farther than the controversy over Clint Eastwood's film *American Sniper*. Its reception exposed a fault line in opinions on the military that the YouGov survey data will help to quantify and clarify.

A Controversial Movie

American Sniper is based on the life of Chris Kyle, a Navy Seal who served four combat tours in Iraq. According to official military records,

Kyle was the deadliest sniper in US history, with 160 confirmed kills. After leaving the service, he wrote a best-selling memoir, extending to the general public the fame he had already achieved in military circles (where he was known as "the Legend," apparently without irony). He was subsequently murdered at a shooting range by a disturbed veteran whom he had sought to help (as he had others) through the challenge of coping with memories of wartime experience and loss and the return to civilian life.

Eastwood's film makes an unambiguous hero of Kyle, and *American Sniper* was a box-office phenomenon. When it opened nationally, it set records for an R-rated film. At this writing, it has grossed more than $349 million domestically and $543 million worldwide. Numerous reports had audiences cheering at its wartime climax, when Kyle, played by Bradley Cooper in an Academy Award–nominated performance, fires an astonishing long-range shot to take out a rival sniper, Mustafa. There were likewise reports of audience members weeping when a title card at the end of the movie informed them of Kyle's death at the hand of someone he was trying to help. The movie concludes with actual newsreel footage of mourners and supporters turning out in large numbers for a memorial service for Kyle at the Dallas Cowboys stadium and along the road of the funeral procession to his burial place at Texas State Cemetery in Austin. Clearly, Eastwood had the choice of making a movie depicting a fictitious American hero of the Iraq war or a real hero, and he chose the latter.

In doing so, the famous actor-director had ample material from Kyle's life on which to draw. Nevertheless, Eastwood introduced a number of fictionalizations, most notably the sniper "Mustafa." Meanwhile, the accuracy of some of Kyle's claims in his memoir and elsewhere has also come into dispute. And it appears Kyle expressed his attitude toward combat and the enemy he faced in harsher terms in the book than the movie depicts, though the movie character does refer to insurgents as "savages." Finally, but not least, Kyle's deeds took place in the midst of a bitterly divisive war, one that a significant majority of

Americans have long judged to be a mistake. Gallup has been asking whether going to war in Iraq was a mistake since 2003, and by mid-2005 majorities started concluding consistently that it was. Only two polls of the more than fifty Gallup has conducted in the past decade show an even divide; it seems likely that they are outliers. A June 2014 put the figure for "yes, a mistake" at 57 percent and "no, not a mistake" at 39 percent.[4]

Some or all of these factors have figured into the negative responses to *American Sniper*. As Matt Taibbi writes in *Rolling Stone*, "to turn the Iraq war into a saccharine, almost PG-rated two-hour cinematic diversion about a killing machine with a heart of gold (is there any film theme more perfectly 2015-America than that?) who slowly, very slowly, starts to feel bad after shooting enough women and children— [*Forrest*] *Gump* notwithstanding, that was a hard one to see coming." He goes on to lament the implications of the movie's success at the box office: "It's the fact that the movie is popular, and actually makes sense to so many people, that's the problem." He notes that when the Chris Kyle character shoots Mustafa—portrayed in the movie as an Olympic gold medal–winning Syrian sharpshooter who has come to Iraq to join the insurgency and has been exacting a fierce long-distance toll on US forces—"even the audiences in the liberal-ass Jersey City theater where I watched the movie stood up and cheered. I can only imagine the response this scene scored in *Soldier of Fortune* country."[5]

Hollywood documentary filmmaker Michael Moore took to Twitter and his Facebook page (January 18, 2015) to denounce the "cowardly" role of the sniper in wartime. He says his uncle had been killed by a German sniper in World War II and adds, "My dad always said, 'Snipers are cowards. They don't believe in a fair fight. Like someone coming up from behind you and coldcocking you. Just isn't right. It's cowardly to shoot a person in the back. Only a coward will shoot someone who can't shoot back.' . . . I think most Americans don't think snipers are heroes."

Chris Hedges, writing at Truthdig, says the movie "lionizes the most despicable aspects of US society—the gun culture, the blind adoration of the military, the belief that we have an innate right as a 'Christian' nation to exterminate the 'lesser breeds' of the earth, a grotesque hypermasculinity that banishes compassion and pity, a denial of inconvenient facts and historical truth, and a belittling of critical thinking and artistic expression."[6] David Adelstein, writing in *New York* magazine, calls the movie "essentially, a propaganda film" and "a Republican platform movie" in its view of the Iraq war.[7]

Others disagreed. Writing in *Salon* to defend the film against that very charge, Andrew O'Hehir said he detected (at least on second viewing) "a level of sardonic commentary at work"—which apparently brought *American Sniper* subtly into line with a view of the war closer to his own: "This is a portrait of an American who thought he knew what he stood for and what his country stood for and never believed he needed to ask questions about that. He drove himself to kill and kill and kill based on that misguided ideological certainty—that brainwashing, though I'm sure Clint Eastwood would never use that word—and then paid the price for it. So did we all, and the reception of this film suggests that the payments keep on coming due."[8]

Unsurprisingly perhaps, the movie also gave rise to controversy on campus. A protest briefly derailed plans to show the movie at UMix, a regular Friday night social gathering at the University of Michigan. Organizers canceled the screening in response to a student-generated open letter claiming, "The movie 'American Sniper' not only tolerates but promotes anti-Muslim and anti-MENA rhetoric and sympathizes with a mass killer."[9] But the decision to cancel quickly generated a counterprotest also organized by students. The latter group got a boost from Michigan football coach Jim Harbaugh, who said in a tweet, "Michigan Football will watch 'American Sniper'! Proud of Chris Kyle & Proud to be an American & if that offends anybody then so be it!"[10] UMix organizers subsequently reversed the cancellation. E. Royster Harper, university vice president for student life, said in a statement, "It was a mistake to cancel. . . . The initial decision . . . was not consistent with the high value the University of Michigan places on freedom of expression and our respect for the right of students to make their own choices in such matters."

Meanwhile, the student-run movie theater at Rensselaer Polytechnic Institute decided to postpone a screening of *American Sniper,* stating, "We realized that this movie has caused heightened tension across communities and campuses nationwide, including violent actions and even murders." (The statement offered no substantiation for the contention that the movie "caused . . . murders.") The student film group said it would reschedule the movie later in the semester in conjunction with "an educational forum."[11]

Some of the critical response focused on a perceived anti-Muslim or anti-Arab bias in portraying Kyle as a hero. But much of it was directed at Kyle as a representative of the military as such and at the military's place in society: hence the references to Kyle as "a mass killer," "a killing machine," and a kind of victim of "brainwashing," as well as the denunciation of "blind adoration of the military."

An AWOL Critical Perspective?

Some of the negative response to *American Sniper* was vitriolic and visceral, as we have seen. But others have presented more thoughtful critical analyses of the military and its high status in American society. James Fallows, writing in *The Atlantic,* is one such critic. He avers that the comments of public officials on the military consist of little more than "[o]verblown, limitless praise, absent the caveats or public skepticism we would apply to other American institutions, especially ones that run on taxpayer money." He described the attitude of the public at large as "reverent but disengaged," a "Chickenhawk nation . . . eager to go to war, as long as someone else is going."[12] The YouGov data do indeed affirm that the military life is not something Americans see as suitable for everyone. Although 43.7 percent of respondents stated that they have considered joining the military, only 26 percent would advise a young person to enlist after high school, and 67 percent of Americans oppose returning to the military draft (CM2T 10; CM1T 35, 36).

As with social criticism, so too in literary circles. The winner of the National Book Critics Circle Award for 2012 was *Billy Lynn's Long Halftime Walk* by Ben Johnson, a story about members of Bravo Squad on a "victory tour" in Texas following a tour in Iraq fighting insurgents and chronicled on Fox News.[13] The *San Francisco Chronicle* found it "a bracing, fearless and uproarious satire of how contemporary war is waged and sold to the American public." The *Washington Post* called it a "masterful echo of 'Catch-22,' with war in Iraq at the center." Yet as Fallows lamented in his *Atlantic* essay, the novel failed to "dent mainstream awareness enough to make anyone self-conscious about continuing the 'salute to the heroes' gestures that do more for the civilian public's self-esteem than for the troops.'"

There is a certain paradox here, however. Those espousing the critical perspective on the military represented in some of the responses to *American Sniper,* in the Fallows essay, and in *Billy Lynn's Long Halftime Walk* generally understand theirs as a minority perspective. Some 57.3 percent of YouGov respondents believe that depictions of the military today are very or somewhat supportive. Conversely, 18.2 percent believe that depictions are somewhat or very hostile (CM2T 13).

The supermajority support for the military among the general public is not something critics deny, but rather regret. Yet it would hardly be accurate to describe those who embrace this critical perspective as marginalized voices in the debate. *The Atlantic,* after all, has long been a leading American publication, known for thoughtful journalism and social criticism. *Rolling Stone* has a similar though edgier reputation. *New York* is the fashionable city's weekly guide to itself. *Billy Lynn* won the National Book Critics Circle Award, a major literary prize, and won praise from the *New York Times* and its *Book Review,* as well as the *Washington Post, San Francisco Chronicle,* and numerous other newspapers and magazines.

This critical perspective is thus able to command a wide hearing in society and culture at large. Nor is there anything particularly new or unusual in this. Since World War I and throughout the twentieth century, a critical perspective on the military has been a salient characteristic of literary and intellectual culture—certainly not to the exclusion of more sympathetic perspectives, but the dominant perspective. As Fallows notes of World War II, "From *Mister Roberts* to *South Pacific* to *Catch-22,* from *The Caine Mutiny* to *The Naked and the Dead* to *From Here to Eternity,* American popular and high culture treated our last mass-mobilization war as an effort deserving deep respect and pride, but not above criticism and lampooning. The collective achievement of the military was heroic, but its members and leaders were still real people, with all the foibles of real life." As to whether *Catch-22* depicts the war as "an effort deserving deep respect and pride" or as, essentially, an absurdity, opinions differ. Fallows also notes the critical perspective of the cultural artifacts of the Vietnam era, such as *M*A*S*H.* He does not fault them for being unbalanced in their criticism of the military, yet it is hard to find in them anything resembling a depiction of the "collective achievement of the military [as] heroic."[14]

And while Fallows insists that the critical perspective of *Catch-22* and the other works he mentions has diminished, as we have seen, it has hardly vanished. Its influence seems to have waned since its heyday in the immediate aftermath of the Vietnam era. But the critical perspective remains a significant strain of public opinion. Note the lead article by Fallows in the January–February 2015 edition of *The Atlantic* and the highly praised fiction winner of the National Book Critics Circle Award for 2012. But exactly how broad a swath of opinion are we talking about? Here, the YouGov survey yields important insights.

Many of the survey questions invite answers indicating either a skeptical view of the military or a beneficent view. Once we have identified such questions, we can look at how the more skeptical viewpoint breaks down based on political ideology. Is a skeptical view (or a beneficent view) common among all respondents, or does it show up in more pronounced form based on ideological convictions? Is the distribution of skepticism a steady slope from left to right or right to left, or does it spike?

For example, questions 25 through 27 ask respondents whether they agree or disagree with statements about the fairness of the military, and questions 31 through 37 ask whether they agree or disagree with statements about the opportunity the military provides to its members (CM2T 25–27, 31–37). Insofar as we are justified in the conclusion that "fairness" and "opportunity" are of sufficiently general normative value among almost all respondents, regardless of ideology, we can further conclude that those who disagree with a statement that the military acts fairly in a particular area or provides opportunity for a particular group take a skeptical view of the military, whereas those who agree take a beneficent view.

Not all of the questions in the survey, of course, are premised on matters of general normative value. The survey asks in question 18, "Do you think the military has different values than the rest of American society?" Since we do not know if a respondent believes the military *should* have values different from the rest of society, the answer produces no reasonable inference about a skeptical versus beneficent attitude toward the military. More of something one regards as bad or wrong or unjust would be a bad thing, whereas more of something one regards as right or good or just would be a good thing. Without knowing the normative value a respondent attaches to the premise of the question, one cannot infer a conclusion about an overall positive or negative attitude toward the military on the question at hand. The answers to this and other such questions are markers for further research into underlying normative attitudes.

What quickly emerges from even a cursory glance is that there is a noteworthy divide in American society on those most inclined to question the institution both in wartime and in peacetime. It is not a divide between civilians and the military. It is not a divide between elite and mass opinion. It is political, but not simply between liberal and conservative, with the attitudes of moderates bridging the gap.

It is actually a divide between people who identify themselves as "very liberal" versus everyone else. Across the political spectrum running from "liberal" to "very conservative," attitudes vary somewhat, and it is possible to say that those who consider themselves "liberal" may, on balance and as a whole, express slightly more skepticism toward the military than those who identify as "conservative" or "very conservative." But the gap there is not very large, and on a number of specific survey questions, it is all but invisible. The clear outliers are the "very liberal."

Those who are "very conservative" are somewhat less likely to question the institution of the military than the median view, but the emphasis has to go on "somewhat"—they are not that far out of alignment. Those who identify as "very liberal," however, are often very far from the mainstream in their tendency to express skepticism toward the military. We can see this in their attitudes toward the military as a social institution, in their view of aspects of warfighting, and in their opinions about civilian control of the military.

The Military as Social Institution

First, let us consider some of the survey questions that probed attitudes toward the military as a social institution. Here, we are considering the military not in its warfighting and war-deterring ways, the key functions that differentiate it from all other social institutions, but as one American institution among many. The question is how it measures up to expectations Americans have for such an institution. Do Americans think the military delivers on such basic matters as fairness and opportunity?

A series of questions asks whether the military is "more fair . . . than the rest of American society," "about as fair as the rest of society," or "less fair" for specified cases. A number of these questions went to the issue of the internal fairness of military procedures in such matters as promotions, opportunity to excel, opportunity for self-improvement, and opportunity for respect. Here, it is noteworthy that very small percentages of Americans expressed a skeptical attitude, and variation based on ideology was minimal.

Let us look at some of the questions on which the skepticism of the "very liberal" is no more pronounced than that to be found among other ideological classifications. Question 26 asks about the fairness of "promotions and recognition" in the military (CM2T 26). Totals for "more fair" than the rest of society are 39.5 percent, "about as fair" 37.0 percent, "less fair" 8.5 percent, with the rest saying they are not sure. No major variation appears along ideological lines. Those saying "less fair" are 9.5 percent for very liberal (VL), 11.2 percent for liberal (L), 8.3 percent for moderate (M), 7.9 percent for conservative (C), 6.3 percent for very conservative (VC). A large majority of Americans all across the political spectrum sees the internal processes by which the military rewards its members as on par with civilian practices or better.

Question 27 asks about "opportunity to excel" (CM2T 27). Totals were 43.4 percent "more fair," 37.1 percent "about as fair," and 7.1 percent "less fair." The ideological breakdown for "less fair" was 11.3 percent VL, 8.5 percent L, 6.4 percent M, 6.8 percent C, and 3.7 percent VC. Again, a large majority of Americans spanning the entire political spectrum believes the military is on par or better than society as a whole in providing individual members with an opportunity to demonstrate their true abilities. The same conclusion holds for question 28, which asks about "opportunity for self-improvement" (CM2T 28). Totals were 48.0 percent "more fair," 33.7 percent "about as fair," and 6.8 percent "less fair." The ideological breakdown for "less fair" was 14.3 percent VL, 8.5 percent L, 7.1 percent M, 6.2 percent C, and 5.2 percent VC.

If the internal *processes* of the military win generally high marks from Americans, with no more than one in seven expressing skepticism in any ideological group, Americans meet some structural elements of the military as an institution with greater skepticism.

Question 25 asks about the treatment of women, and 14.0 percent find the military "more fair," 38.1 percent "about as fair," and 35.0 percent "less fair" than society as a whole (CM2T 25). Among those who say "less fair," a sharp gradation on ideological lines is apparent: 66.9 percent of VLs, 60.6 percent of Ls, 34.8 percent of Ms, 20.9 percent of Cs, 11.7 percent of VCs. Notably, gender is the outlier, as one might expect given military restrictions on women in combat. Those who say the military offers "less opportunity" to minorities "than the rest of American society" amount to only 6.9 percent of all respondents, although that does includes 18.4 percent of VLs, somewhat of an outlier but not a high percentage of that ideological group.

A significant gap between the VLs and others does emerge in one potentially revealing institutional aspect, however. Two questions illustrate it, both asking whether the military provides more opportunity than the rest of American society, about the same, or less. For question 35, the group at issue is "the well-educated," and for question 37, it's "high-achieving people, regardless of background" (CM2T 35, 37). For the former, the overall response was 28.3 percent "more," 48.5 percent "same," and 13.4 percent "less." But in this case, more than one in three VLs expressed skepticism: 34.1 percent VL, 21.7 percent L, 14.4 percent M, 7.2 percent C, 8.0 percent VC.

For "high-achieving people," the totals were 33.3 percent "more," 45.1 percent "same," 10.6 percent "less"—but here just over one in four VLs expressed skepticism: 26.7 percent VL, 13.6 percent L, 9.8 percent M, 7.0 percent C, 9.6 percent VC. Here, it is interesting to look at the educational attainment levels (CM2T 92). Overall, 30.1 percent of respondents had a high school education or less, 30.4 percent "some college," 23.3 percent college degrees, and 16.2 percent postgraduate education. The ideological breakdown for those who said they had a postgraduate degree was 24.4 percent VL, 18.0 percent L, 12.8 percent M, 12.9 percent C, and 16.2 percent VC. It seems likely that some well educated VLs see little opportunity for themselves in the military and accordingly express skepticism at greater levels about opportunity for the well educated in general—and by extension, perhaps, "high-achieving people"—a mirror imaging of their own attitudes.

A series of questions asks, "If a military person brings discredit upon the country, should that person go to jail in the following cases?" (CM2T 38–44) One interesting case from the culture wars is "opposing women or homosexuals serving with them." Overall, the response was 22.7 percent "yes" and 57.4 percent "no," with the rest undecided. VLs, however, divided equally on the question, at 43.0 percent on each side; otherwise, "yes" was 35.4 percent L, 27.6 percent M, 13.3 percent C, and 9.3 percent VC. VLs are clearly the most willing to mete out serious punishment to those who disagree with their normative views on how the military should be more inclusive.

The survey also asked respondents whether they agreed with the statement, "The military has more sexual harassment and assault than the rest of society," a view with which 35.5 percent of all respondents agreed (CM2T 48). For VLs, however, the figure was 78.5 percent agreement, with 62.3 percent L, 39.2 percent M, 18.3 percent C, 18.3 percent VC. Emerging from this and the previous question is a broadly shared view among VLs of the military as a sexist institution in which women are at risk.

And in the prevalent VL view, the military must change to accord more with their normative preferences. Overall, fewer than 1 in 4 (23.3 percent) agreed that "the military needs to change to become more like American society" (CM2T 48). But that was the majority view among VLs, 51.5 percent, compared to 39.6 percent L, 29.1 percent M, 7.8 percent C, and 4.1 percent VC.

Given the attachment within the military to ideas and practices VLs regard as retrograde and in need of reform, it is perhaps unsurprising that VLs tend to see a mirror image of their normative disapproval of the military in military attitudes toward the society at large. Overall, 63.9 percent of respondents agreed that "most members of the military have a great deal of respect for civilian society" (CM2T 50). Yet this is a minority view among VLs at 42.1 percent, compared to 53.3 percent L, 63.8 percent M, 71.4 percent C, and 83.7 percent VC.

What, then, do VLs think of those who emerge from an institution some of whose fundamental characteristics they find very troubling? Overall, 65.9 percent of respondents agreed that "veterans are more reliable and hard-working than the rest of society" (CM2T 48) But among VLs, this statement mustered the support of only 49.8 percent, versus 55.0 percent L, 60.8 percent M, 79.1 percent C, and 81.3 percent VC.

On some questions, VLs and Ls do not diverge as much, and the division that emerges is more starkly liberal-conservative. Question 63 is one of a series that asks whether a particular situation might help or hurt the effectiveness of the military in wartime (CM2T 63). In this case, it's "the military trying to hold on to old-fashioned views of morality." Respondents had the option of saying the proposition being tested "is not happening at all," and across the ideological spectrum, few did. For VLs, the figure is 7.1 percent and for VCs, 6.2 percent, with Ls, Ms, and Cs in the middle. The overall response to the question is 29.5 percent "hurts effectiveness" and 30.9 percent "helps effectiveness"—a fairly even split indicating no great skepticism. But the ideological distribution here is quite striking, as the military's "old-fashioned views of morality . . . hurt effectiveness" in the view of 56.9 percent of VLs and 59.9 percent of Ls, versus 14.6 percent of Cs and 6.2 percent of VCs (with Ms at 29.1 percent). The "helps effectiveness" figures are the mirror image, at 2.8 percent among VLs and 9.0 percent among Ls, versus 49.5 percent of Cs and 67.9 percent of VCs (with Ms at 25.3 percent). Perhaps the starkness of the term "old-fashioned views of morality" invites Ls here to close the gap with the VLs rather than to move in the direction of the M view, where presumably "old-fashioned views of morality" meet less disapprobrium.

Wartime Issues

Most of the YouGov survey questions go to views of the military as an institution. Yet several expose fault lines in views of the military's essential function, to deter and when necessary wage war.

And it is a fact of war that bad things happen in wartime, at times accidentally, at times on purpose. A series of questions asks, "If a military person brings discredit upon the country, should that person go to jail in the following cases?" One is for "offending the sensibilities of other cultures (for example, burning Korans)" (CM2T 40). Responding yes overall were 26.1 percent, no 50.2 percent. Among VLs, however, the yes response was 47.6 percent, compared to 33.4 percent L, 32.7 percent M, 16.3 percent C, and 6.9 percent VC. What we see here—in addition to conservative indifference to clearly prohibited conduct—is perhaps an extension of the broader VL view in opposition to intolerance of diversity.

In the series of questions that asks whether a condition "helps effectiveness" or "hurts effectiveness" during wartime, one issue resonates ideologically with contemporary debates about alleged media bias: question 66 asks whether "inaccurate reporting about the military and military affairs by the news media" hurts effectiveness (CM2T 66). Overall, 73.3 percent say it hurts effectiveness, which is perhaps unsurprising in light of the premise of the question, namely, inaccurate reporting. Yet respondents also have the option of disagreeing with the premise by indicating the posited condition "is not happening." For this question, VLs are more than three times as likely as the next closest ideological classification (Ms) to say inaccurate reporting "is not happening," albeit at rather low levels (12.6 percent VL, 4.1 percent M). Ls, Ms, Cs, and VCs believe inaccurate reporting hurts effectiveness by very large margins (respectively, 70.1 percent, 67.8 percent, 82.8 percent, 89.5 percent). Among VLs, however, the percentage who say inaccurate reporting hurts effectiveness is a bare majority, 52.9 percent. This view may reflect a higher level of identification among VLs with those who are trying to report the news accurately but sometimes err than with those who might claim to be "victims" of media errors (a frequent complaint heard from conservatives).

Questions 79 and 80 ranked respondent agreement and disagreement, respectively, with a number of statements about the use of force and military intervention (CM2T 79, 80). Ambivalence about the use of force is pronounced among VLs, though the distribution from VL to VC often seems to be more a continuum along a relatively straight line. One statement for agreement or disagreement was: "Military force should only be used in pursuit of the goal of total victory." Overall, 24.4 percent disagreed with this statement, but of those who did, VLs were the highest, at 44.0 percent compared to 39.6 percent L, 23.6 percent M, 19.1 percent C, and 9.6 percent VC. Another was: "The use of force in foreign interventions should be applied quickly and massively rather than by gradual escalation." Overall, 15.2 percent disagreed. VLs, however, were more than twice as likely to disagree, at 32.4 percent, compared to 24.0 percent L, 20.9 percent M, 5.7 percent C, and 4.9 percent VC.

Finally, the same question assessed overall views of sources of security by asking respondents if they agreed or disagreed with the statement "American national security depends more on international trade and a strong domestic economy than on our military strength." Switching lenses to look at agreement here, we see that this was the view of merely 37.6 percent of respondents overall (those disagreeing were a plurality at 44.1 percent)—but of 68.8 percent of VLs, compared to a bare majority of Ls at 51.1 percent, a plurality of Ms (42.6 percent), and minorities of Cs (24.7 percent) and VCs (17.9 percent). VLs are far less likely to see "hard" security as central to US national security.

Question 61 is one of the series that asks whether a particular situation might help or hurt the effectiveness of the military in wartime (CM2T 61). In this case, the question asks about "nonmilitary people getting too involved in purely military affairs." The question as formulated is somewhat tendentious, referencing a group already "too involved." And overall, 61.5 percent of respondents said "hurts effectiveness." This was majority sentiment among Ls (50.7 percent), Ms (55.1 percent), Cs (76.3 percent), and VCs (81.1 percent), but not among VLs (43.9 percent), who were also nearly twice as likely as Ls to say that "nonmilitary people getting too involved" actually "helps effectiveness" in wartime (18.2 percent to 9.5 percent). Again, we can see a marked propensity among VLs toward the view that the military needs outside supervision.

Command and Civilian Control Issues

The US and other modern, Western-style systems of civil-military relations are based on the fundamental proposition that civilian authorities control the military, not the other way around. In the United States, Congress is responsible for legislation establishing and regulating the armed services, and the president has the constitutional power of commander in chief. Although military leaders have considerable influence over defense policy, including decisions about whether and how to go to war, the command authority belongs with the president, who has been elected by the people.

The deference military leaders owe to civilian authorities is something that seems well understood by the military itself and by the American public. Although military leaders have opinions of their own, if they are critical of the civilian leadership, especially of the president, there is an expectation that they will keep these opinions to themselves—at a minimum, that such criticism will not become public. In the event of a breech, there will be consequences. President Obama relieved General Stanley McChrystal of his command of the Afghanistan war following publication of an article in *Rolling Stone* magazine in which officers on McChrystal's staff made disparaging comments about senior administration officials. The president's decision drew bipartisan and military support, notwithstanding the esteem in which most close observers held McChrystal's abilities as a wartime commander.

An indication of the nearly creedal status across ideological lines of the principle of civilian control can be seen in the survey's question 74, which asks, "When the president makes a policy decision on the wars, does the military have a responsibility to support the policy?" (CM2T 74) Overall, the answer was 72.3 percent yes, breaking down 78.8 percent VL, 85.9 percent L, 67.1 percent M, 70.7 percent C, 73.8 percent VC. Question 75 applies the general principle to a specific case, with results not too far at variance (CM2T 75). A series of questions gauges what action by the military might be appropriate if "the President decides to withdraw completely from the Afghan war in 2014"—a previous survey question (CM2T 73) having informed respondents of "the military's support for continued involvement in Afghanistan after 2014." Question 75 asks if the military "has a responsibility to . . . support the policy despite any concerns to the contrary" (CM2T 75). Overall, those responding yes are 63.0 percent, breaking down as 80.2 percent of VLs, 76.0 percent of Ls, 60.0 percent of Ms, 62.7 percent of Cs, and 61.4 percent of VCs.

But as to how much latitude the military should have in expressing its views in opposition to the president's policy, the ideological divide reasserts itself. Question 78 asks if the military should "educate the public about their concerns" (CM2T 78). Overall, 50.4 percent of respondents said yes, 33.0 percent no. But a clear majority of VLs, 56.2 percent, said no, far outstripping the no tally in other ideological groups: 37.5 percent L, 33.8 percent M, 27.9 percent C, 35.2 percent VC. Question 76 asks if the military should "testify to Congress on their concerns," to which 61.3 percent of respondents overall said yes (CM2T 76). This was a clear majority view among Ls at 53.0 percent, Ms at 59.2 percent, Cs at 73.8 percent, and VCs at 69.3 percent—but not among VLs at 42.1 percent. A presumably less drastic step than testifying publicly, but potentially perceived by some as more underhanded, namely, "privately explain their concerns to Congress," skewed similarly, with 57.7 percent of respondents overall saying yes, including majorities of Ls (54.2 percent), Ms (53.3 percent), Cs (65.7 percent), and VCs (73.7 percent)—but not VLs at 46.4 percent.

The "Very Liberal" View in Sum

What emerges from these survey findings is a group of people, the very liberal, who are much more inclined to express skeptical attitudes toward the military. Though they do not tend to dispute the internal processes of the military in matters such as awards and promotions, they perceive an institution less fair to women and gays and are more likely to see punishable conduct in the expression of opposing views within the military. They tend to think the military should become more like the rest of society. They are more inclined to see members of the military as disrespectful of the rest of society. They tend to think the military's attachment to old-fashioned moral structures under-mines the institution and its effectiveness. They tend to see little place for highly educated and high-achieving individuals in the military, perhaps a reflection of their own high levels of educational attainment. They are more skeptical than others about service in the military making veterans more reliable and hardworking.

The very liberal tend to think that the importance of military power is overrated compared to the economy in assessing national security. In cases of the use of force, they are less inclined to see a need for its overwhelming application and to insist on clear victory as an objective. They are disinclined to worry about the effects of poor news reporting on military effectiveness in wartime. And they tend to judge miscon-duct by US service members more harshly.

The very liberal of the present day are not much more likely to sup-port civilian control over the military than others, but they are less inclined to support public or private expressions of disagreement within and from the military over policy questions. They tend not to be very worried about the effects of the involvement of nonmilitary people in military affairs. Despite the fact that most of the very liberal are themselves nonmilitary people—yet have a decided view of the need for the military to change in accordance with their normative preferences—they are self-confident in their ability to reform the military without diminishing its effectiveness.

It seems plausible that the very liberal view, were it widespread throughout the US population, might indicate a gathering problem for civil-military relations. Given the very liberal view of the primacy of the economy in national security, for example, one might expect proposals to gain traction for an extended period of much lower levels of defense spending.

However, the military has also shown itself able to accommodate, at least to some degree, views originating on the left side of the ideological spectrum by changing policies. Expanded opportunities for women and the end of the ban on gays serving openly are prime examples. So, too, is the military's increasing commitment to investigating and prosecuting sexual harassment and assault. And in fact, under the budget sequester, military spending *has* gone through a period of pronounced contraction. The military is hardly indifferent to the concerns most prevalent in the very liberal point of view, though, perhaps unsurprisingly, the very liberal tend to be skeptical about the sincerity and sufficiency of these efforts.

The next thing that must be remarked, however, is how tiny a fraction of the US population identifies as "very liberal" (CM2T 93). Of the total sample, 4.8 percent described themselves that way, as against 16.4 percent "liberal," 30.7 percent "moderate," 30.3 percent "conservative," and 10.1 percent "very conservative" (7.6 percent did not know). Thus the category of those most likely to take a skeptical rather than a beneficent attitude toward the military is quite a small segment of the American population, notwithstanding its considerable cultural influence.

The raw numbers may tell only a part of the story, however. In the first place, even among those who call themselves "very liberal," a skeptical attitude toward the military is hardly uniform. The "very liberal" are not unanimous in agreeing on X, Y, and Z. It would be interesting to look in detail at the answers from each individual identifying as "very liberal" to see if the generally expressed skepticism toward the military divides between a larger group that *almost always* expresses a skeptical view of the military and a smaller group that *almost always* expresses a beneficent view of the institution—or if the beneficent view of the military pops up from those who call themselves "very liberal" more randomly depending on the survey question. If it is the former, then the category of skeptics represents an even smaller segment of the population than the 4.8 percent of the population calling themselves "very liberal."

It is also possible that different attitudes toward the act of classifying oneself politically may be a factor in the results. To declare oneself "very liberal" or "very conservative," it seems to me, is to *make a statement* in a way that classifying oneself as "liberal," "moderate," or "conservative" may not be. If this is so, then there may be a significant segment of those identifying as "liberal" and "conservative" who are actually (subjectively or by some notional objective measure of policy views) "very liberal" or "very conservative" but unwilling to identify itself as such. I would expect that this is largely a one-way phenomenon, that is, that there are relatively fewer individuals who claim to be "very conservative" or "very liberal" when they are "actually" merely "conservative" or "liberal."

If an effect such as this is in play in the responses, its implications would be asymmetric. The reason for this is that in response to most questions, the difference between the views of those identifying as "conservative" versus "very conservative" is significantly smaller than the difference between "liberal" and "very liberal." As noted, the "very conservative" view is much closer to the view of the sample as a whole than the "very liberal" view. If some who identify as "liberal" are "actually" "very liberal," then of course the segment of the population that is "very liberal" is larger. But it would accordingly be even farther out of line with mainstream opinion on the military. If one could somehow properly sort "very liberal" respondents from "liberal" respondents, on this analysis, the respondents one would be moving from the "liberal" to the "very liberal" category would tend to be more skeptical about the military than those who remain. This would skew the aggregate "very liberal" view even further in the direction of skepticism toward the military, while moving the aggregate "liberal" view closer to the mainstream.

We should also note that this survey took place against a backdrop of a country at war for well over a decade, led now by a Democratic president. The situational element of the responses is something the YouGov survey has not assessed. For example, suppose a conservative Republican were president and in favor of a wartime escalation of troop strength to advance military objectives (an example would be the "surge" strategy in Iraq from 2006 to 2007). Suppose some senior military officials held the view that the escalation would be ineffectual at best, leading only to a protracted commitment and more US casualties. Would the very liberal be as intolerant of expressions of dissent from Congress under such circumstances? In this context, respondents' perceptions of the question might not be along the axis of civil (presidential) authority versus military (uniformed) authority, but rather along an axis of bellicosity running from more (the president) to less (the military brass). More research will be necessary to distinguish views of the military as an *instrument* of bellicosity as opposed to a source of bellicosity.

It is undeniable that the skeptical view of the US military was once considerably more socially and culturally influential, especially in the aftermath of the Vietnam War. It is likewise important, as Fallows says, for outsiders as well as the military itself to scrutinize its conduct and its institutional structure.

The range of opinions on military matters revealed in the YouGov survey data does indeed seem to suggest that the cultural reach of the "very liberal" skepticism of the military as an institution of American society and as an instrument of national policy is out of proportion to its share of public opinion as a whole. Contrary to Fallows, however, the skeptical view would seem to have *more* rather than *less* influence given the 5 percent share of the population the "very liberal" view commands.

This disproportionate cultural influence of the "very liberal" view could be contributing to an exaggerated sense of conflict between civilian and military perspectives. We are likely seeing evidence of this in the responses to many survey questions of those who identify as "conservative" and "very conservative"—an impression on the right side of the political spectrum of a culturally embattled military. This impression is arguably well-founded with regard to the skeptical view of the military among the very liberal, but arguably ill-founded with regard to the *prevalence* of this skepticism among the general public. Conservatives are not wrong to conclude that an influential strain of public opinion is highly skeptical of the military, an institution they hold in high esteem—as do a large majority of Americans, who are perhaps less inclined to publicize their views beyond occasionally thanking members of the military for their service or giving them a round of applause when called upon to do so at sporting events.

In sum, a very tiny percentage of Americans go to see *American Sniper* and emerge from the theater so repulsed by its portrayal of Chris Kyle that they are moved to denounce the movie, the man, and the institution in which he served. A large majority of Americans emerge from the theater saddened by Kyle's untimely death while trying to help a fellow veteran, but pleased by the film's depiction of a hero.

Notes

1. Gallup, "Confidence in Institutions," June 2–7, 2015, http://www.gallup.com /poll/1597/confidence-institutions.aspx.
2. References to the YouGov data by question number appear in parentheses throughout this essay with the abbreviations CM1T and CM2T indicating the 2013 and 2014 surveys, respectively. The complete results are available

at http://www.hoover.org/warriors-and-citizens-crosstabs-1 (CM1T) and http://www.hoover.org/warriors-and-citizens-crosstabs-2 (CM2T).

3. Institute of Politics, Harvard University, "Survey of Young Americans' Attitudes toward Politics and Public Service: 25th Edition," April 29, 2014.

4. Gallup, "Iraq," http://www.gallup.com/poll/1633/iraq.aspx, accessed April 16, 2015.

5. Matt Taibbi, "*American Sniper* Is Almost Too Dumb to Criticize: Almost," Rolling Stone, January 21, 2015, http://www.rollingstone.com/politics/news /american-sniper-is-almost-too-dumb-to-criticize-20150121.

6. Chris Hedges, "Killing Ragheads for Jesus," Truthdig, January 15, 2015, http://www.truthdig.com/report/item/killing_ragheads_for_jesus_20150125.

7. David Adelstein, "Clint Eastwood Turns *American Sniper* into a Republican Platform Movie," *New York Magazine,* December 29, 2014, available at http://www.vulture.com/2014/12/movie-review-american-sniper.html#.

8. Andrew O'Hehir, "*American Sniper* and the Culture Wars: Why the Movie's Not What You Think It Is." *Salon,* January 20, 2015, http://www.salon.com /2015/01/21/american_sniper_and_the_culture_wars_why_the_movies _not_what_you_think_it_is.

9. Laura Moehlman, "Umix Won't Screen Film in Wake of Complaints," *Michigan Daily,* April 5, 2015.

10. Emma Kibery, "University Plans to Show Both *American Sniper* and *Paddington* on Friday," *Michigan Daily,* April 8, 2015.

11. See Jessica Chasmar, "Rensselaer Polytechnic Institute Postpones *American Sniper* Showing after Muslim Outcry," *Washington Times,* April 13, 2015.

12. James Fallows, "The Tragedy of the American Military," *Atlantic,* January–February 2015.

13. Ben Johnson, *Billy Lynn's Long Halftime Walk,* Ecco Press, 2012.

14. Fallows, "Tragedy of the American Military."

CHAPTER 9

Young Person's Game
Connecting with Millennials

Matthew Colford and Alec J. Sugarman

Introduction

In April 2011, just over forty years after the Stanford University faculty voted to kick the Reserve Officer Training Corps (ROTC) program off campus, the Faculty Senate voted in favor of inviting ROTC programs back.[1] The vote followed a yearlong process of study and heated debate that engaged a wide array of student groups, faculty, and the university administration in conversations over issues such as the military's inclusiveness and the academic rigor of ROTC programs. Faculty luminaries such as former secretary of defense William Perry, former secretary of state Condoleezza Rice, and historian David Kennedy led the push to reconsider and reinvite ROTC to campus, while student groups such as Stanford Students for Queer Liberation (SSQL) and Stanford Says No to War (SSNW) led the opposition to reintegration.[2]

The result of the 1970 vote to remove ROTC from Stanford was ostensibly due to concerns over whether the academic rigor of ROTC's military science classes was sufficient to merit the granting of university credit, but it came in the larger context of the Vietnam War and the broad antimilitary sentiment it inspired amongst the students and many faculty members. Considering the vehemence of the antiwar protesters, who torched both the Naval ROTC building and the university president's office in 1969, it would have been shocking if the university had maintained its support for the program.[3]

As Stanford students at the time of the most recent ROTC controversy, we noticed a phenomenon that distinguished this debate from what we knew of the Vietnam-era environment: while a few students passionately opposed inviting ROTC back, most students did not share their zeal, and most of the discussion among the faculty and administration focused not on whether to invite the services back, but on how to make it work. Somewhere in the previous decades, the default position of the university and its students had shifted from opposition to engagement with the military. The proximate cause of this shift in campus opinion was the repeal of the "Don't Ask, Don't Tell" (DADT) law, which barred homosexuals from serving in the military and was often invoked to justify excluding the military from college campuses on the grounds that DADT constituted illegal discrimination.[4] The law's repeal lent momentum to the nascent push for a reconsideration of ROTC and Stanford's relationship with the military and also precipitated similar discussions at Harvard, which was to welcome back ROTC at around the same time.

While DADT's repeal made possible Stanford's formal reinvitation of ROTC by eliminating a major source of discrimination in the military, it cannot explain the broader feeling around campus, particularly among the faculty and administration, that engagement with the military would be good for both the military and the university. Even some students who were personally and ideologically close with those opposed to ROTC's return spoke in favor of it as bringing a diverse and underrepresented perspective to campus. Speaking before the Faculty Senate, a student representative to that body noted that she "[knew] little to nothing about military lifestyles" and that "most of [her] knowledge of the military came from watching *Pearl Harbor*. That is not okay." She went on to argue that "military perspectives have been invisible on this campus" and that allowing ROTC back could "humanize the people who fight our wars."

Four decades on from Stanford's expulsion of ROTC, much has changed in our nation's civil-military relations, yet the stereotype of young people—especially those at elite universities—as antiwar radicals still persists in some quarters. All the more surprising, then, that when the student body voted on whether to support the Faculty Senate's decision to invite ROTC back, those in favor won a plurality of the vote. The shift in opinions towards the military in the Stanford case highlights the need to update our understanding of how millennials view the military. The survey data collected for this book provide an excellent opportunity to explore empirically what millennials think of the military and what experience and knowledge they have of it.

As the United States military begins its final drawdown from Afghanistan and reassesses its strategy and legacy in Iraq, millennials will begin to witness the end of a period that for most has comprised the majority of their lifetimes. This age group has, after all, come to be known as the 9/11 generation, and rightly so: young Americans between 18 and 29 have made the transition into adulthood during the single longest period of continuous war in American history. They are as accustomed to news stories of al Qaeda, the Taliban, and the war on terror as they are to stories of perhaps all other foreign-policy issues combined. A significantly greater portion of their tax dollars has gone towards the wars in the Middle East than to federally funded higher education subsidies (that is, Pell Grants).[5] As of 2011, the number of countries with some form of US military presence was up to nearly 150.[6]

And yet there is an inherent contradiction in the lives of millennials: despite growing up in an age of continuous war, this generation is broadly unfamiliar with the military, its culture, its basic structure, and its function. Millennials do not exhibit the same open antagonism towards service members that many of their parents or grandparents might have during the Vietnam era, yet neither do many of them understand the difference between a sailor, a soldier, an airman, and a Marine. They understand that the military is a very hierarchical organization but may not be able to explain the difference between a second lieutenant and a lieutenant colonel. When they interact with service members or are asked their opinions of the military and its role in American foreign policy, then, they may not appreciate how much autonomy and responsibility an enlisted "grunt" may actually have had while deployed to an Afghan village, or how little influence even a high-ranking officer may have had in planning the war in Iraq. Without understanding the basics of military structure and culture, millennials are liable to underappreciate the positive contributions of some service members, misattribute blame for failures to others, and, overall, fundamentally misconceive the nature of the military and its relationship with civilian policymakers and civil society.

In this chapter, we will argue that this disconnect is largely a function of a lack of awareness and exposure. Using survey data collected for this volume by YouGov for James Mattis and Kori Schake, we will outline and analyze the statistics that underlie this dynamic. Throughout this analysis, we will also offer observations from our own experiences as students at Stanford University teaching student-initiated courses on civil-military relations and leading a group of students to the United States Naval Academy and Washington DC. We conclude by offering a list of policies that can be adopted to bring millennials closer to their peers in the military. Underlying this chapter is a sincere optimism on both our parts: there is an openness among millennials to greater familiarity with the US military, belying claims that millennials generally want to distance themselves from America's largest institution. The reality is that most millennials simply lack the information and experience necessary to understand the military.

Analysis

Using the data, which breaks down public attitudes towards the military by age, socioeconomic status, race, and various other categories, we make two broad observations. First, millennials generally trust the military and its people. Though they disagree with a number of specific policies, the military leadership is viewed far more favorably by millennials than political leaders are. Millennials also have a high opinion of veterans' work ethic and see the military as providing opportunities for the poor and minorities. Second, millennials are not knowledgeable about the military's basic characteristics. They dramatically overestimate its size, are not familiar with the myriad roles service members may play outside of combat, and frequently respond with uncertainty to other factual questions, suggesting a self-awareness about their lack of familiarity.

A Trusted Institution?

One of the primary conclusions we draw from the YouGov data is that millennials exhibit some skepticism about the US military as an institution while showing notable respect for men and women in uniform. We see this distinction between supporting the troops and supporting the military as an institution in questions of policy and of trust in military messaging. A majority of millennials believes the military's public portrayal of the progress made in the war in Afghanistan is either "very" or "somewhat" inaccurate, while just one in five millennials thinks it is "mostly" accurate, and only 1 percent believe it is "completely" accurate.

With respect to overall military pay, 33 percent of 18- to 29-year-olds favor increasing military pay, while only 6 percent favor decreasing it (57 percent believe it should be kept the same). A plurality of millennials believe enlisted service members are taking a pay cut, implying a recognition of the pecuniary sacrifice they made in enlisting, or perhaps a belief that troops are high-quality private-sector job candidates. However, no other category of the military budget addressed in the survey was received this favorably, with support for increasing the operations and training budget coming in second at only 14 percent. When asked about overall defense spending, only

12 percent of millennials think it should be increased, while 50 percent think it should be decreased, and a similar pattern holds for the military operations budget, which 50 percent of millennials believe should be decreased.

Millennials' views also clash with military policies on "social" issues, with 75 percent of young people supportive of allowing homosexuals to serve in the military and a majority disagreeing either "somewhat" or "strongly" with excluding women from the infantry. Despite the furor over these topics and resistance to changes from within the military, though, only 41 percent of millennials believe the military's treatment of women and homosexuals is unfair, lower than any other generation (CM1T 43).[7] Likewise, 45 percent of millennials have confidence in the meritocratic nature of the military hierarchy. These findings are especially interesting in light of the public discussions over DADT and sexual assault and the media coverage these issues have received. Though millennials are substantially more progressive on these issues than the military as an institution, the data suggest that their faith in the military as basically fair is resilient, even in the face of policies that run counter to their principles.

Millennials are not militaristic, and do not, as a single group, "put the military on a pedestal." Though 60 percent believe veterans are harder working and more reliable than the rest of society, millennials do not believe that they should be privileged over more qualified applicants in private-sector hiring (CM1T 48). Millennials are also the only demographic of which a majority does not support raising taxes to provide veterans with "the best health and retirement benefits" (CM1T 47). But focusing on these issue-specific disagreements risks missing the proverbial forest for the trees.

Forty percent of millennials believe the president should manage only the broad objectives of war, leaving the details to the generals, in line with classic theories of civil-military relations. Nearly half of millennials believe that military leaders share the values of the American people, compared to only 12.5 percent who believe that political leaders do (CM2T 16, 17). Pluralities of millennials believe the military provides more opportunity for the poor and for immigrants than the rest of American society, and millennials are more likely than any other age group to believe that the military is more progressive than the rest of society (CM2T 31, 34, 19). All of this is to say that despite disagreements and occasional mistrust over specific issues, young people have faith in the institution of the military.

Unfortunately, the data do not point to an obvious explanation for why the military seems to receive the benefit of the doubt from young people. Speculatively, though, we suggest that millennial faith in the military begins with the fact that it is a volunteer force. During the Vietnam era, when scores of young people were coerced (or faced the risk of coercion) via the draft into joining the military against their will, their opinions of the institution may have been poisoned from the very beginning. Today's service members choose to join of their own volition. For millennials who are not radically antimilitary but have no interest in serving, the transition to an all-volunteer force affords them an intellectual and emotional distance from the perceived "negative" aspects of military life—the risk of injury or death, the regimented lifestyle, and the general lack of independence—not afforded their predecessors in the 1960s and 1970s. The basic fairness of the all-volunteer force, and the concomitant elimination of the risk of coerced service, may have created space for young people to respect the military in the abstract without worrying that it would unduly intrude on their lives.

There is likely more to this story than simple self-interest, however. In a period characterized by shockingly low levels of trust in our fundamental institutions, the military has consistently been the most trusted. A recent poll released by the Harvard Institute of Politics finds that 53 percent of millennials trust the military to "do the right thing" at least some of the time; the second most trusted institution is the Supreme Court, at just 42 percent, and just 17 percent of millennials have any faith that Congress will do the right thing.[8] The military, as a nonpartisan, service-oriented institution, may have become relatively more attractive as a source of national pride and hope.

The Knowledge Deficit

We observed anecdotally during the ROTC debate at Stanford that even students who were passionate about the issue displayed an ignorance of the basic organization, demographics, and principles of the military. Claims that allowing ROTC to return would support an institution that murders innocents and preys on the poor and uneducated for recruits were met with the response (from civilian students, of course) that civilians should not question military policies because they could not possibly understand it without having served.

This lack of basic knowledge comes through clearly in the survey data. When millennials are asked directly about their familiarity with the military, 45 percent say "somewhat familiar" while another 32 percent are "not very familiar." Only 15 percent claim to be "very familiar" with the US military. Relative to all other age groups, millennials are the least likely to self-identify as "very familiar" and most likely to identify as "not very familiar" (CM1T 39). On factual questions, millennials are not much better: their mean estimate of the Marine Corps' manpower was upwards of 3 million—off by a factor of twenty (CM1T 57). Likewise, millennials estimated the overall strength of the military to be nearly 11 million, or roughly one in 30 Americans of all ages, when in reality the number is closer to 2.3 million, or roughly one in 140 (CM1T 58). Millennials also frequently respond with "not sure" to survey questions that involve factual knowledge of the military, suggesting a combination of ignorance and humility regarding these issues (CM1T 51, 40).

In addition to a dearth of factual knowledge of the military, there is also a general lack of awareness among millennials that service members fulfill duties other than combat. We have encountered many young people who were unaware that it is possible to be a lawyer, or a nurse, or a priest, or an electrician and have a significant role within the US military (whether on active duty or as a reserve billet). On a college campus, students are particularly shocked to find active-duty officers enrolled in graduate programs. In the YouGov survey, 73 percent of millennials agree with the statement that "many veterans" have difficulty adjusting to civilian life because of stresses they experienced in the military (CM1T 47). This finding could be interpreted in many ways, especially when juxtaposed with the responses of other generations, all of which were even higher than those of millennials. In the context of millennial unfamiliarity with the military, though, this may be further evidence of it not being common knowledge that a relatively small number of troops actually experience combat, while the vast majority will never be in a firefight.

For a generation that, by virtue of the Internet, has access to exponentially more information than its parents or grandparents, what might be the reason for millennials' ignorance? First, they may simply not be interested in the military. Twelve percent of millennials report that a military isolated from society is a good thing, more than any other age group (CM2T 24). Millennials are the demographic least interested in news and public affairs, and, though television is the primary source of news for a plurality of millennials, nearly a quarter get their news from pop-culture sites such as BuzzFeed or social media sites such as Facebook or Twitter rather than from major news organizations directly (CM1T 66, 34). When it comes to the military specifically, millennials are the least likely demographic to advise a close friend to join the military, perhaps suggesting that it is not seen as an attractive career option (CM2T 11).

The second explanation is that millennials, even those who are curious about the military, do not have enough opportunities to learn about it. Millennials generally have more interaction with current service members than other age groups do, as one might expect given that most service members are themselves millennials (CM2T 3, 5, 6, 7). On almost every other measure of personal connection to the military, however, millennials lag behind the rest of society. They are least likely to work with a veteran (CM2T 4). They are the least likely demographic to have served in the military themselves, and they are most likely to have no family members who have served (CM1T 52, 53).

While both these explanations probably have some truth to them, the second offers a much clearer path to improving the civil-military relationship amongst millennials, one that we explored at Stanford. Rather than just trying to generate millennials' interest in the military, as seemingly every advertising agency, NGO, and political party is trying to do for their own purposes, we believe that providing opportunities to meet the demand of those already curious about the military but lacking a way to engage with it is the most promising path towards closing the millennial-military divide.

Experiential Learning

In the spring of 2012, we designed and taught a survey course for undergraduates, The US Military in International Security. The purpose of the course was to give interested students a broad overview of the history and role of the US military in American society and ongoing armed conflicts. Two years later, having identified a desire for more hands-on engagement with military issues—even among students whom one might not expect to be interested in civil-military relations (for example, students with nonmilitary families and little academic background in academic international security issues)—we decided to develop a course that would culminate in an Alternative Spring Break trip. After sifting through applications, we selected twelve students to enroll in our course, Bridging the Civil-Military Divide: Military Service as Public Service in the 21st Century. Through a variety of media, from guest lectures to film screenings to a poetry performance by student veterans, the course exposed the students to basic facts about the US military and a variety of issues in civil-military relations.

After ten weeks in the classroom, the course culminated in a one-week trip to the Washington DC area. Our group spent the first portion of the trip at the U.S. Naval Academy (USNA) in Annapolis, Maryland. There, with the help of a group of student leaders equally committed to increasing civil-military dialogue, we paired our students up with midshipmen to be fully immersed in the Annapolis experience, from morning physical training to classes to extracurricular activities. The second portion of the trip involved meetings with senior Pentagon officials, a visit to Andrews Air Force Base, Marine Corps Base Quantico, the House Armed Services Committee, and the White House Office of Public Engagement.

While the second portion of the trip exposed students to high-level thinking and discourse about civil-military relations, the first portion actually allowed them to live it on a personal level and, as we will describe below, turned out to be much more impactful for them.

There were several important takeaways from the course and accompanying trip. Firstly, it confirmed our intuition that there was some unmet demand for more avenues to engage with the issue of civil-military relations and the supposed civil-military divide. Not only did the number of applications for the course and trip far exceed the resources we had at our disposal, but there were also no other structured courses or programs on Stanford's campus to which we could point where students so unfamiliar with the military could learn and engage on these issues.

Secondly, we noticed that the human connection between our students and our military hosts was the most significant aspect of the trip. When we followed up with our counterparts at Annapolis, we were told that there was similarly strong feedback from the USNA midshipmen who were paired up with our students. The trip, unlike a more sterile classroom setting, was an opportunity for interesting conversations and exchanges of views, sometimes uncomfortable but very human.

The biggest and most important takeaway, therefore, was this: if there is indeed a millennial-military divide, the key to closing it is not in forcing millennials to learn more facts about the military or in studying American military history. Rather, it is in enabling interpersonal connections between young people and their peers in the military—connections that can inspire interest and important discussions about military and civilian values and the differences and commonalities between both groups.

Policy Prescriptions

Though we hear the occasional call for reinstating the draft or requiring young people to perform a year of public service, such large-scale policy changes are, at present, unpopular and probably infeasible. There are, however, several ways to increase mutual understanding and respect between young civilians and their military counterparts. Some of the ideas we propose below are straightforward and relatively easy to implement, while others might be slightly more controversial and difficult to execute. We present these ideas in order to spark conversation and thought, not as polished proposals for reform, but we believe their implementation would contribute positively to tightening the relationship between civilians and the military at all levels.

1. New Ways to Fulfill Service Obligations

As of now, newly commissioned officers are placed within their respective service branch's hierarchy, usually in a junior management position in which they interact only with their enlisted subordinates and commissioned supervisors. Whether it is in commanding an infantry platoon or a small flight, these young officers have very little exposure to civilians working on issues of defense and international security. Flag officers, on the other hand, interact much more frequently with their civilian counterparts. Even mid-to-senior-level officers (O-4 to O-7) have the opportunity to do Pentagon rotations and engage with civilian defense officials. One alternative to the existing model, therefore, would be to allow a select group of newly commissioned officers from each military academy to fulfill a portion of their initial service obligation through a rotation at a civilian institution. Allowing a second lieutenant to work alongside a junior CIA analyst, for instance, or to serve alongside a junior foreign service officer at one of our embassies would give each an insight into the other. While spending one or two years working outside the military carries the risk that these junior officers would miss important milestones in their early careers, the experience they would gain would pay great dividends down the road, especially if they were required to work in a joint or interagency environment. Additionally, as a few high-achieving academy graduates are already able to earn a graduate degree between receiving their commissions and continuing their training, there exists a model for reintegrating junior officers into the pipeline after a year or two away.

Another option would be to allow active-duty service members to participate in long-term civilian service programs while stationed stateside. During peacetime, service members could apply to spend six months or one year working as instructors with Teach for America or builders with Habitat for Humanity, serving side-by-side with civic-minded civilians. Combined with a civil-society-based effort to engage civilian young people in national service, such a program would allow civilians and service members to bond not just through words but through actions that demonstrate their shared commitment to serving their country. The Aspen Institute's Franklin Project, whose mission is to enable and encourage all young adults to spend a year doing public service, could be a potential partner in this endeavor.[9]

2. University Fellowships for Senior Noncommissioned Officers

Presently, midcareer officers (usually at the O-4 and O-5 level) are given the opportunity to spend a year at a civilian institution for leadership development, introspection, and research (Stanford's Hoover Institution and Harvard's Kennedy School, for instance, both have year-long National Security Fellows programs with a participant from each service). As of now, these programs are restricted to officers. Allowing a select number of senior noncommissioned officers to participate in such a program would give college students a perspective on the largest and arguably most critical component of the military: the enlisted ranks. Just as they can learn a great deal from a lieutenant colonel, students could learn a great deal from a sergeant major with twenty years of experience literally making the planes run on time.

3. Exchange Programs

Just as our students at Stanford benefitted from a short period at the Naval Academy, so other college students would gain important insights by spending some time at one of the US military academies, and vice versa. American universities and the military academies should do more to establish formal exchange programs with one another, to include faculty members and administrators if possible. There are several universities that are already engaged in such efforts, such as Tufts University and Boston University, but there is certainly room for many more to become involved.

Semester-long exchanges between civilian schools and military academies would be ideal. The extended time frame would allow the exchange students not only to get a glimpse of life at their new institutions but also to integrate into the academic, social, and athletic routines and to come away with substantive achievements, such as completion of courses, participation on an athletic team, and a network of new friends. However, the practical realities of life at the military academies—with their intense, intricately planned schedules of classes and military training—may make such an extended exchange impossible. In that case, shorter exchanges, such as the week-long program we developed, can still be immensely valuable. Students in such programs would get to know their peers at the institution they were visiting and gain exposure to the different routines and culture, even if they were not able to get the in-depth experience a longer program would allow. Ultimately, exchange programs of any length are an essential tool for exposing future military officers to the independent, innovative thinking taught at the best civilian schools and for exposing civilian students to some of their most disciplined, driven, and service-oriented peers in the country.

4. More Courses on Military History, Strategy, and Civil-Military Relations

Watching the ROTC campus debate unfold, we were simultaneously inspired by the passion and underwhelmed by the knowledge displayed by the participants. Convinced that there was a market for studying military issues, we started organizing. Our first attempt to address the campus civil-military gap was leading a student-initiated course in 2012 on US military history and policy. The course was conceived the prior year by two ROTC students, and we assumed leadership after they graduated. Designed to cover the basics—what someone new to the topic might want to learn about how the military works—the class consisted of lectures from officers, professors, and former policymakers with wide-ranging experience.

We received generally positive feedback from the students, but the course had a smaller impact than we had hoped, as most of the students did not involve themselves further with military issues after the class. Lectures and PowerPoint, however well designed and presented, can only be so inspiring. The highlight of the course was a virtual staff ride through the Battle of Wanat, led by a researcher from the Combat Studies Institute at Fort Leavenworth. Using software that generated a virtual landscape of Wanat, complete with virtual trees and army positions, we were able to move through the battlefield as the presenter explained the situation on the ground and what decisions were being made. This class session struck a chord because it went beyond the classroom, in feeling at least, and into the mindset of the soldiers making decisions under fire. Far more than just learning about army tactics and the facts of one of the bloodiest battles of the war in Afghanistan, through this immersive presentation we gained some small insight into the human aspect of war.

At civilian institutions of higher education, most courses on military strategy are in the context of ancient warfare, and discussion centers on strategic theory and accounts of battles long past. While these are important topics worthy of scholarly attention in their own right, if they are to be more than interesting intellectual exercises, curricula must be redesigned (or new classes added) that emphasize interactivity in the classroom and interaction with service members through, for example, class trips to nearby bases or meetings on campus with visiting officers and enlisted personnel.

5. Active-Duty Officers Teach Full Time at Civilian Institutions

In our college careers, we benefitted immensely from the presence of "warrior-scholars" on campus. Lieutenant General Karl Eikenberry (Ret.), General James Mattis (Ret.), and Colonel Joseph Felter (Ret.), among others, provided invaluable guidance and perspective for us as students and citizens. As the military draws down from Afghanistan and shifts to a peacetime posture (the ongoing operations in Iraq, Syria, and elsewhere notwithstanding), providing more active-duty service members the opportunity to pursue higher education and then teach at civilian institutions would allow students around the country to benefit from their leadership and enable the service members to bring lessons learned in civilian institutions back into their services as they ascend the ranks. The instruction should cover traditional topics such as political science and history but could be expanded to include, say, allowing nuclear submariners to teach introductory courses in engineering and mathematics or having an army trauma surgeon teach a medical school course on emergency medicine. This would allow them to both share their perspectives as operators of finely tuned systems and make clear that there are many paths in the military other than that of the traditional infantry "grunt." The service members, in turn, would bring to their next assignments a deeper knowledge of their field of study and a broader intellectual perspective; teaching skills, which are crucial to good leadership; and an understanding of the civilians they serve.

6. More Civilians Teaching at Military Institutions

Conversely, the students at military institutions could benefit from civilian instructors. As of now, the faculties of the US military academies are made up mostly of active duty or retired officers.[10] with a few civilians in the mix whose subjects may be seen as too "soft" for those in the military profession.[11] Elizabeth Samet, a civilian English professor at West Point, has written about her experience helping cadets find meaning in literature and how the lessons they learned in her classroom stuck with them as they deployed and returned home. (She has also described how much the experience has influenced her own views and beliefs.) If we could move past the fear that civilian instructors would compromise the rigor and focus of service academy curricula, increasing the number of civilian instructors could introduce service academy students to broader perspectives and even complement the lessons they learn from their military instructors, in the classroom and in the field.

7. Recruiting Veterans to Universities and Increased Funding for Veteran Scholarships

Admissions offices at American universities should improve their outreach to veterans, who would bring a unique perspective to any incoming freshman class, and, accordingly, veteran representation should be considered an integral part of a diverse student body.

Additionally, institutions of higher education, from state community colleges to private four-year universities, should create funds to help subsidize veteran enrollment. While the post-9/11 GI bill provides education benefits to veterans, it only covers the cost up to that of the state's most expensive public university, and only does so for four academic years (thirty-six months). As the average American takes far more than four years to complete his or her undergraduate degree and most private universities cost far more than the public ones, it is reasonable to expect that veterans might require additional financial assistance beyond what the post-9/11 GI bill provides.[12]

Furthermore, there are several for-profit universities that can only be described as predatory in their targeting of veterans. As Captain Tim Hsia (Ret.) and Anna Ivey point out in their *New York Times* op-ed "Fix the New G.I. Bill," the predatory practices of these institutions are leading to higher rates of student loan defaults, an issue that only complicates a veteran's smooth entry into the civilian workforce.[13] Service to School, a nonprofit founded by Augusto Giacoman, Tim Hsia, Khalil Tawil, and Anna Ivey, provides free application counseling to veterans and has so far assisted over one hundred applicants in gaining admission to elite universities such as Harvard, Stanford, Northwestern, Columbia, and Notre Dame. This model should be replicated on a larger scale to encourage more veterans to apply to four-year colleges and universities.

Conclusion

The issue of civil-military relations, particularly millennial-military relations, is one that merits further investigation and consideration, both in a scholarly sense and in the context of a broader societal discussion. We do not purport to have all of the answers as to why the civil-military divide exists, nor a silver bullet to achieve perfect under-standing between millennials and the military. Given the particular nature of the military profession, there will always be a gap between service members and civilians of every demographic, and this is not necessarily a bad thing. But in making an effort to understand the military and our peers serving in it, we have been fortunate to have our assumptions challenged, to build meaningful relationships with people we otherwise may never have encountered, and to gain insight into the sacrifices our fellow citizens have made—and stand ready to make again—on our behalf. Our work on this issue has done much to shape our sense of what it means to be a young person in the United States and our understanding of what opportunities and responsibili-ties our citizenship entails. We hope that this book and projects like it will inspire our peers—civilian and military alike—to undertake similar efforts toward mutual understanding and appreciation.

Notes

1. Kate Abbott, "Faculty Senate Votes 'Yes' on ROTC Return," *Stanford Daily*, April 29, 2011, http://www.stanforddaily.com/2011/04/29/breaking-faculty -senate-votes-on-rotc.
2. "ROTC: The Debate in Review," *Stanford Daily*, April 29, 2011, http://www.stanforddaily.com/2011/04/29/rotc-the-debate-in-review.
3. "A Mad, Mad, Mad World," *Stanford Magazine*, January–February 2009, https://alumni.stanford.edu/get/page/magazine/article/?article_id=30520.
4. Kurt Chirbus, "'Don't Ask' Repeal Jumpstarts ROTC Debate," *Stanford Daily*, January 5, 2011, http://www.stanforddaily.com/2011/01/05/dont-ask-repeal -jumpstarts-rotc-debate.
5. New America Foundation Federal Education Budget Project, "Federal Pell Grant Program," March 10, 2015.
6. "US Military Personnel by Country," CNN, 2011, http://www.cnn.com /interactive/2012/04/us/table.military.troops.
7. References to the YouGov data by question number appear in parentheses throughout this essay with the abbreviations CM1T and CM2T indicating the 2013 and 2014 surveys, respectively. The complete results are available

at http://www.hoover.org/warriors-and-citizens-crosstabs-1 (CM1T) and http://www.hoover.org/warriors-and-citizens-crosstabs-2 (CM2T).

8. Della Volpe, John Robo, and Ellen Robo, "Survey of Young Americans' Attitudes toward Politics and Public Service: Executive Summary," Harvard University Institute of Politics, 29 April 2015.

9. David Ignatius, "The Case for National Service," *Washington Post,* November 27, 2014, http://www.washingtonpost.com/opinions/david -ignatius-the-benefits-of-national-service/2014/11/27/f8e69038-75a1 -11e4-a755-e32227229e7b_story.html.

10. Kristen M. Keller et al., "The Mix of Military and Civilian Faculty at the United States Air Force Academy," Rand Corporation, 2013, http://www .rand.org/content/dam/rand/pubs/monographs/MG1200/MG1237/RAND _MG1237.pdf.

11. The Naval Academy is a notable exception, as its faculty is split roughly evenly between officers and civilian instructors. See http://www.usna.edu /Academics/Faculty-Information.

12. National Center for Education Statistics, "Fast Facts: Time to Degree," Institute of Education Sciences, 2011, https://nces.ed.gov/fastfacts/display .asp?id=569.

13. National Center for Education Statistics, "Fast Facts: Time to Degree," Institute of Education Sciences, 2011, https://nces.ed.gov/fastfacts/display .asp?id=569.

CHAPTER 10

A Model for Connecting Civilians and the Military

Jim Hake

It has been said that 1 percent of our citizens serve and go to war while 99 percent go to the mall. The YouGov poll confirms the disconnect: only 15.6 percent of Americans have served or had an immediate family member serve since 9/11 (CM2T 2).[1] This gap may explain why most Americans think the military gets less respect than it deserves (CM2T 18)—but the issue has importance far beyond respect or gratitude for the military. The disconnect between civilians and the military undermines our nation's security and jeopardizes the health of the American Experiment. The bond formed when a high school teacher and student helped Marines in Afghanistan points the way to a solution. After this encounter, Ethel Gullette, Director of Community Service Learning, Windward School, summed up her impressions thus, "There are all kinds of good things I could say about the Marines. They were articulate, intelligent, well read, historically savvy. They conveyed a real sense of caring about the Afghan people and their well being." Brice Green, a senior at the Windward School, reported that he "learned the most when the Marines came and talked about their experience on the ground. It's so much less filtered than a video on some media channel or reading some op/ed in *The New York Times*."

It was spring 2011, during the height of the US military mission in Afghanistan. Ethel and Brice had just completed videoconferencing with Afghan students at the Kodoala Drab School in Helmand Province—a school established and protected by the U.S. Marines.

The Afghan students lived in mud homes with no electricity or running water. They were as far away—culturally and geographically—as one can get from West Los Angeles, which is home to Windward School. Yet what was most remarkable to Ethel and Brice were the Marines they had gotten to know—the first members of the armed forces to visit Windward in the school's forty year history. Along with dozens of other Windward students, parents, and teachers, Ethel and Brice had come to understand who the Marines are, what the Marines do, and why they do it. The videoconference was organized by Spirit of America, a citizen-funded nonprofit. The project reflects a new model for connecting civilians and the military, a model in which the American people are partners in US missions abroad.

This chapter provides a framework for connecting civilians and the military. It examines the value of, and the barriers to, connecting civilians and the military. The chapter concludes with recommendations for citizens and policymakers.

Origins of a New Model

Like most Americans, after the 9/11 terrorist attacks I wanted to do something to help. I had no military or government experience. I had no nonprofit, nongovernmental organization (NGO), or international aid and assistance experience. My background was as a technology and Internet entrepreneur, including founding and selling one of the early Internet media ventures. My experience with the military was comparable to that of many Americans—only 8.3 percent work with someone currently in the military (CM2T 3).

It took eighteen months to find a meaningful way to help. It happened when I stumbled upon a *National Geographic* show about a U.S. Army Special Forces team in Orgune, Afghanistan—a small village near the border with Pakistan. The scene that caught my eye was Sergeant First Class Jay Smith and US soldiers playing baseball with Afghan boys and girls.

When he deployed, Jay took his baseball glove for his own use but soon children in the village were using it and having fun playing catch. Inspired, Jay called his wife, Dianne, and asked her to send enough bats, balls, and mitts for the Afghan kids to play a real game. With donations from friends, family, coworkers and her church group, Dianne bought the gear and sent it to Jay. Then Jay and his soldiers taught the whole village how to play baseball. It all happened because of Jay's initiative and his desire to make life better for the villagers. Jay's initiative was supported by the generosity of people back home.

That was my light-bulb moment. I thought there must be others like Sergeant Smith serving on the front lines who, as part of their difficult missions, needed something to help the local population but could not get it through government channels. I knew there were other Americans who, like me, would jump at the chance to help, if only they knew what was needed. And, I knew I could use the Internet to connect the two—to connect supply and demand, connect civilians and the military.

I tracked down Jay and met with him and his Special Forces team at Fort Bragg. Jay told me that baseball gear was only one of the ways he and his team had helped the villagers of Orgune. They provided other small-scale, highly targeted humanitarian assistance—shoes, blankets, school supplies. Everything was in response to what the villagers needed and all provided by people back home who wanted to help.

I told them my idea: when troops needed something to help the local population, they could tell me and I would use the Internet to get people to help. Jay said this idea would save lives. He explained that when he and his team were in Orgune, al Qaeda was crossing the Pakistan border at night and firing rockets on their camp. Then, purely because of the strong relationship and trust our soldiers had built with the villagers, the villagers formed a nighttime patrol to protect our soldiers. The rocket attacks stopped. Lives were saved. After hearing that, I committed myself to carrying out my plan. In this way, connecting civilians and the military became my personal mission.

I was part of the 71 percent of Americans who consider themselves only somewhat or not very familiar with the US military (CM1T 39). However, my lack of government or military experience gave me a helpful naiveté: I thought that if the idea made sense to me, and if it made sense to Jay and his fellow soldiers, then I could figure out everything in between.

After meeting Sergeant Smith at Fort Bragg, I founded a 501c3 nonprofit organization to execute the idea. I called it Spirit of America to reflect the initiative, generosity, and optimism that define the American character. Spirit of America (SOA) has provided assistance to support the missions of US troops in thirty-four countries. Everything SOA has provided is in direct response to what American troops say is needed to help local people and partners and is in support of the troops' missions: sewing machines to empower Iraqi women and help them provide for their families; tools to support seaweed farming in Mindanao in the Philippines; GPS devices, metal detectors and tourniquets to support the Peshmerga in their fight against ISIS.

In providing opportunities for Americans who want to help, SOA has been the catalyst for new policy that enables greater collaboration between the private sector and the military. It has defined a new type of "not neutral" nongovernmental organization and a new category of philanthropy in which charitable giving supports national security objectives. Spirit of America's trials and tribulations offer lessons for those who seek to build connections between civilians and those who serve in uniform.

Reasons for Connecting Civilians and the Military

As many as 32.5 percent of Americans believe the military is isolated from society (CM2T 23). And, 59.6 percent see such isolation as a "bad thing" (CM2T 24). They are right.

There are two primary reasons why America needs to connect civilians and military. First, a strong connection is vital to the safety of our troops, the success of their missions, and, more broadly, national security. Second, a strong connection leads to a better-informed public, which is the foundation for better-informed policy, stronger political will, and more effective American engagement in the world.

Safety of Our Troops and the Success of Their Missions

The Windward-Kodoala Drab videoconference project had all the appearance of a feel-good charitable effort. But there was a deeper motivation that illustrates the impact civilians can have on the safety and success of our troops. Spirit of America organized the videoconference to help the Marines with specific security-related objectives and mission requirements.

Beginning in December 2010, Spirit of America had a field operations representative on the ground, working within and alongside Marine units in Helmand Province. Our field rep, Matt Valkovic, was an army veteran who had served in Iraq. His job was to understand the Marines' objectives and what they needed and determine ways to apply private assistance to help.

Matt learned the Taliban had been spreading propaganda to turn the population against the Marines. In one case, the Taliban created composition notebooks that had covers with images of a Christian crusader from the Middle Ages, a brandy snifter half filled with liquor, and a flower. The Taliban distributed these notebooks to students and their parents, saying they were from the Marines. The message was clear: the Marines intended to conquer Afghanistan's Muslims, corrupt them, and convert them to Christianity.

This was a crude attempt at propaganda in rural Afghanistan, but the Taliban efforts were having an effect on relations and security The Marines needed ways to build trust with the local Afghans. The Marines also knew that increased school attendance would improve security, for when Afghan teenagers were in the classroom they could not be on the battlefield. With this backdrop, the videoconference project was conceived as a way to get more local children in school and to build trust between the Marines and the Afghans, especially the teenage boys most likely to be used by the Taliban against the Marines (for example, to plant roadside bombs).

Prior to the videoconference, Windward students filled backpacks with school supplies to give as gifts of friendship to the students at Kodoala Drab. Spirit of America arranged for shipment. The Windward students also received a background briefing from Lieutenant Colonel Ben Watson. Lieutenant Colonel Watson had recently returned from Afghanistan where he commanded the battalion of Marines deployed to Garmsir.

Watson gave his talk during lunch period. More than one hundred Windward students missed lunch to hear what he had to say. Watson had prepared a twenty-slide PowerPoint briefing, but only a minute into his talk, he was fielding questions. The Windward students were fully engaged, asking about every detail of what he and his Marines did in Afghanistan.

When lunch period ended, many students skipped their next class and stayed, crowding around Watson to ask more questions. Ninety minutes later, when Lieutenant Colonel Watson had to leave Windward to return to Camp Pendleton, he had not gone beyond his briefing's title slide with only his name and "Garmsir" on it. This student interest is particularly noteworthy in a time when only 26 percent of Americans would recommend enlisting in the US military after graduating from high school (CM1T 35).

The videoconference was scheduled after the backpacks and school supplies from Windward were received by the Marines in Garmsir. Spirit of America's Matt Valkovic set up the connection at Kodoala Drab using a Broadband Global Area Network (BGAN) satellite Internet terminal, a laptop, and Skype. Nearly two hundred Afghan boys and teachers were assembled, along with a dozen Marines. At Windward, the assembly room was packed with students, parents, and teachers. It was early morning in Afghanistan and just past dinnertime in Los Angeles.

Afghan students sang their national anthem; one Windward student played a saxophone; another sang John Lennon's "Imagine." Windward students showed photos of their pets and families. A Windward girl showed a photo of her playing soccer. The best part was the simple conversation, the questions and answers, between the two groups of students. The most striking thing was how normal and natural the interactions were. The videoconference concluded with Afghan boys presenting flowers to Windward students and the Marines distributing the backpacks and school supplies to the Afghan students.

For all the civilians assembled at Windward, it was the most encouraging thing they had seen or heard in the nearly ten years America had been at war in Afghanistan. For the Marines, the key measure of success was that attendance at Kodoala Drab doubled in the week following the videoconference and held steady after that for as long as the Marines were deployed to Garmsir. The videoconference project had a direct impact on the safety of the Marines and the success of their mission, and the Windward community was a direct participant in the outcome.

With the help of civilians from all fifty of the United States, Spirit of America implemented hundreds of other projects to support the US mission in Afghanistan. The Marines reported that radios provided by

SOA to the Afghan border patrol led to a reduction by 60 percent in Improvised Explosive Devices (IEDs) found in the Helmand Province/ Pakistan border area. An army sergeant reported that Afghan Local Police at one checkpoint found more than forty IEDs in just one week using metal detectors donated by Spirit of America. Each of these projects provided opportunities for civilians to connect with US troops in Afghanistan and support their difficult missions.

This civilian-military connection also works in support of the military's small-footprint conflict-prevention operations. In Mauritania, West Africa, to help a US military team counter al Qaeda in the Islamic Maghreb (AQIM), Spirit of America provided funding, training, and equipment to enable village men to go into business as veterinarians. Improved livestock health provided villagers with more meat, milk, and money, and made it more difficult for AQIM to exploit poverty as a recruiting tool.

With a $500 billion Department of Defense annual budget, the idea that relatively small-scale private assistance can contribute to mission success is counterintuitive. But the unconventional threats America faces place a premium on speed, flexibility, and innovation. And that is where the resources and brainpower of our citizens—unfettered by bureaucracy and the inevitable restrictions on the use of taxpayer funds—can have an off-scale impact. Civilian support is akin to venture capital: risk tolerant, responsive, and able to help military personnel capitalize on windows of opportunity. In our economy, venture capital is very small (early-stage venture capital is a mere 0.05 percent of GDP) yet it fuels the innovation that drives our $17 trillion economy.

A More Informed Public, More Informed Policy, and Stronger Political Will

Few decisions our political leaders make are as consequential to our nation as the decision to send the men and women of our military to serve abroad. And few things are as difficult as maintaining the steadfastness to follow through once that decision has been made. However, a majority of Americans think our political leaders are not very knowledgeable or not knowledgeable at all about the military (CM2T 15). A well-informed public is ultimately the best hope for well-informed policy and the political will needed to persist and prevail.

Unfortunately, the public is not well informed now. According to the YouGov poll, Americans' estimates of how many service members are in all five branches of the military were on average wrong by a count of over five million (CM1T 58). Guesses on specific branches of the military, such as the Army and Marine Corps, were incorrect by hundreds of thousands of people (CM1T 56, 57).[2]

A strong connection to the military—one based on helping military personnel in a meaningful way—is the best way for the public to become better informed. This type of connection gives civilians more insight directly, and it motivates them to learn more because they are engaged participants, not merely recipients of a message.

A strong civilian-military connection is especially important because the issues regarding the use of the military are more difficult to understand than other areas of public policy. Very few civilians have a direct experience of the military. Military events take place thousands of miles away. In every other field of national importance—education, health care, crime, employment—there is something relevant to it happening in a citizen's own neighborhood. This is not so with foreign affairs and national security. As a result, civilians must rely on the news media, which tends to focus on the sensational or simplistic. As Windward student Brice Green said, although he read the newspaper, he learned the most from the unfiltered information from the Marines. Similarly, after participating in the videoconference and helping the Marines and Afghan students, Windward's Ethel Gullette said, with tears in her eyes, "there is hope."

At the present, there is overwhelming public support for increasing or maintaining spending levels on military pay, operations and training, construction, weapons procurement, and war operations budgets (CM1T 10–15). However, 69 percent of respondents want to decrease slightly, or decrease a lot, spending on foreign aid, and 68 percent want to decrease assistance to foreign militaries (CM1T 7, 16, 38). A better connected public might be more supportive of increasing foreign assistance or personally participating in the military.

Ways of Connecting Civilians and the Military

Discussion of connecting civilians and the military often focuses on media and messaging with the idea that there must be something people can be told that will get them engaged and connected. However, information campaigns will not do it; today's media environment is too crowded and consumers are too cynical.

The way to build an enduring civilian-military connection is to give civilians a way to help—something they can do—and to provide feedback on the impact of what they have done. It is essential that the help requested meet real, meaningful needs.

Taking action transforms people from passive, often distracted observers into participants and investors. The ability to take action is a primary reason behind the growth of social media. Users can participate and not merely consume media, creating a stronger connection—or "stickiness"—than that enjoyed through any other form of media. Similarly, the act of buying shares in Google makes one far more interested in everything that affects Google's success. Taking action is especially important with respect to the complex security challenges faced by our nation and military. Having some way to help is an antidote to the helplessness and hopelessness that undermine America's engagements abroad. Civilians must be given feedback on the impact of the help they have provided. Social media's feedback loop has been essential to its success. People can easily track who likes, shares, or comments on their Facebook posts and who re-tweets or favorites their tweets.

The action/feedback approach was used in World War II to mobilize and engage the American home front. Civilians were asked to help in a multitude of ways. They bought war bonds. Calls to "Get in the Scrap" inspired nationwide drives to collect tin, rubber, and steel. People tore down their fences to provide wood used to build barracks. Feedback was provided through newsreels and posters.

In contrast, after 9/11, President Bush told Americans to get on with their lives as normal and go shopping. This was neither a way to directly help the military, nor was it meaningful. While there was logic to it—our national security ultimately depends on the health of our economy—it failed to create a connection between Americans and the military or the mission. This was a significant missed opportunity of the Bush presidency. Unfortunately, the Obama administration has not done better.

Privately funded, citizen-led nonprofit organizations have stepped in to provide an outlet for Americans who want to help. At Operation Gratitude, civilians gather to assemble and ship care packages to deployed military personnel. Civilians can include personal notes in the packages. Operation Gratitude provides feedback through photographs and emails from troops who receive the care packages.

The Navy SEAL Foundation provides opportunities for citizens to help the Navy Special Warfare community. People can give to fund scholarships for the children of Navy SEALs killed in action or to provide assistance to wounded SEALs and their families. Feedback is provided through YouTube videos, Facebook, and Twitter, including testimonials by SEAL veterans and family members.

Project HOPE (Health Opportunities for People Everywhere) sends civilian medical volunteers aboard U.S. Navy ships to provide medical assistance, health education, and vaccinations in support of navy humanitarian missions. The feedback is immediate: volunteers see firsthand how their assistance has impacted the lives of those suffering from illness, poverty, and natural disasters.

Spirit of America uses crowd-funding to enable citizens to help deployed military personnel, support their missions, and assist local populations. People visit the SOA website, choose a project, and make a donation. Supporters receive updates on their projects via email, blog posts, and social media. When a project is completed, supporters receive an impact summary and an accounting to the dollar of how their money was spent.

The diversity of ways to help represented by these organizations, and many others, is important. They provide different entry points—each with a unique appeal and value proposition—for civilians to connect with the military.

Barriers to Connecting Civilians and the Military

Spirit of America's experience illustrates the barriers that impede efforts to connect civilians and the military.

Department of Defense Legal and Policy Barriers

In 2010, seven years after its founding, Spirit of America encountered a variety of military legal objections to its operations. In discussions with Marines deploying to Afghanistan, the idea arose of having Spirit of America personnel on the ground in Afghanistan working within and alongside Marine units. SOA personnel would look at the Marines' missions and local needs from the standpoint of how private assistance could help and do things that could not be done with US government resources. SOA personnel would rotate among the Marine units in Helmand Province that were interested in having SOA conduct assessments and provide assistance in support of their missions.

Up to this point all Spirit of America assistance was provided remotely. SOA would communicate with deployed military personnel regarding local needs via email. SOA would then purchase goods and arrange for delivery to the point of need. The new approach of forward-deployed Spirit of America field personnel in Afghanistan required legal review at U.S. Central Command (CENTCOM). Unfortunately, the attorneys at CENTCOM saw a number of problems with Spirit of America's existing and proposed operations.

In order to assess needs and provide assistance on the ground in Afghanistan, SOA personnel would need to sleep on Forward Operating Bases (FOBs) and Combat Outposts (COPs), eat military chow, and occasionally ride in military vehicles. CENTCOM attorneys ruled that there was no legal basis for providing such support to a non-Federal entity (NFE) and doing so would be a violation of the Joint Ethics Regulation. Moreover, even though Spirit of America was providing assistance that military personnel said was needed and helpful to military missions, the attorneys viewed military personnel receiving goods donated by Spirit of America and delivering them to the local population as the military providing support to SOA. Again, CENTCOM attorneys saw this as improper support for a non-Federal entity.

CENTCOM attorneys also saw a problem with how Spirit of America had operated since 2003. The attorneys said that if a soldier or Marine told Spirit of America that certain Afghan women needed sewing machines to provide for their families that would constitute an improper solicitation of gifts that violated ethics regulations.

Ironically, US policy calls for partnership and collaboration with the private sector. A Department of Defense (DOD) issuance, for example, instructs DOD personnel to "collaborate with . . . nongovernmental organizations, and private sector firms as appropriate to plan, prepare for, and conduct stability operations" (DODI number 3000.05). Similarly, the 2010 U.S. "National Security Strategy" called for increased public-private partnerships: "[W]e must tap the ingenuity outside government through strategic partnerships with the private sector, nongovernmental organizations, foundations, and community-based organizations. Such partnerships are critical to U.S. success at home and abroad, and we will support them through enhanced opportunities for engagement, coordination, transparency, and information sharing." However, these calls for partnership and collaboration did not have much effect outside Washington. The prevailing interpretation of the Joint Ethics Regulation (JER) at the Unified Combatant Command level and below created a disconnect between policy and operations.

The effect of the CENTCOM legal interpretations in 2010 would have been to end Spirit of America's operations and its model of connecting civilians with the military. However, John Bellinger, an attorney with Arnold and Porter, took on Spirit of America as a pro bono client in an effort to craft a solution. Mr. Bellinger had held several senior presidential appointments in the US government, including positions as the legal adviser to the Department of State from 2005 to 2009 and as senior associate counsel to the president and legal adviser to the National Security Council (NSC) at the White House from 2001 to 2005. He was well versed in US government ethics issues.

Bellinger arranged a meeting with the Department of Defense general counsel, Jeh Johnson, and the head of the DOD Standards of Conduct Office, Leigh Bradley. After describing Spirit of America's work and the legal objections that had been raised at CENTCOM, Mr. Johnson and Ms. Bradley indicated it should be possible to create a legal framework that would allow military personnel to continue to utilize Spirit of America's assistance. As a result of this meeting, CENTCOM requested and received guidance from the DoD Office of General Counsel (OGC) on the range of legal concerns that had been raised by Spirit of America's work: gift solicitation, support for a non-Federal entity, preferential treatment, and improper endorsement. For example, on the issue of perceived gift solicitation, OGC said, "If SOA

had an open request for the identification of the needs" of local people, it "might easily resolve the concern." In other words, if Spirit of
America requested information and asked What is needed? military
personnel would be permitted to respond.

In November 2010, using the guidance provided by OGC,
CENTCOM attorneys created a new regulation—U.S. Central Command Regulation 27-14 (CCR 27-14)—that provided the legal framework that allowed Spirit of America's operations to proceed and
enabled SOA to have field personnel forward-deployed on the ground
with military units in Afghanistan.

CCR 27-14 specifies fourteen requirements an NFE must meet
in order to be eligible to receive support in the CENTCOM Area of
Responsibility. One of the requirements is that an NFE must be registered as a USAID Private Voluntary Organization; this, in turn,
requires an organization like Spirit of America to meet nineteen other
conditions.

In January 2012, based on the positive impact of CCR 27-14, in a
"twelve-star memo," generals James Mattis, James Amos, and Raymond
Odierno recommended to Secretary of Defense Leon Panetta that "the
DOD implement guidance in a Department-wide regulation similar
to CCR 27-14 in order to facilitate a common understanding amongst
battlefield commanders concerning the depth and breadth of support to NFEs and NGOs." In May 2012, Admiral William McRaven,
Commander of the U.S. Special Operations Command, added backing
to the recommendation for DOD consolidated guidance. In August
2012, Secretary Panetta agreed with the need for consolidated guidance. He wrote to generals Mattis, Amos, and Odierno and Admiral
McRaven, "I support your proposal to consolidate existing guidance related to Non-Federal Entities (NFEs) and Nongovernmental
Organizations (NGOs) during contingency operations and am committed to fulfilling the needs you outlined in your letter." As of June
2015, the requested regulation had not emerged from the Department
of Defense. Nonetheless, the legal framework provided by CCR 27-14

has had a positive effect outside CENTCOM and has enabled Spirit of America operations in support of other military commands.

However, barriers remain. The guidance provided by DOD OGC and the legal framework provided by CCR 27-14 are not broadly understood by DOD personnel. On occasion, this lack of familiarity requires previously resolved issues to be revisited, resulting in delay and additional expense for both the military and civilian organizations. And, although CCR 27-14 made it possible for civilians to provide assistance in response to needs identified by military personnel, the barriers to providing feedback to those who help are far more difficult to resolve.

To provide feedback, an organization like Spirit of America must report on the impact of the assistance it provides. The military personnel involved—those who identified the need and witness the results—are the most qualified to provide this information. However, concern over violating the Joint Ethics Regulation often prevents military personnel and their commands from providing feedback that can be used on the record.

As it should, the JER prohibits preferential treatment and endorsement.[3] The fairness of government employees is critical to the confidence of our citizens and the credibility of our government and military. The difficulty is that interpretations of what constitutes preferential treatment and endorsement can vary widely—especially since military personnel must avoid both *actual* preferential treatment and the *appearance* of preferential treatment. Accordingly, military personnel must consider how things might appear to, or be perceived by, someone in the vast DOD system. Making matters worse, military personnel must also consider the potential misperceptions of those outside the DOD system, including the press and Congress. The current "gotcha" media and political environment creates enormous uncertainty and risk. To avoid all the distraction and the risk of being charged with creating the *appearance* of wrongdoing, it is rational to say, and do, nothing.

Thus, SOA information products often do not include even factual statements by military personnel about assistance provided by SOA, making it difficult to provide any meaningful feedback to American citizens. Additionally, Spirit of America obtains review and approval of its public information products by the military personnel directly involved in our operations, as well as the relevant command's public affairs office. This process is essential, but it delays the feedback loop, making it more difficult to establish and maintain the connection between civilians and the military. Spirit of America media also feature the disclaimer "no endorsement of Spirit of America by the US Department of Defense or its personnel is intended or implied."

The military itself encounters the legal and policy barriers that handicap citizens and non-Federal entities. In a study of private-public collaboration in the Department of Defense, the Defense Business Board (DBB) surveyed US combatant commands, military services, and defense agencies. Some 71 percent said they encounter "significant obstacles" to private-public collaboration (PPC)."[4] The DBB study noted, "The single most frequently cited issue preventing the advancement of PPCs is the absence (actual or perceived) of legal authority" and "a strong aversion to risk results in most [DOD] attorneys, finding it easier to say no."[5]

Organizations without a deep commitment to helping the military may find these barriers too challenging and time consuming to overcome and, as result, may not follow through on their desire to connect.

Universal Humanitarian Principles

Organizations that provide humanitarian assistance overseas would seem natural candidates for providing opportunities for civilians to connect with the military. However, the dominant paradigm of providing international assistance prevents the close collaboration with, and connection to, the military pioneered by Spirit of America.

This barrier to connecting civilians and military came to light in the spring of 2013 when Spirit of America applied for membership in Inter-Action. InterAction is a member organization of NGOs that provide international aid and assistance. InterAction's members include many well-known NGOs—such as CARE, Catholic Relief Services, Save the Children, Feed the Children, World Vision, and Heifer International.[6] Spirit of America sought to join InterAction in order to access experts in other organizations who could provide advice on SOA projects and to have a platform from which to encourage other NGOs to collaborate with the US military. InterAction rejected SOA's application for membership. It was right to do so because, by intentionally supporting the safety and success of US troops, Spirit of America "takes a side," and "taking a side" violates "universal humanitarian principles" to which InterAction members must adhere.

SOA was familiar with the uneasy relationship many NGOs have with the US military, and, as a way to make clear Spirit of America's approach, we had long described SOA "not neutral" in briefings to US troops. However, we were not familiar with the full meaning and implications of "universal humanitarian principles." These principles are specified in two United Nations General Assembly resolutions. One resolution (46/182) was adopted by the General Assembly in 1991, the other (58/114) was adopted in 2004.[7] Tens of billions of dollars flow into the international aid and assistance system according to these four principles:

- Neutrality: Humanitarian actors must not take sides in hostilities or engage in controversies of a political, racial, religious or ideological nature.

- Independence: Humanitarian action must be autonomous from the political, economic, military or other objectives that any actor may hold with regard to areas where humanitarian action is being implemented.

- Impartiality: Humanitarian action must be carried out on the basis of need alone, giving priority to the most urgent cases of distress and making no distinctions on the basis of nationality, race, gender, religious belief, class or political opinions.

- Humanity: Human suffering must be addressed wherever it is found. The purpose of humanitarian action is to protect life and health and ensure respect for human beings.

Spirit of America adheres to the principle of humanity but SOA's close collaboration with, and strong connection to, the US military violates the three other principles: neutrality, independence, and impartiality.

Organizations that adhere to this code of universal humanitarian principles do noble, critically important, and often courageous work. However, the principles create an institutional barrier to connecting civilians and the military. Organizations that wish to connect to, and collaborate with, the US military may find that violating this code of universal humanitarian principles creates challenges with donors and partner organizations.

Recommendations

Spirit of America's experience can serve as a model for new efforts to connect civilians and the military. The legal framework provided by CENTCOM Regulation 27-14 enables other private organizations and non-Federal entities to provide assistance in response to needs identified by deployed military personnel. CCR 27-14 also specifies the steps NFEs must take in order to be validated as eligible to receive logistical support in a CENTCOM Area of Responsibility.

To be successful, citizen-led efforts must focus on identifying real, meaningful need that the military and government cannot otherwise meet. This is harder than it sounds. Too many charitable efforts are supply driven—driven by the supply of good intentions or the availability of donated goods. Efforts to help the military must be need driven. Finding the needs and determining what will be useful requires going to the point of need, talking to the military personnel who are there, and listening to what they say. This will most likely involve travel outside the Washington DC area.

Organizations that are prevented by their adherence to the NGO code of universal humanitarian principles from directly connecting with the military could consider creating subsidiary organizations. These subsidiaries could have greater freedom to collaborate with, and support, military personnel. Alternatively, humanitarian organizations can create affiliate or liaison relationships with the organizations that directly work with the military. Such relationships could enable information sharing, better alignment of operations, and mutual support.

In the nonprofit arena the strong desire to help leads to a tendency to reinvent the wheel. The Bush Institute at the George W. Bush Presidential Center estimates there are 45,000 organizations that serve the needs of veterans.[8] Those who are motivated to help the military should carefully evaluate whether they will add more value with a new initiative or by lending their support to an existing effort.

Policymakers can play a critical role in fostering connections between civilians and the military. The goal is to greatly expand these connections without creating processes that stultify them. Finding and meeting needs, organizing people who want to help, and providing feedback on results are entrepreneurial endeavors that are more suited to our citizens and private sector than to our government bureaucracies. Policymakers should thus focus on two tasks: enable and encourage.

Policymakers should think in terms of making it possible for civilians to engage with and help the military when their engagement and help support military objectives. This will set the conditions for the desired civilian-military connections to be created. Removing legal and policy barriers should be the priority so that the military has the clear ability to identify needs and utilize assistance from non-Federal entities. No special privileges should be afforded to NFEs. The military must determine if, and when, civilian assistance is appropriate.

The Department of Defense should issue the consolidated guidance based on CCR 27-14 that was requested in 2012 by generals Mattis, Amos, and Odierno and Admiral McRaven. Concerns over gift solicitation have been a primary impediment to civilian-military connections and have prevented civilians from providing mission-critical assistance in every theatre. Thus, even a narrow regulation that simply addresses gift solicitation would have a profound impact.

The Defense Business Board recommends that DOD create a "collaboration cell" within the Joint Staff to take the lead on private-public collaboration and report to either the chairman or assistant to the chairman of the Joint Chiefs of Staff.[9] If the collaboration cell serves as a facilitator and not as a controlling or centralizing mechanism, this recommendation should be implemented

Policymakers should find ways to spotlight best practices and successful civilian efforts to help the military. Congress could play a special role in this regard.

Conclusion

Although the military is deserving, connecting civilians with the military is not about respect, gratitude, or warm feelings. Faced with proliferating security challenges and declining resources, our government and military cannot do it all alone. Fortunately, Americans want to help, and when assistance from civilians is connected with the military it has a significant impact on the safety and success of our troops and on national security. The connection created when civilians help the military also leads to a better-informed public and, ultimately, to the better-informed policy and political will America needs to maintain its leadership and influence abroad.

Civilians who want to help must ensure their good intentions meet real military needs. Humanitarian organizations should reevaluate policies and principles that prevent them from collaborating with the military. Policymakers must provide clear guidance and legal authorities that enable private-public collaboration in the Department of Defense and that remove the well-understood, yet persistent, barriers that impede the military from using assistance from civilians.

Notes

1. References to the YouGov data by question number appear in parentheses throughout this essay with the abbreviations CM1T and CM2T indicating the 2013 and 2014 surveys, respectively. The complete results are available at http://www.hoover.org/warriors-and-citizens-crosstabs-1 (CM1T) and http://www.hoover.org/warriors-and-citizens-crosstabs-2 (CM2T).
2. Cf. Defense Manpower Data Center, "Active Duty Military Strength by Service: Current Strength," https://www.dmdc.osd.mil/appj/dwp/dwp_reports.jsp.
3. U.S. Dept. of Defense, *The Joint Ethics Regulation* (JER), 5500.07-R, http://www.dtic.mil/whs/directives/corres/pdf/550007r.pdf.
4. Defense Business Board, "Public-Private Collaboration in the Department of Defense," 2012, http://dbb.defense.gov/Portals/35/Documents/Reports/2012/FY12-4_Public_Private_Collaboration_in_the_Department_of_Defense_2012-7.pdf, p. 6.
5. Defense Business Board, "Public-Private Collaboration," p. 7.
6. InterAction, "Our Members," http://www.interaction.org/member-directory.
7. United Nations Office for the Coordination of Humanitarian Affairs, "OCHA on Message: Humanitarian Principles," April 2010, https://docs.unocha.org/sites/dms/Documents/OOM_HumPrinciple_English.pdf.
8. Bush Institute at the George W. Bush Presidential Center, "Serving Our Post-9/11 Veterans: Leading Practices among Nonprofit Organizations," 2015, http://www.bushcenter.org/essays/serveourvets.
9. Defense Business Board, "Public-Private Collaboration," p. 9.

CHAPTER 11

Ensuring a Civil-Military Connection

Kori Schake and Jim Mattis

We undertook this project to better understand attitudes of the American public about their military forty years into having an all-volunteer force and after fifteen years of being continuously at war. The project's goal was to produce data to inform both scholarship on civil-military relations and policy debates about a wide range of defense issues. We were looking to develop data that could help define salient gaps between the American military and the public it serves. Armed with the data from the YouGov surveys we commissioned, authors of the essays in this book explored whether American attitudes are changing toward our military and, if so, what potential consequences of those changes might be. This concluding chapter seeks to highlight and synthesize commonalities in the authors' findings, provide our thoughts on the issues, and identify potential areas of inquiry emerging from the data that were not taken up by any of the other authors.

In our judgment and that of the authors contributing to this volume, the relationship between America's military and its civilian society is fundamentally strong and healthy. Coming from varied areas of expertise and different political viewpoints, none of us saw cause for concern. We believe this to be a huge success for a democratic country fighting its fifteenth year of war with an all-volunteer force that was never designed to sustain that burden.[1]

Gaps certainly exist between our civilian society and our military, some of them important. Respect for the American military is widespread, but the public's knowledge of the military is shallow. Our initial reaction was that an uninformed public does not matter much; it could even be understood as a measure of success that the public does not perceive a need to carefully supervise its military. We have become persuaded by our colleagues in this project, however, that public ignorance about the military is problematic. It contributes to strategic incoherence, encouraging politicians to consider their strategic choices hemmed in by public opposition and to shift responsibility for winning policy arguments onto the military; impedes sustained support for the war effort; permits the imposition of social policies that erode battlefield lethality; fosters a sense of victimization towards veterans that skews defense spending toward pay and benefits; and distances veterans from our broader community.

Scholars of civil-military relations are always fixated on the risk of military insubordination to civilian control.[2] The contributors to this volume saw no evidence that frictions between civilian leaders and our military are at historically high levels. In fact, they appear less contentious than when the last large-scale data were collected in the 1998 Triangle study, despite the fact that public support for elected leaders has plummeted while public respect for the military has remained resiliently strong.

The collapse of public confidence in policy elites is consequential far beyond civil-military issues, but it has important effects on those relations, as well.[3] The changed balance between civilians and the military illustrated in the YouGov data may be informally shifting their respective weights in the policy process, with politicians both pushing the military to take a greater public role but also possibly distrusting military advice as politicized. Survey data show that political elites believe the military behave as politicians, whereas the military's public standing depends on them not doing so.[4]

In fact, some gaps appear to be wider and more salient between the public and its political leadership than between civilians and the military. Assessments of civil-military relations would thus benefit from something not explored in this project: a better understanding of which frictions are unique to the military's role in our political structure and which parallel other changes in American society.

An Uninformed but Admiring Public

The most striking data were those that show how reluctant Americans are to express an opinion about military issues (something uncharacteristic of Americans). The YouGov polls provide ample basis for concluding that wide swaths of the public know little about their military or are hesitant to venture an opinion on military matters. Responses to many key questions included high rates of "don't know" or "no opinion" answers (see table 11.1 for examples).[5]

These are not small numbers; nor are they inconsequential, especially when military issues are frequently prominent in the news, as they have been since 9/11. The high incidence of "don't know" responses indicates a public not bothering to be informed even when information is plentiful and easily available. Even where respondents perceive themselves as knowledgeable, they were often incorrect: 48 percent of respondents rated themselves knowledgeable about the military, yet the median response to the basic question about the size of our armed forces was off by a factor of six (CM1T 39, 56–58). The uncertainty was highest among women, minorities, those under 30 years of age, those with incomes under $40,000 per year, those living in metropolitan centers, and self-described Democrats. In each case, the percentage of "don't know" responses ranged between 30 percent and 40 percent for these groups.[6]

Survey Prompt	"Don't know"/ "no opinion" responses (%)
Most members of the military have a great deal of respect for civilian society (CM2T 50)	45
Military force should be used only in pursuit of the goal of total victory (CM2T 79)	42
When force is used, military rather than political goals should determine its application (CM2T 79)	40
The American public will not tolerate large numbers of US casualties in military operations (CM2T 79)	52
You have confidence in the ability of our military to perform well in wartime (CM2T 50)	55
Veterans are more reliable and hardworking than the rest of society (CM2T 48)	51
What percentage of young men today can qualify to enlist in the army as a private? (CM2T 12)	48
In general, do you think military leaders share the same values as the American people? (CM2T 16)	24
Even if civilian society did not always appreciate the essential military values of commitment and unselfishness, our armed forces could still maintain required traditional standards (CM2T 50)	44
Would you advise a close friend or the child of a close friend to join the military? (CM2T 11)	28
The American people understand the sacrifices made by people who serve in the US military (CM2T 50)	38
The military should choose its leaders with an eye to diversity (CM2T 48)	42
Help or hurt military effectiveness: a military culture and way of life that are very different from the culture and way of life of the rest of society (CM2T 64)	25
Help or hurt military effectiveness: the military trying to hold on to old-fashioned views of morality (CM2T 63)	19
An effective military depends on a very structured organization and a clear chain of command (CM2T 67)	57
The US military has done a much better job of eliminating racial discrimination within the military than American society has in general (CM2T 68)	25
Overall, how does military pay compare to civilian pay for similar jobs? (CM1T 51)	28
The military has more sexual harassment and assault than the rest of society (CM2T 48)	27
Help or hurt military effectiveness: a ban on language and behavior that encourages camaraderie among soldiers (CM2T 59)	24

TABLE 11.1 "Don't Know"/"No Opinion" Responses in YouGov Civil-Military Surveys

Every single author contributing to this book worried about the effect of public ignorance on the issues within their particular focus. Such high levels of admitted ignorance and unwillingness to venture opinions illustrate that Americans have to a significant degree dissociated themselves from defense issues.

Wide as is the breadth of public ignorance about the military, we noticed several heartening things in the YouGov data. The first is that the public's judgment is fundamentally sound. Where people are willing to express views (excluding the "don't know" respondents), the vast majority of them hold views consistent with a sturdy and positive civil-military relationship. From our general public's perspective, there is no crisis of civil-military relations in America.

The substantial segment of respondents who did not believe they knew enough to answer data questions about the military exhibited sound judgment in questions phrased to test for logic rather than knowledge. When asked a series of questions that increased their knowledge as the questions progressed, responses showed a strong grasp of the fundamental principles on which the American model of civil-military interaction is based. This was particularly true of the respective responsibilities of civilian and military leaders. For example, the majority of respondents rightly affix responsibility for setting war strategy with political leaders, informed by, but not subject to, the judgments of military leaders.

The majority of Americans have a very high opinion of their military, as well. Eighty-eight percent of respondents describe themselves as proud of the men and women who serve in the American military. On the central issue of the military profession, 93 percent of elites and 81 percent of the general public are confident in the wartime performance of the American military. These are huge majorities, cause for great satisfaction about the civil-military bond in our country.

Our impression from the initial survey that a wide gulf existed between elites and the general public on military issues was not borne out. We had seen hints in the 2013 YouGov survey that public attitudes hewed closely to those common in the military and explicitly designed the second survey to probe for differences between elites and the general public. In fact, elite attitudes were better informed and in many important ways more supportive of the military than were the general public.

For example, one third of the general public thinks the reason the military is less progressive than society relates to the function of warfighting; an equal number in the general public think this is because the military draws people who are more conservative than our broader society. By contrast 53 percent of elites make the association between organizational conservatism and the military's function. More elites also think the military provides greater opportunities for self-improvement than our broader society (62 percent), while only 41 percent of the general public does (and when "or equal to" opportunities are added in, the proportions are 94 percent of elites and 76 percent of the general public) (CM2T 28). And the better educated elites are, the more likely they are to believe the military provides opportunities to excel (CM2T 50).

Since the Triangle study in 1998, it appears that respect for the military among elites has increased substantially. There are many possible explanations for this change: the well educated are likeliest to be informed, so the increased news coverage about military issues since 9/11 may have affected them more than it has the less knowledge-hungry public; and this group may experience greater concern about foreign affairs due to travel or business exposure (both education level and elite signifiers are associated with higher concern about global threats than appears in the general public across a variety of questions) (CM2T 69–72). This was an unexpected finding, one meriting further exploration.

Both elites and the general public believe the military has handled racial integration better than the rest of our society has. Two thirds of the American public believes opportunities for women are greater in the military than in broader society. Three fourths of the public thinks the military provides greater opportunities for the well-educated than does the civilian economy. Sixty percent of respondents believe the military cares more about the people under them than does civilian society (CM2T 25–37). Fifty-two percent believe the military should be paid more; more respondents favored increasing military pay than pay to firefighters, nurses, or police (CM1T 10, 18–29). By contrast, the same respondents considered many other professions overpaid, including elected officials (77 percent of respondents), corporate executives (74 percent), doctors (34 percent), university professors (34 percent), public employees (25 percent), and computer programmers (21 percent).

America is unquestionably a society supportive of its military. The data reveal consistently high levels of support across a wide swath of issues and throughout a cross-section of the public. Moreover, 51 percent of the general public and 53 percent of elites believe the military gets even less respect than it deserves. Only about half of respondents believe the American people understand the sacrifices made by people who serve in our military. Sixty-nine percent of elites believe that veterans are more reliable and hard working than the rest of society (CM2T 50). These are astronomically high levels of approval, unmatched by any other profession or segment of society in America, and unusual internationally.

The YouGov data provide some hints that attitudes may be polarizing, though, as with many other issues in American politics. The survey found more elites concerned about the military getting less respect than it deserves, while the general population is moving in the opposite direction, believing the military gets more respect than it deserves.[7] While still small percentages of the population, public belief that the military gets more respect than it deserves has doubled among veterans and tripled among the general public (9 percent and 12 percent respectively) since the 1998 study. However, these hints are swamped by the high levels of "don't know" responses, and the field has too little time-series data to judge significance.

As Matthew Colford and A.J. Sugarman suggested in their chapter, the attitudes of 18- to 25-year-olds are closest in some important ways to those of over-65-year-olds. By a substantial margin, fewer respondents in the 18 to 25 age bracket felt the military was out of step with society, which might be the natural result of most active personnel being their age mates, making personal association with someone currently in the military more likely, or the result of military issues being more a part of public discourse while the country has been at war their entire adult lives. Perhaps coming of age during the 2008 financial crisis also shaded 18- to 25-year-old's attitudes similar to the way in which the Great Depression shaped its generation. Or, a more likely explanation is simply that both cohorts came of age in wartime. The similarities in response between the youngest and the eldest groups raise the prospect that many of the attitudes of civilians toward the military in America may not be unidirectional. That is, the attitudes associated with baby boomers may be unique to their experience rather than a trend in society going forward. And the attitudes of 18- to 25-year-olds may signify a pendulum swinging back in the other direction, as so often happens in American politics.

Seven Days in May?

Scholars of civil-military relations worry inordinately about the prospect of an American military growing resentful of its civilian masters.[8] There is historical basis for this concern, military men having been a threat to civilian governance at least since Caesar crossed the Rubicon with his army in violation of the Roman Senate's restriction. Historian T. R. Fehrenbach, for example, cautions against an army so professional it looks down on others.

Even in contemporary America, where the military is so reliably subordinate to civilian control, concerns sometimes arise about our military coming to believe itself a praetorian guard to an undeserving civilian society. The 1998 Triangle study authors were alert to this possibility, worried that a military more socially and religiously conservative than governing elites was emerging. In a mild form, this attitude is captured in Phil Klay's short story "Psychological Operations": "The weird thing with being a veteran, at least for me, is that you do feel better than most people. You risked your life for something bigger than yourself. How many people can say that? You chose to serve. Maybe you didn't understand American foreign policy or why we were at war. Maybe you never will. But it doesn't matter. You held up your hand and said, 'I'm willing to die for these worthless civilians.' "[9]

Resentments between civilian leaders and the military are natural, given their respective spheres of responsibility, especially in a country with friction built into its government in the form of distributed power and institutional checks and balances. And, as Eliot Cohen reminds us, the dialogue is an unequal one in America, with civilians being paramount. When civilian leaders seem ill informed or are seen by the military to be making decisions insensitive to military concerns, resentment increases. It may also be intensified now for structural reasons, since our military is small (encompassing only one half of one percent of our citizenry), voluntary, and having entrance standards that exclude all but 20 percent of applicants from admission—by definition a select group.[10] Entrance standards associated with physical fitness alone exclude more than 27 percent of applicants. Moreover, American society has been little affected by fifteen years at war, in stark contrast to the demands on servicemen and women and their families since 9/11. And, it must be admitted, democracy in action is often an unedifying spectacle, perhaps even more than ordinarily so in our current American politics.

Feaver, Golby, and Cohn are concerned that public ignorance coupled with respect for the military and disrespect for elected political leaders could cause a shifting of weight on the civil-military scales, resulting in the military having too great an influence on policy issues for which responsibility rightly rests with elected civilian leaders. We agree that this would be a worrisome outcome: military leaders lack the public mandate to make necessary trade-offs between, for example, security and civil liberties. This is a legitimate issue to watch, but we see little evidence of it materializing in contemporary policy debates. In fact, the opposite is more in evidence. In recent policy debates—such as those about allowing homosexuals to serve openly, retaining a residual force in Iraq and Afghanistan, cutting military spending, and assigning women to combat units—military leaders' counsel and the opinions of rank and file servicemen and women have been dismissed by political leaders and the public.[11]

Moreover, there is an enormous distance between routine tensions and the military usurping civilian authority. Post-9/11 presidents have fired even very popular and well-regarded military leaders without any rumblings of insubordination from the ranks. The Obama administration has imposed onto the military services over explicit objections of military leaders numerous progressive social policies, which are also often unpopular in the ranks, yet they have all been crisply carried out. The most direct recent challenge to civilian authority, the 2005 campaign against Secretary of Defense Donald Rumsfeld's stewardship of the Iraq war, came from retired military, not those on active duty.[12] Responses in the YouGov surveys from those who had had military service hewed more closely to textbook responsibilities for civilians and military than did those of the general public, suggesting greater restraint, not less, among our military.

One of the key precursors to alienation would be the military considering itself separate from society. Such separation has always been a tension. Samuel Adams observed in the 1770s that "soldiers are apt to consider themselves as a Body distinct from the rest of the Citizens." Oliver Wendell Holmes, Jr., a veteran of the Civil War, described it more poignantly, in a speech delivered on Memorial Day in 1895, as a natural result of "the incommunicable experience of war."[13] The YouGov data indicate that the American public is concerned about its military becoming isolated from broader society but not overly so: 60 percent think it would be bad for the country were the military to become isolated, and only 32 percent believe the military is isolated (CM2T 23). Of course, it is the military's attitude, not the public's, about isolation from society that would be cause for concern, and this project did not explicitly poll active duty military, but attitudes of veterans among the respondents suggest little basis for concern.

Another precursor to an alienated military would be a perception of disrespect from the public it serves. But the proportion of veterans who are concerned the public does not respect them enough has increased only slightly since the 1998 study—a remarkably small shift, given how great have been the wartime burdens on many in our military forces and their families and how little affected has been our broader society. While neither veterans nor civil society believe the other adequately respects them, this belief is largely consistent across time.[14] Overall, we find little justification in the data or in contemporary civil-military interaction for the academic preoccupation with a military restive about civilian control.

The first YouGov poll suggested that some gaps that had been thought of as being between civilians and the military are in fact between elites and the general public. That is, the public's attitudes were more in line with those of the military than they were with those of civilian elites. This seemed apparent, for example, in questions about whether military or civilian leaders better represented respondents' values.

Based on that first poll, the second YouGov poll was designed specifically to establish attitudes of elites for comparison to those of the general public. The survey separated out elites from the general population and further disaggregated elites in general (by education, profession, income) from those influential in policy (legislators and staffers, journalists and opinion shapers), allowing us to determine whether the greater chasm was between the public and policy elites rather than between civilians and the military. The distinction is between elites who shape the culture versus those who directly affect government policy. The data turned up little distinction in attitudes between policy elites and the general public but significant differences with cultural elites. Those people making decisions about military issues are generally in line with public attitudes, but those elites who shape the cultural environment create pressure on politicians to make choices not in line with the traditional values of military culture or the attitudes of the general public.

This is where public ignorance of the military again becomes salient. With few Americans directly affected by changes in the military, cultural elites' desires for our military to become indistinct from the broader society, and politicians naturally responsive to activism, we could be moving toward a military that is more representative of the values of the 5 percent of very liberal Americans than those of the vast majority of our fellow citizens, liberal and conservative. Such an outcome would distance the military from American society. It would also force the military to sacrifice practices it perpetuates not for reasons of social conservatism but for reasons of military practicality and battle-field success. To the extent that sustaining a military is fundamental to sustaining the American Experiment, decisions made for nonmilitary reasons and against military advice are potentially reckless.

The YouGov data show a dramatic drop in confidence that political leaders share the public's values when compared with the 1998 study. While the data do not reveal differences in attitudes between policy elites and the public, the perception is that the military is not diverging from American society but rather policy elites are diverging from American society. Civilian elites do consider political leaders' values different from the values of the public, and only a quarter of civilian elites believe they share political leaders' values.[15] We are seeing a crisis of confidence among the public about policy elites.

Veterans voice a concern similar to the general public's about political leaders: about a third believe political elites do not share their values. The military's leaders are slightly less likely to believe political leaders are out of step with their values than are enlisted troops—the belief is stronger among rank-and-file than elite military respondents.[16]

Disaffection toward elites is thus not unique to the relationship between the military and society; it is part of a more general discrediting of elites.[17] But even if alienation from political elites is occurring across the spectrum of American life, it may still have important effects on the civil-military relationship: it could informally change the relationship between military leaders and their civilian superiors, even as civilians retain their constitutional and statutory primacy.

For example, 83 percent of civilians without military experience believe civilian leaders do not rely sufficiently on military advice.[18] The last two Republican presidential nominees stridently criticized the sitting presidents (both Bush and Obama) for not taking the military's advice, reinforcing the misperception that the commander in chief has an obligation to accept the military's recommendations. Scholars of civil-military relations—including those in the military—emphasize that the president has no such responsibility. The president is elected to determine the amount of effort to direct toward a war and has the right to disregard the military's counsel. Military leaders lack the public mandate to make necessary trade-offs between, for example, security and civil liberties.

In the YouGov data, more veteran respondents than civilians were concerned about the military becoming too involved in nonmilitary policies such as social issues affecting the broader public or budgetary matters.[19] Civilian respondents were much more willing than they have been previously to give the military a broader role than our traditions of civil-military relations and the restraining professionalism of our military allow. It turns out that the American military itself is currently a better guardian of the restraints on policy activism by the military than is the American public.[20] From this it is possible to conclude that our military is policing itself: it understands better than do civilians that its high stature with the American public depends on respecting the prohibition on activism beyond the military realm.

But is the military standing guard at its own boundaries an adequate or enduring check on its influence? Juvenal cautioned about entrusting the guardians of the republic to guard themselves.[21] The disparity between the public's attitude toward political leaders and their attitude toward the military is a strong incentive for change in the traditional scope of involvement by the American military. Peter Feaver, Jim Golby, and Lindsay Cohn conclude from the YouGov data that attitudes once anathema to the American military are eroding. For example, the data from veteran respondents about resigning in protest of civilian leaders' policies, not carrying out orders they do not agree with, or leaking internal government deliberations to the media all show significant change since the 1998 TISS study. In these authors' view, relying solely on the military's professionalism encourages use of the military for political purposes in what are properly civilian roles, incentivizing the military to behave just like civilian politicians with parochial, partisan interests.

Like so much else in the American system of federal government, civil-military relations are a negotiation. Leverage shifts to the military in wartime and away in peacetime. Adroit politicians in suits or uniforms are highly advantaged because the system is fundamentally political, not technical. The process of budgeting and war planning, which requires the input of political objectives and resource parameters, is likely to receive legislative scrutiny—a process in which military leaders have loyalty to the Congress as well as to the president—and relitigation in the media. In our view, if there is a contemporary departure from the American norm, it is that military commanders are more, not less, hemmed in by political leaders because the wars we are fighting are more removed from the everyday experience of most Americans.

Whether or not military views are effective in public debates, Cohn, Feaver, and Golby suggest that concern by political elites about public deference to military attitudes may be causing political elites to scorn the advice of military leaders. This dynamic, also suggested by Mackubin Owens, is borne out by some aspects of the YouGov data: only 7 percent of the public consider political leaders very knowledgeable about military issues and elites are more concerned than the general public is about the military educating the public on their concerns with the president's policies (CM2T 18, 75, 77). The combined effect is worrying, since elites without military experience alienated from the advice offered by the military are more likely to use military force ineffectively. We believe we have been seeing exactly this in American national security policies over the last dozen years.

Strategic Atrophy

The YouGov data show that Americans understand fundamental responsibility for war strategy lies with elected political leaders. It also shows that the public is dissatisfied with their leaders' performance in developing coherent strategy. The public sees policy elites incapable of winning our ill-defined wars, implausibly expecting military force to produce sophisticated political, economic, and cultural outcomes.[22]

Strategy divorced from politics is unsustainable.[23] As Colin Gray instructs us in *The Future of Strategy,* "the core challenge of strategy is the attempt to control action so that it has the politically desired effect."[24] There is no abstract purpose, or practice, of strategy from which politics can be effectively leeched. It is inherently a political undertaking. In free societies, politicians must choose the political ends. They must also determine what price—in blood, treasure, and national credibility—to pay for those ends.

Yet Nadia Schadlow argues that political leaders wrongly believe themselves to be constrained by public attitudes on defense issues. Politicians fear public opposition to their policies—and especially public reaction to casualties—as though attitudes were immutable. President Obama's vacillation over enforcement of his Syrian red line is said by his supporters to have been significantly affected by the belief that the public would not back another war in the Middle East.[25] Yet the

YouGov data demonstrate that public attitudes are actually quite malleable. Political leaders just are not expending the effort to change attitudes; they are instead decrying their lack of public support to justify inaction. But by expending political capital to engage and educate the public, political leaders could create larger decision space: they could expand their strategic options by fostering an educated public and choosing strategically sound courses of action that would draw and sustain public support.

Benjamin Wittes and Cody Poplin raise the related point that an uninformed public is less likely to sustain over time policies necessary to succeed at the wars we are fighting. They view the YouGov data as illustrating numerous contradictory attitudes that, while not uncommon in surveys of public opinion, impinge on policies ranging from domestic surveillance to military justice. They emphasize that the types of threats America currently faces are low in visibility for the public but long in duration, thereby putting a premium on sustained effort—and, unguided by political leaders routinely educating the public about threats and policy trade-offs, the public is unlikely to sustain support.

We share these concerns about political leaders shying away from their responsibility to shape public attitudes. There has developed a tendency for political leaders to rely on the credibility of their military commanders to garner support for their policies. President Bush left to General David Petraeus the task of overcoming Congressional opposition to the 2006 Iraq surge. President Obama has been mostly silent on the war in Afghanistan since 2009; the case for continuing American troop presence has been made entirely by the military. And while we believe military commanders have a responsibility not only to carry out, but also to advocate for, a president's policies, this does not remove elected officials from their responsibility to win political arguments instead of depending on the military to do so.

Relying so heavily on military credibility to deliver their policy preferences only further erodes the public standing of elected officials.

It sets up military leaders as the guarantors of public support, something that should be anathema to the long-standing balance of civil-military roles in America. And the near-term gain of public support for a particular policy may result in a long-term erosion of the military's standing with the American public if the people come to see military leaders as politicized.

Public attitudes are especially inconsistent about legal issues associated with the use of military force. Law being an area the public has direct experience with, Benjamin Wittes and Cody Poplin suggest there is a tendency by the public to overstate its comparability: the data suggest the public struggles to understand why laws governing our military are different from those governing civilian society. They have no comprehension of whether the laws of war are applicable in other circumstances nor of how to ethically balance the humanitarian issues that arise with the military necessity also recognized under international law.

Our enemies have structural advantages in our current wars because they are fighting a total war, and we only limited wars. They are also proving adept at establishing a higher standard of battlefield conduct for us than for them. We are limiting ourselves beyond what the law of war calls for because our vibrant civil society recoils from the inexorable human suffering that is intrinsic to achieving political aims by military force. We believe this is influenced by the fact that so few Americans have experience of warfare. We have people in policy circles who are as familiar with the humanitarian and legal aspects of human interaction as they are unfamiliar with military necessity and battlefield realities, including what is permitted, from military necessity, under international law and conventions.[26] And we often lack people at the top level of policymaking who have an innate, studied appreciation for what it takes to win wars and who are willing to expend the political capital to build a sound basis for sustained public support. Here again, political leaders are creating the very conditions they decry for limiting their strategic options by not explaining and defending views for which survey data suggest there is a bedrock of opinion among the public on which broader support could be built.

Acting strategically does not require intellectual elegance; it requires political leaders making clear but difficult decisions to use military force effectively. As Carl von Clausewitz wrote in *On War,* "in warfare everything is simple, but the simple is exceptionally difficult." An American public unknowledgeable about military issues gives political leaders a pass on their essential function in wartime. It is not good enough in a free society to shift that responsibility to the military, which is what the YouGov polling suggests the public supports doing. To do so would absolve the political leadership of their responsibility to aggregate societal preferences within the dictates of sound geopolitical judgment. That judgment is rightly exercised by elected and politically appointed civilian leaders who weigh strategic choices and make decisions about when to employ military force. It is their job.

Defense spending is another military tool that is atrophying due to the public's ignorance and political elites' reticence. Rosa Brooks argues that the combination of ignorance about, and admiration for, our military inclines the public and the Congress toward funneling defense spending disproportionately toward pay and benefits rather than training or the development and purchase of equipment.

While military compensation exceeds that of 90 percent of civilian counterparts, 70 percent of respondents to the YouGov polls believe pay for officers is either too low or about right; 82 percent consider enlisted pay too little.[27] Members of Congress fear looking as though they do not support the troops by not voting for pay raises and benefit increases, even when (as for the past four years) the Pentagon's civilian and military leadership oppose the expense. The U.S. Army chief of staff testified in 2013 that at current pace within a decade 80 percent of the army's spending will be for personnel.[28]

A volunteer force requires the government to pay the market rate for military personnel. That rate fluctuates with the rate of unemployment and degree of uncertainty about funding for defense but is certainly higher than required to produce a conscripted force. The rate is also rising dramatically, because some elements of personnel policy (such as twenty-year retirement) were deemed unaffordable by the architects of the all-volunteer force but have never been changed.[29] This is not unrelated to public attitudes about the military, since Congressional unwillingness to reduce pay and benefits to servicemen and women has become a major problem for the sustainability of the all-volunteer force.[30] And the data from the YouGov poll illustrate that the public knows very little about the cost of the American military. When combined with high levels of public support for the military, the public ignorance creates a political dynamic in which apportionment of the defense budget skews strongly toward pay and benefits to the detriment of training, equipment, and numbers in the force, key factors in sustaining a strong military capable of winning battles and bringing more troops home alive from war.

Ken Harbaugh characterizes the effect thus: "a political class with almost no military experience that feels it lacks the moral authority to say no."[31] As the YouGov poll illustrates, the American public is generally ignorant of the facts about pay and benefits in the military *and* generally supportive of greater personnel spending. Representative Adam Kinzinger, himself a combat veteran, reinforces this view: "The average person who has never been in the military is scared to death of talking about it because they're afraid of being labeled anti-veteran or anti-military."[32] The problem gets exacerbated by the huge drop in confidence among the public that political leaders share their values, now hovering between 25 percent and 30 percent, as evident in the YouGov data.

Our views accord closely with those of former Joint Chiefs of Staff chairman General Martin Dempsey: "We owe much to our veterans and their families, but we shouldn't view all proposed defense cuts as an attack on them. Modest reforms to pay and compensation will improve readiness and modernization. They will help keep our all-volunteer force sustainable and strong. Keeping faith also means investing sufficient resources so that we can uphold our sacred obligations to defend the nation and to send our sons and daughters to war with only the best training, leadership and equipment."[33]

Martial Values

Attitudes on social issues, in particular, show significant differences between the public and the military—and especially between the public and those veterans who are classified in the YouGov surveys as elites (a designation based on factors such as education, income, and profession after military service).[34] For example, 49 percent of veteran elites consider the male-dominated aspects of the military important to its culture; civilian elite and veteran nonelites both clock in at 37 percent support for this view, but only 21 percent of the civilian public agrees (Golby, Cohn, Feaver Crosstabs 41C). The pattern holds across issues of military language and behavior that instill camaraderie and whether military leaders share the public's values. It would seem the military has figured out how to persuade civilian elites of the reasons for maintaining a distinct culture in the military but has not similarly persuaded the general public—or perhaps the public is tone-deaf or insufficiently interested in military matters to consider the impact of the battlefield on military culture.

Public attitudes are deeply divided on whether the military attempting to hold on to "old-fashioned values" helps or hurts the war effort. Almost as many respondents thought it helps the war effort for the military to become less male dominated.

But what is most interesting for us is that even among Americans critical of our military's conduct, the majority believes the military may need different and less egalitarian standards than civilian society.

Even on issues where the public is skeptical of military actions, the majority still believes the military should have the latitude to set its own standards. So, for example, 35 percent of respondents consider the military's treatment of women less fair and 54 percent believe homosexuals should be able to service openly; only 25 percent of respondents believed the military should have to change and become more like society (CM2T 25, 54, 48). There remains an underlying deference by the public to allow the military to operate by its own rules, an interesting factor since our political leadership has not advocated for such a difference. In recent years political leaders have instead often used the military as a vehicle to lead social change in the broader society.

The YouGov data reveal an American public much more willing than we had expected to tolerate our military continuing to have different practices and even different values than our broader society. Public debates about allowing open homosexuals to serve and opening combat assignments to women show civilian attitudes strongly at variance with those of the military (especially those serving in ground-combat units, where the atavistic nature of warfare is most pronounced). And yet the YouGov surveys show the public deferential to the military's differences from civilian society. Seventy percent of civilians believe that the military's "bonds of loyalty" are different and therefore the military is entitled to retain different values from civilian society. Elites are even more convinced of the case for a military culture distinct from that of our broader society. The YouGov survey shows a general acknowledgement that the military is different from society and support for it remaining so.

The underlying public deference is in keeping with what the founding fathers—whose political liberties and even lives relied closely and immediately on the warfighting abilities of their military—established for our republic: military jurisprudence was to remain separate from the civilian justice system, allowing the military to establish and enforce codes of conduct appropriate to the demands of the battlefield.

A significant proportion of Americans, roughly one third, believe the military is diverging from society but are unconcerned; respondents who had had military service were even less concerned.[35] In fact, the surveys suggest the public is less concerned about the academic preoccupation of undue military influence in politics than it is of undue political influence over the military: 84 percent of civilian elites and 48 percent of the general public worry about too much civilian intrusion into the military (CM2T 61). Strong majorities of veterans and 44 percent of civilian elites do not think the military should become more like society (Golby, Cohn, Feaver Crosstabs 8D).

Contemporary public attitudes displayed in the YouGov surveys suggest the public understands that what our military does demands different practices from those we enjoy in civil society. The data show a 30 percent jump in support for military policies when respondents were told the policy served a functional military purpose. Glimpses of that understanding also come through in specific questions about military practices; for example, very high percentages of the public—96 percent of civilian elites and 71 percent of the general public—consider the infantry's opposition to including women important (Golby, Cohn, Feaver Crosstabs 51). When informed, the public tends to support military policies it would not tolerate in civilian society.

If the public is willing to indulge our military in operating by different rules, sustaining a culture at variance with our broader society, why then are civilian leaders imposing so many changes the military as an institution is clearly uncomfortable with? Tod Lindberg posits a partisan answer drawn from the YouGov data, which is that people who identified themselves as "very liberal" for the poll are disproportionately influential in shaping the culture. Mackubin Thomas Owens concludes that a more ominous force is at work: public ignorance about military issues allows elected leaders to utilize the military for progressive social purposes. Having so small a military that only one half of one percent of the public will be directly affected and so inattentive a public ensures that political leaders pay no real price for diminishing combat effectiveness. At least there is no visible, near-term price.

We are persuaded by Lindberg's and Owens's arguments that public ignorance or indifference to military issues provides leeway for liberal shapers of culture and politicians with a progressive agenda to impose their ideas on the military. The command hierarchy and subordination to civilian superiors so deeply engrained in our military make it responsive in ways much more difficult to enforce in our broader society and therefore provide a controlled environment in which to advance social change.

In addition to the arguments put forward by Lindberg and Owens, we think the superior fighting force of America's military is also contributing to this activism. Since the end of the cold war, the United States has not faced in battle a military of equivalent combat power. Our dominance has driven the strategy of our enemies away from fighting symmetrically, because they could have no hope of winning; instead, America's enemies have been driven to the ends of the combat spectrum rather than being allowed to contest for primacy at its center. Our political leaders and public have lost the consciousness of military defeat. They do not operate in fear of the degradation of thousands of American prisoners of war starving in captivity, as at Bataan. Casualty counts in the hundreds are sufficient to cause reconsideration by political leaders of the worthiness of the war effort. The idea of an enemy subjugating our country to its political will is unimaginable for our political leadership. It is increasingly difficult for our political leaders and our public to understand that an undefeated army can lose a war.[36] So wide is our margin for error that political leaders and the public think little of chipping away at it by our own choice, as if American victory is preordained.

We believe the American public is not nearly as concerned as it should be that changes to military policies are accruing risk to our force. We fear that an uninformed public is permitting political leaders to impose an accretion of social conventions that are diminishing the combat power of our military, disregarding our warfighting practitioners' advice. These demands impose a burden the public and political leaders refuse to acknowledge and will only be evident in the aftermath of military failure. We vociferously support the standard for determining military policies outlined by U.S. Marine Corps general John F. Kelly (Ret.): every change to established practice should be judged on whether it increases battlefield lethality.[37] Americans ought to fear more than we do the consequences of our prevalent lassitude about warfare.

Post-traumatic Strength

Tom Donnelly suggests that the public's unfamiliarity with our military has another worrisome effect: that unfamiliarity leads to pity rather than respect. One of the most important gaps that seems to have emerged during our current wars is the perception that most veterans suffer from post-traumatic stress, even that they pose a danger to themselves and others as a result. This has been disproven (only about 15 percent of veterans experience post-traumatic stress disorder [PTSD]) and is inconsistent with recent attitudes of employers, for whom veterans are generally preferred hires.[38] Only 6 percent of respondents disagreed with the statement that "veterans have a very strong work ethic" (CM1T 48), yet concern about PTSD contributed to higher rates of young veteran unemployment from 2005 to 2013.[39] And data from the YouGov surveys show that 78 percent of respondents still in 2014 agreed with the statement that "many veterans have difficulty adjusting to civilian life because of stresses they have experienced in the military" (CM1T 47). Yet this is at wide variance with the experience of most veterans: 89 percent of post-9/11 veterans would join the military again if they had the chance.[40]

For at least the first six years of President Obama's term of office, when ending American involvement in Iraq and Afghanistan was his principal foreign policy objective, he was more likely to visit Bethesda Naval Hospital than Fort Hood, with its 52,280 active duty soldiers.[41] The criticism is not intended to discourage the president from condoling with wounded servicemen and women or from grieving the costs of any president's policies. But emphasizing the wounded to the exclusion of those still in the fight, without conveying to the wounded and to the broader public the crucial importance of what they were trying to achieve, is to send a cultural message that casualties are more important than what we are fighting for.

Encouragement of victimization is also evident in well-meaning government programs intended to benefit servicemen and women. The Veterans Administration (VA) now coaches men and women transitioning out of military service to maximize their benefits, specifically for disabilities that bring payments even when some, such as sleep apnea for example, seem unconnected to any specific military activity. Forty-three percent of veterans now receive some disability rating, with an average of 6.3 medical conditions per veteran.[42] Suffering or witnessing violence is no longer required for the VA to categorize a veteran as suffering from post-traumatic stress disorder; and claims once made are almost never downgraded with time.[43] Disability payments to veterans—not the cost of medical treatment for injuries but the compensation for an assumed inability to work—have doubled, and the average payout has increased by 60 percent since 2000.[44] Removing veterans from the workforce further isolates them from broader society, whether we do so by classifying them as disabled, paying for disabilities that are questionable, or removing the work incentive that characterized previous generations of veterans returning from war.

There has been an explosion of news stories about a crisis of suicides in the military, nearly all of which suggest the trauma of war is the cause, when in fact suicides among servicemen and women do not correlate with combat, with frequency or length of deployment, or with military culture.[45] Suicides in the military correlate with the same factors that drive suicides in our broader society.[46] By treating military suicides as an epidemic unique to military service, we discourage recruitment into the military and hiring of veterans when they leave the military and encourage their isolation from their fellow citizens. As with many other aspects of contemporary civil-military relations, well-intentioned attention but ill-designed programs and processes work to the detriment both of our national security and the well-being of our veterans.[47]

We disagree with Rosa Brooks's suggestion that the military needs to change to better reflect American society. YouGov data show that the public is actually pretty tolerant of sustaining a military organized along different lines from those of civilian society. And the large segment of the public that hesitates to even venture opinions on military issues is a winnable constituency. A nonmilitarized society—one in which human aspirations are enabled to craft a fairer, inclusive, and friendly environment—is fundamentally different from the battlefield, which is the auditor of our military. The public seems to sense the danger of imposing kinder values on a force that exists to preserve our freedoms by winning on an unkind battlefield.

But it is not just our military's job to remain visible to our broader public. It is our civic responsibility as beneficiaries of a free society to understand our military and reward their sacrifices by giving them the gift of inclusion, of living among us and being organically connected to us, without making them into comic book heroes or treating them like victims irreparably damaged by their service.

Jim Hake encourages Americans to close the distance between the American public and its military and has modeled this in Spirit of America, a nongovernmental organization unapologetically committed to bringing private support to our troops and diplomats in foreign service. Our military are part and parcel of our society, deserving of special attention, to be sure, for their sacrifices but also deserving of unexceptional attention that will knit them more closely with the rest of us. The very best kind of civil-military relationship in a free society is one in which we celebrate those who serve by holding them close to us.

Conclusion

The great experiment of a free society eschewing compulsory military service has unquestionably produced a superior fighting force for the United States of America. Soldiers, sailors, airmen, Marines, and coastguardsmen serve by choice, which makes them more motivated to join and also more accepting of the burdens of service than those forced into the military are. The American military managed in the 1970s the difficult transition to a volunteer force, increasing professionalization in the noncommissioned officer ranks at the same time such that the institution became more proficient and also rose in the esteem of the general public. Competitive pay made it a viable option for higher quality enlistees to join and remain in the service for a career.

Even quite recently in American history, military service has not always been respected by our public. We tend to think that Americans have always had a close and affectionate relationship with their military. In part, this construction is consistent with our national self-image as a society forged in military rebellion, one with strong state militia balancing the power of the federal government, Constitutional protection of the right to bear arms, and an elegiac attraction to the conquest of the American west. We are culturally a more militaristic society than most of the developed world. But these attributes mask considerable friction that has also been central to the American civil-military relationship, a phenomenon that Mackubin Thomas Owens's chapter reviews.

Our widespread contemporary practice of thanking those in uniform for their military service was anathema to Americans forty years ago, when, during the Vietnam War, colleges shuttered Reserve Officer Training Corps programs on campuses (many of which—including Stanford University's—remained closed until very recently, another reminder of the persistent friction between civilian institutions and the military). Veterans returning from the Vietnam War were cautioned against wearing their uniforms to avoid public scorn. But the period of the unpopular war in Vietnam is just one of many examples of a time when the relationship between the American public and its military has been frayed. Most often, friction has resulted from controversy over not just the cause but the conduct of a war: draft riots in New York City during the Civil War had their roots in the magnitude of the levy, unfairness of some being able to purchase indemnity from conscription, resistance by new immigrants to involvement in the war, sympathy for the confederate cause by many New Yorkers (the reflex of a commercial hub toward neutrality in wartime), and seeming stalemate in the war's progress. This underscores how important are the government's choices about defense policy for the civil-military relationship.

Political leaders now take for granted an abiding respect by the public for our military, as though it were immune to any effect from their policy choices. This is a deeply flawed, and potentially deeply costly, mistake. American public respect for our military has ebbed and flowed over time. These tidal changes have been significantly affected by the uses to which political leaders have put our military and the responsibility those leaders take—or fail to take—for their policy decisions.

Our central concern about America's civil-military relationship is that the combination of public ignorance of and public admiration for our military is accruing unexamined risk that will not be apparent until it is revealed in war. As a political culture, we are becoming insensitive to the trade-offs between effectiveness of our fighting forces and the nonfighting demands we place upon them. Public ignorance allows political leaders to put military forces into action with little prospect for success. The public has so strong a belief that our military can achieve anything it sets out to do that we inadequately prepare to avoid failure. We are so far removed from outcomes such as the fall of Corregidor or tens of thousands of American prisoners of war being held by North Korea that political leaders are inadequately fearful of bad outcomes.

In short, because the American public holds its military in such high regard, we are putting it at greater risk. We have allowed our strategic thinking to atrophy, allowed our policymaking to become flabby because our military's high level of performance has lulled our sensibilities. This is both a policy failure and a moral one. And we should not avert our eyes from the very real consequences of these failures, such as those we have experienced in recent wars that lacked clear political objectives and carried self-imposed limitations such as troop caps, campaign end-dates disconnected from conditions on the ground, and restrictions on using ground troops at all (or that allowed them in only incremental numbers).

In addition to illuminating the civil-military gaps in American society, the YouGov surveys also point toward successful policy redress of the concerning gaps. For example, one solution to the disproportionate influence of "very liberal" cultural elites is, of course, for the other 95 percent of Americans to compete in those arenas. What is needed is not necessarily a diminution of liberal views but their diffusion in a broader mix of cultural influences that is more knowledgeable about, and less wary of, military experiences. We believe we are beginning to see this occur with the renaissance of literature by veterans of the Iraq and Afghanistan wars.[48] We believe it is also beginning to occur in politics, with a disproportionate number of recent veterans running for political office.[49] It also is occurring in civil society, and for similar reasons: veterans have a strong sense of civic obligation. Eric Greitens, founder of The Mission Continues and author of *Resilience,* counsels veterans that civic involvement is a natural transition from the military: "You have to make this transition because your community still needs you, because your country still needs what you have to offer."[50]

Veterans groups such as Team Rubicon, Team Red, White and Blue, and The Mission Continues all serve the function that Veterans of Foreign Wars and American Legion did for earlier generations of veterans, namely, giving them the comradeship of their fellow veterans. As Bernard Trainor argues, "often the best medicine for bruised bodies and psyches is communion with those who have supped from the same bitter cup."[51] But the new generation of organizations founded by veterans from our current wars also serves to get veterans out into, and contributing to, our broader society. As Eric Greitens says, "They realize that they know how to inspire people in difficult circumstances, which is useful not only in Afghanistan, but in helping third graders who are struggling to read. They realize that they have what it takes to bring together a team of people who have no common background."[52] We believe this is important not only for reintegrating our veterans but also for rebuilding a sense of common purpose and a capacity to solve our problems in American society.

Veterans have a leading role to play in bridging the civil-military divide by showing civilian society new ways to address domestic concerns. Sustained pressure from military leaders will be required before Congress slows the rate of increase in military pay and benefits and veterans are developing test programs that, for example, provide disability assistance while incentivizing work—something important for disabled veterans to reintegrate with American society.[53] Currently, civilian and military leaders are relying on sheer political courage in Congress to do the right thing for national defense when it exposes them to charges of having "voted against the troops," which is seldom a winning strategy in American politics.

There exists a general belief, as evidenced in the YouGov data and castigation of the VA, that our current approach is making the all-volunteer force unaffordable and is badly failing our veterans. This perception can be worked with to build support for an approach that reins in personnel spending in order to serve our forces well by training and equipping them better. It can also be worked with to smash Veterans Administration practices, such as restricting veterans to care at VA facilities, that are destructive to the welfare of our servicemen and women. Creative approaches should be experimented with, such as the Independence Fund, which would retool disabled veterans services to be more empowering, creating "personal rehabilitation accounts" of $10,000 to $20,000 for veterans to use for education or starting a business or whatever path they are drawn to and providing wage support that incentivizes getting out into the work force.[54]

All these developments make us hopeful that the gaps between civil society and the military in America can be bridged. The bridging is not solely or even principally the military's job, as Jim Hake points out. We as citizens need to find, take, or make opportunities to involve ourselves in the war effort and with our veterans. With the end of conscription and the much smaller size of our military forces, most Americans are not organically connected to the military through service by family members. Political leaders have encouraged dissociation—think of President Bush trying to reassure the country of normalcy after 9/11 instead of binding the public into sharing the burdens of a long war or President Obama declining to make the public case for his war policies.

The dissociation between civilian society and the military has served short-term political ends (preventing panic after a terrorist attack, rebalancing attention from foreign to domestic priorities). However, it has several detrimental long-term effects—even in narrowly political terms—for the country's political leaders. As Benjamin Wittes and Cody Poplin point out, an uninformed public is ill prepared for the steady, long-term commitment necessary to fight wars whose progress will not be immediately evident. We will overreact to incidents (ISIS executions, for example) and undervalue endurance (progress in Iraq that by 2010 needed only a modicum of US forces to be sustained, for example). As Pakistan's former ambassador to the United States summarized the problem, "America doesn't lose wars, it loses interest."[55] These are predominantly the kinds of wars American will be confronted with, but politicians have not yet become convinced they have a self-interested reason to rebuild a closer, more organic relationship between our military and our broader society. Wartime presidents—commanders in chief—including Lincoln, Wilson, Franklin D. Roosevelt, Johnson, Nixon, and both presidents Bush, led by engaging the country with its military.

In any event, we ought not expect political leaders to solve what problems exist in civil-military relations in America. As Thomas Jefferson instructs us, "Every government degenerates when trusted to the rulers of the people alone. The people themselves are its only safe depositories."[56] We, the people, are the only safe repository of sound civil-military relations.

Civic activism is the long suit of American society. During the Barbary Wars, privateers were at least as important a factor as the Navy. In the War of 1812, citizens raised private funds for Navy ships. Jim Hake's Spirit of America is only the latest example of our tradition of civic involvement with active military, allowing Americans to directly support deployed troops outside government channels.

The question that animates this study is whether a free society can maintain the strong military necessary for defending that free society, despite their often differing values. We believe that it can, but only if the broader society understands and accepts why its military is organized differently and rewards behavior at odds with the very society it protects.

The YouGov data show that too much of American society does not understand this, although the broader public has an underlying disposition to accept the military's arguments for its differences. Some of the authors in this study (Peter Feaver, Jim Golby, and Lindsay Cohn; Rosa Brooks) have concerns that this underlying disposition, when coupled with public disaffection for elected political leaders, could thrust military leaders into too influential a role in policy decisions properly made by elected political leaders.

Conversely, others (Thomas Donnelly, Mackubin Thomas Owens, and ourselves) worry that it has lead political leaders to distrust military advice—and the YouGov polls show there is continuing support from the public for aggrandizement by the military of more political roles. As Owens persuasively argues, the American system of civil-military affairs relies on a high degree of trust between civilians and the military; this trust is eroding. Senior military leaders have a right to be heard on military and warfighting policy; they do not have the right to be obeyed. The question today is more whether they are being heard by the political leadership as this trust is eroding.

America's founding fathers had great concern about military heroes subverting civilian power; yet they accepted that an effective fighting force would require separate rules governing the military's conduct and order. They wrote into the Constitution a completely separate military justice system, autonomous from civilian oversight. The wrenching experience of the Civil War and the danger and physical exertion of settling the West meant that martial virtues were never remote from Americans' reality. Mobilization of ten million Americans into military service during World War II likewise kept a consciousness of the military's differences from society—and their purposes—as general knowledge. But these events are past, and the decision to maintain, even during America's longest war, an all-volunteer force, has removed a sense of shared danger from 99 percent of American families.

We now find ourselves as a society in circumstances in which our national security does not require mass mobilization of our citizens, and we have elected a voluntary system of military service. We have not truly felt that our way of life is at risk since well back into the cold war. We fear terrorist attacks, rightly, but not ISIS flags flying over the Capitol or an enemy being able to impose their manner of governance or social organization on America. We sense that our military is strong enough to keep us free and maintain our way of life unfazed by external danger.

Military presence is a novelty on many college campuses, especially the most effete, and military history largely purged from college curricula. These and many other factors have created a nonchalant attitude among the public about warfare, leaving absent in our scholarship the grim consequences of failure on any battlefield. Few Americans recall the surrender of our troops to Japan and their brutal treatment on the Bataan Death March. The failures of our forces, from the battles of Kasserine Pass to Osan, are known only within military circles today. It is difficult to imagine a time when negotiations took years before American prisoners of war were repatriated from North Korea. We are treating our wars as though they have no strategic consequence— we elected defeat in Iraq and Afghanistan. As a society, we are underestimating the profound consequences of failures on the battlefield. Theodore Roosevelt's caution rings even more true today: "Despise that pseudo-humanitarianism which treats advance of civilization as necessarily and rightfully implying a weakening of the fighting spirit and which therefore invites destruction of the advanced civilization by some less advanced type."[57]

Notes

1. In fact, the TISS study's authors predicted a civil-military relationship under severe stress as "dangerous schisms and trends" exacerbated the underlying cleavages. See Peter D. Feaver and Richard H. Kohn, "Soldiers and Civilians: The Civil-Military Gap and American National Security," *Foreign Affairs,* March 1, 2002.
2. A 2007 survey of the literature by the RAND Corporation concluded that "there is a potential for a civil-military gap to undermine military effectiveness by reducing support for defense budgets, increasing the difficulties of recruiting quality people to join the military, and dwindling public support for using military force, particularly where high casualties are likely. Some

observers even worried that a growing civilian-military gap could undermine the principle of civilian control of the military." Thomas S. Szayna, Kevin F. McCarthy, Jerry M. Sollinger, Linda J. Demaine, Jefferson P. Marquis, and Brett Steele, "The Civil-Military Gap in the United States: Does It Exist, Why, and Does It Matter?" RAND Corportation, 2007, p. xiii.

3.   Rigorously defining "elites" is a difficult task. The 1998 Triangle study was criticized by Pew pollster Andrew Kohut for relying on self-selection (such as appearance in a *Who's Who*) and not controlling for conflation of profession, income, and political affiliation. The dataset for these surveys conducted by YouGov includes 500 interviews with a sample of elites designed to represent opinion leaders in professional areas of expertise: media, business and finance, state and local government, nongovernmental organizations (NGOs), think tanks and academia, religious organizations, and federal government. In the sectors of business and finance, academia, and religious organizations, the elite sample was randomly drawn from publicly available lists of leaders. Academics were selected from the National Academy of Sciences, executives from the largest 500 US companies ranked by total annual revenue as of June 1 of the current year, journalists from the 2013 list of best state-based political reports, and religious figures from a database of religious institutions compiled from the Pluralism Project at Harvard University. Congressional staff, NGO leaders, and think-tank staff were recruited via YouGov's DC Insider recruiter.

4.   Conservative commentators suggest that there is an incapacity among liberals to understand the military's culture of honor, but the attitude dates back at least to Chairman of the Joint Chiefs of Staff Colin Powell's public advocacy on the Balkans wars and was prevalent in the Bush administration Pentagon as well. See Michael Gerson, "White House Bergdahl Mess," RealClearPolitics, June 10, 2014; Rosa Brooks, "Obama vs. the Generals," *Politico Magazine*, November 2013; and James Taranto, "Suck It Up and Salute," *Wall Street Journal*, June 4, 2014.

5.   References to the YouGov data by question number appear in parentheses throughout this essay with the abbreviations CM1T and CM2T indicating the 2013 and 2014 surveys, respectively. The complete results are available at http://www.hoover.org/warriors-and-citizens-crosstabs-1 (CM1T) and http://www.hoover.org/warriors-and-citizens-crosstabs-2 (CM2T).

6.   General rates of "don't know" responses in these categories were 37 percent among women, 35 percent among Hispanics, 31 percent among blacks, 40 percent among respondents under 30 and also among those with incomes less than $40,000, and 30 percent among self-described Democrats.

7.   The view that the military gets more respect than it deserves has increased since the Triangle study by more than 15 percent among veteran elites and

by 10 percent among nonveteran elites, but it has decreased among nonelites by less than 7 percent among veterans and by 13 percent among nonveteran respondents.

8. See, for example, David M. Kennedy, ed., *The Modern American Military,* Oxford: Oxford University Press, 2013. See especially the chapter by Robert L. Goldich, "American Military Culture from Colony to Empire."

9. Phil Klay, *Redeployment,* New York: Penguin, 2014, p. 203.

10. "80% of Military Recruitments Turned Down," *Military Times,* May 14, 2014.

11. Micah Zenko, "The Soldier and the State Go Public," *Foreign Policy,* September 26, 2013, http://foreignpolicy.com/2013/09/26/the-soldier-and -the-state-go-public.

12. Moreover, according to former national security advisor Steven Hadley in a personal interview, this campaign extended, rather than shortened, Secretary Rumsfeld's tenure, because in order to uphold the norm of civilian control, President Bush did not want to be seen as capitulating to even retired military pressure on the secretary of defense.

13. Oliver Wendell Holmes, Jr., "The Soldier's Faith," address, Harvard University, May 30, 1895.

14. The data from the TISS survey and the YouGov surveys were disaggregated and tabulated by Golby, Cohn, and Feaver. These cross-tabulations are available at http://www.hoover.org/warriors-and-citizens-crosstabs-3. Throughout this essay, references to this source are indicated with the phrase Golby, Cohn, Feaver Crosstabs; a subsequent number indicates the relevant question in their cross-tabulation. According to Golby, Cohn, and Feaver's cross-tabulations, 15 percent more elites than veterans believe society respects the military; more than 30 percent of veteran respondents disagreed with the claim that society has a great deal of respect for the military; and 10 percent more veterans than civilians believe the military respects civilian society (33A–B).

15. Twenty-five percent of civilian elites and 27 percent of the general public did not believe political leaders shared their values.

16. The phrase "elite veteran" applies to those respondents who specified veteran status and were also coded as elites according to the YouGov methodology. It does not refer to servicemen and women who were officers holding especially senior ranks or prestigious positions or who were career military. Thirty-one percent of elite veterans and 36 percent of nonelite veterans believe that political leaders do not share their values (Golby, Cohn, Feaver Crosstabs 25).

17. Robert A. Lerner, Althea K. Nagai, and Stanley Rothman, *American Elites,* New Haven: Yale University Press, 1996, p. 108; Robert Presthus, *Elites in the Policy Process,* Cambridge: Cambridge University Press, 1974, p. 360.

18. While fewer veterans than civilians believe leaders should rely more on military counsel, the figure is still a very high 75 percent and has remained

constant since the 1998 TISS study. Concern about civilian leadership has increased by more than 18 percent since the 1998 study (Golby, Cohn, Feaver Crosstabs 48D–R).

19.   Seventy-five percent of veteran elites and 60 percent of nonelite veterans versus 64 percent of civilian elites and 46 percent of the general-public respondents were concerned about the military becoming too involved in nonmilitary policies (Golby, Cohn, Feaver Crosstabs 41D).

20.   Concern among the professional military of overstepping its bounds into civilian realms in the YouGov results is consistent with earlier findings by the TISS study.

21.   Juvenal, *Satire VI,* lines 347–48.

22.   See Hew Strachan, *The Direction of War: Contemporary Strategy in Historical Perspective,* New York: Cambridge University Press, 2013, p. 97. Strachan argues that "we have tended to assume that the danger is a military *coup d'état,* when the real danger for western democracies today is the failure to develop coherent strategy."

23.   Lawrence Freedman illustrates that the divorce between politics and military force occurs during the Napoleonic era. He considers it strategic folly. See his *Strategy: A History,* Oxford: Oxford University Press, 2013, p. 103. Freedman also makes this argument in "Coping with Disorder: The Use and Limits of Military Force," *World Politics Review,* October 27, 2015.

24.   Colin S. Gray, *The Future of Strategy,* Cambridge, UK: Polity, 2015, p. 1.

25.   Barack Obama, "Address to the Nation by the President," December 6, 2015; see also "Obama At War," *Frontline,* PBS, May 26, 2015.

26.   For a thorough discussion of the issues, see Michael Howard, George J. Andreopoulos, and Mark R. Shulman, *The Laws of War: Constraints on Warfare in the Western World,* New Haven: Yale University Press, 1997; Michael Gross, *Moral Dilemmas of Modern War: Torture, Assassination, and Blackmail in an Age of Asymmetric Conflict,* Cambridge: Cambridge University Press, 2009; Peter Berkowitz, *Israel and the Struggle over the International Laws of War,* Stanford: Hoover Institution Press, 2012; and High Level Military Group, *Our Military Forces' Struggle against Lawless, Media Savvy Terrorist Adversaries: A Comparative Study,* Friends of Israel Initiative, February 2016.

27.   Dept. of Defense, *Quadrennial Review of Military Compensation,* 2014, http://www.defense.gov/Portals/1/features/defenseReviews/QDR /2014_Quadrennial_Defense_Review.pdf.

28.   Raymond Odierno, quoted in Sydney Freedberg, "Pay Raise, Sequester Cut Will Eat Army Budget, GCV at Risk: Gen. Odierno," *Breaking Defense,* July 29, 2103, http://breakingdefense.com/?s=Pay+Raise%2C+Sequester +Cut+Will+Eat+Army+Budget%2C+GCV+At+Risk%3A+Gen.+Odierno&sub mit=Search.

29. Tim Kane, "Military Retirement: Too Sweet a Deal?" *War on the Rocks,*
    March 2, 2015, http://warontherocks.com/2015/03/military-retirement-too
    -sweet-a-deal.

30. "Putting Military Pay on the Table," *New York Times,* November 30, 2013.

31. Ken Harbaugh, "The Risk of Over-Thanking Our Veterans," *New York Times,*
    June 1, 2015.

32. Quoted in John T. Bennett and Aaron Mehta, "House Armed Services
    Member Blasts 'Arrogance' of DoD," *Defense News,* November 14, 2013.

33. Martin Dempsey, "The Military Needs to Reach Out to Civilians," *Washington
    Post,* July 3, 2013.

34. Civilian elites and veteran nonelites form the center of attitudes.

35. Fifty-three percent of veteran elite and 47 percent of nonelite veteran
    respondents were unconcerned about the military diverging from society
    (Golby, Cohn, Feaver Crosstabs 41J).

36. Robert G. K. Thompson, "Regular Armies and Insurgency," in *Regular
    Armies and Insurgency,* edited by Ronald Haycock, London: Routledge, 2015,
    pp. 9–20.

37. John F. Kelly, cited in Kristina Wong, "Marine General Predicts Lower
    Combat Standards for Women," *The Hill,* January 8, 2016, http://thehill.com
    /policy/defense/265294-marine-general-predicts-combat-standards-will-be
    -lowered-for-women.

38. David Morris, "Surviving War Doesn't Turn All Veterans into Victims,
    Sometimes It Helps Them Grow," *Daily Beast,* May 18, 2014, http://www
    .thedailybeast.com/articles/2014/05/18/surviving-war-doesn-t-turn-all
    -veterans-into-victims-sometimes-it-helps-them-grow.html.

39. Brad Plumer, "The Unemployment Rate for Recent Veterans Is Incredibly
    High," *Washington Post,* November 11, 2013.

40. Rebecca Shabad, "Post-9/11 War Vets: Bush over Obama," *The Hill,* April 2,
    2014, http://itk.thehill.com/policy/defense/202451-post-9-11-war-vets-prefer
    -bush-as-commander-in-chief.

41. "The World's Biggest Military Bases," *army-technology.com,* September 4,
    2013, http://www.army-technology.com/features/feature-largest-military
    -bases-world-united-states.

42. Alan Zarembo, "With US Encouragement, VA Disability Claims Rise
    Sharply," *Virginian-Pilot/PilotOnline.com,* July 18, 2014, http://pilotonline
    .com/news/military/with-us-encouragement-va-disability-claims-rise
    -sharply/article_14ce5c95-f0e2-5ef1-9480-af30b0f70f23.html.

43. Alan Zarembo, "As Disability Awards Grow, So Do Concerns with Veracity
    of PTSD Claims," *Los Angeles Times,* August 3, 2014.

44. Ken Harbaugh, "The Risk of Over-Thanking Our Veterans," *New York Times,*
    June 1, 2015.

45. Cynthia A. Leard-Mann et al., "Risk Factors Associated with Suicide in Current and Former U.S. Military Personnel," *Journal of the American Medical Association,* 310.5, 2013, 496–506.

46. Yochi Dreazen, "Five Myths about Military Suicides," *Washington Post,* November 7, 2014.

47. Benjamin Summers, "Hero Worship of the Military Is Getting in the Way of Good Policy," *Washington Post,* June 20, 2014, http://www.washingtonpost.com/opinions/hero-worship-of-the-military-presents-an-obstacle-to-good-policy/2014/06/20/053d932a-f0ed-11e3-bf76-447a5df6411f_story.html.

48. See, for example, Phil Klay's collection of short stories *Redeployment,* Eliot Ackerman's novel *Green on Blue,* Kevin Powers's novel *The Yellow Birds* and poetry collection *Letter Composed During a Lull in the Fighting,* Brian Turner's poetry collections *Here, Bullet and Phantom Noise* and his memoir *My Life as a Foreign Country,* Benjamin Busch's memoir *Dust to Dust,* Nathanial Fick's memoir *One Bullet Away,* and the numerous books penned by and about Navy SEALs. The literary journal *0-Dark-Thirty,* the Library of Congress, and the Veterans Writing Project also encourage and promote veterans' literature. University writers' programs such as Stanford University's, which was founded by Wallace Stegner to encourage World War II veterans to write about their experiences as a means of transition back to civilian life, are also playing an important role. For an overview, see George Packer, "Home Fires," *New Yorker,* April 7, 2014, and Dexter Filkins, "The Long Road Home," *New York Times,* March 6, 2014.

49. The number of veterans in Congress had been declining since 1980 until 2012, when 189 veterans received their parties' nominations. While the smaller size of our military means Congress is unlikely to again see 75 percent of its membership be veterans (as was the case in the 1950s and 1960s), organizations such as the Center for Second Service at George Washington University, Combat Veterans for Congress, Iraq and Afghanistan Veterans of America, and the Veterans Campaign provide training for veterans seeking to run for political office. Joyce Tsai, "Veterans of Recent Wars Running for Office in Record Numbers," *Stars and Stripes,* November 5, 2012; Jeremy Herb, "Veterans Vanishing from Congress," *Politico,* July 8, 2014, http://www.politico.com/story/2014/07/veterans-congress-108687; Anna Mulrine, "More Iraq, Afghan Vets Going from Service Member to Member of Congress," *Christian Science Monitor,* November 11, 2013.

50. Eric Greitens, Interview, *Philanthropy,* Summer 2015, available at *PhilanthropyRoundtable,* http://www.philanthropyroundtable.org/topic/excellence_in_philanthropy/interview_with_eric_greitens.

51. Bernard E. Trainor, "A Healing in Sharing War Experiences," *Washington Post,* November 29, 2013.

52. Greitens, Interview.

53. Dave Philipps, "Iraq Veteran, Now a West Point Professor, Seeks to Rein In Disability Pay," *New York Times,* January 7, 2015.

54. See http://www.independencefund.org.

55. Hussain Haqqani, Twitter post, December 30, 2013, 10:59 am, https://twitter .com/husainhaqqani/status/417731772781047808.

56. Thomas Jefferson, Letter to William C. Jarvis, September 28, 1820, *Writings of Thomas Jefferson,* edited by A. A. Lipscomb and A. E. Bergh, Washington: Thomas Jefferson Memorial Association, 1907, 15:278.

57. Theodore Roosevelt, quoted in Adam Quinn, *U.S. Foreign Policy in Context: National Ideology from the Founders to the Bush Doctrine,* London: Routledge, 2010, p. 68.

CONTRIBUTORS

ROSA BROOKS is a professor of law at Georgetown University, a senior fellow at the New America Foundation, and a columnist for *Foreign Policy*. From 2009 to 2011, Brooks took a public service leave of absence from Georgetown University during which she served as counselor to the Under Secretary of Defense for Policy, receiving the Secretary of Defense Medal for Outstanding Public Service for her work. Brooks is the coauthor of *Can Might Make Rights? Building the Rule of Law after Military Interventions* (with Jane Stromseth and David Wippman; Cambridge University Press, 2006), and her next book, *War Everywhere: How Everything Became War and the Military Became Everything,* will be published in 2016 by Simon & Schuster.

LINDSAY P. COHN is currently a senior assistant professor of national security affairs at the U.S. Naval War College, where she teaches policy analysis, strategy, and civil-military relations. She holds a PhD in political science from Duke University and has held fellowships from Harvard's Olin Institute for Strategic Studies, the Alexander von Humboldt Foundation, the Stiftung Wissenschaft und Politik in Berlin, and the Johns Hopkins School of Advanced International Studies Center for Transatlantic Relations. Most recently, as a Council on

Foreign Relations International Affairs Fellow, she has been working on building-partner-capacity programs in the Office of the Secretary of Defense. Her research focuses on comparative civil-military relations, military law, and military organization.

MATTHEW COLFORD graduated from Stanford University in 2014, where he and Alec Sugarman co–taught and co–led several initiatives on civil-military relations and participated in the Military Service as Public Service Program. After graduation, he spent a year as a policy advisor and special assistant to Ambassador Samantha Power at the U.S. Mission to the United Nations, serving as Ambassador Power's representative to the National Security Council and the US interagency on a variety of issues. He has also served in the White House Office of Intergovernmental Affairs and U.S. Embassy Rabat.

THOMAS DONNELLY is a resident fellow in foreign and defense policy and codirector of the Marilyn Ware Center for Security Studies at the American Enterprise Institute. His numerous writings on military affairs include *Operation Just Cause: The Storming of Panama* and *Clash of Chariots: A History of Armored Warfare* as well as the forthcoming *Sources of American Conduct,* a study of the strategic culture of the United States. He served as the policy group director on the staff of the House Armed Services Committee and, while a journalist, was editor of *Army Times, Defense News,* and *Armed Forces Journal.*

PETER D. FEAVER (PhD Harvard, 1990) is a professor of political science and public policy at Duke University. Feaver is author of *Armed Servants* (Harvard 2003) and of *Guarding the Guardians* (Cornell 1992). He is coauthor, with Christopher Gelpi and Jason Reifler, of *Paying the Human Costs of War* (Princeton 2009) and, with Christopher Gelpi, of *Choosing Your Battles* (Princeton 2004). He is coeditor, with Richard H. Kohn, of *Soldiers and Civilians* (MIT 2001). He has published numerous other monographs, articles, book chapters, and policy pieces on grand strategy, American foreign policy, public opinion, nuclear proliferation, civil-military relations, and cybersecurity.

MAJOR JIM GOLBY is an active duty army strategist currently serving as an International Affairs Fellow with the Council on Foreign Relations. He previously served as a special assistant to the chairman of the Joint Chiefs of Staff and as an assistant professor in the Department of Social Sciences at West Point Military Academy. Major Golby holds a PhD in political science from Stanford University and has published numerous articles on American foreign policy, public opinion, and civil-military relations. His dissertation, titled "Duty, Honor, Party: Ideology, Institutions, and the Use of Military Force," examines how domestic political institutions structure American civil-military relations.

JIM HAKE is the founder and CEO of Spirit of America—a privately funded nonprofit that provides assistance that supports the safety and success of deployed US troops and the local people and partners they seek to help. Prior to founding Spirit of America, Jim was a technology and Internet entrepreneur. He founded and sold Access Media, Inc.— one of the first Internet media companies—and was twice named a Technology Pioneer by the World Economic Forum. Jim is a member of the Council on Foreign Relations and an honorary member of the U.S. Army Civil Affairs Regiment. He is a graduate of Dartmouth College and the Stanford University Graduate School of Business.

TOD LINDBERG is a research fellow at the Hoover Institution, Stanford University. He is the author of *The Heroic Heart: Greatness Ancient and Modern*, *The Political Teachings of Jesus*, and *Means to an End: US Interest in the International Criminal Court* (with Lee Feinstein). He is editor of *Beyond Paradise and Power: Europe, America, and the Future of a Troubled Partnership* and *Bridging the Foreign Policy Divide* (with

Derek Chollet and David Shorr). From 1999 to 2013, he was editor of *Policy Review.* He teaches a graduate seminar on ethics in international politics at Georgetown University.

JIM MATTIS is the Davies Family Fellow at the Hoover Institution. His only previous employer was the United States Marine Corps.

MACKUBIN THOMAS OWENS is the dean of academics of the Institute of World Politics (IWP) in Washington DC, a position he assumed after retiring in 2014 from the Naval War College, where he had taught national security affairs since 1987. He is also the editor of *Orbis,* the quarterly journal of the Foreign Policy Research Institute (FPRI) in Philadelphia. He is the author of *US Civil-Military Relations after 9/11: Renegotiating the Civil-Military Bargain* (2011). He is a thirty-year veteran of the Marine Corps and Marine Corps reserve.

CODY POPLIN is a research assistant at the Brookings Institution where he focuses on national security law and policy. He is also the associate editor of *Lawfare.* A former Henry Luce scholar at the Centre for Policy Research in New Delhi, India, he graduated from the University of North Carolina at Chapel Hill with majors in political science and peace, war, and defense. He was also Herbert Scoville, Jr, fellow in Washington DC.

DR. NADIA SCHADLOW is a senior program officer in the International Security and Foreign Policy Program of the Smith Richardson Foundation. She received a BA from Cornell University and an MA and PhD from Johns Hopkins School of Advanced International Studies. Her articles have appeared in *War on the Rocks, Parameters, American Interest, Wall Street Journal, Armed Forces Journal, Small Wars Journal,* and several edited volumes. She recently completed a book manuscript on the U.S. Army's experiences with political and economic reconstruction during war. She has served on the Defense Policy Board and is a member of the Council on Foreign Relations.

KORI SCHAKE is a research fellow at the Hoover Institution. She has had many previous employers.

ALEC J. SUGARMAN recently completed a Junior Fellowship in the South Asia program of the Carnegie Endowment for International Peace. He graduated from Stanford University in 2014 with a degree in political science and a minor in Middle Eastern languages, literatures, and cultures. While at Stanford, he and his coauthor, Matthew Colford, taught a course on civil-military relations that culminated in a weeklong class trip to the U.S. Naval Academy, the White House, and multiple military installations in the Washington DC area. He has worked for the Department of the Army and the House Armed Services Committee as an intern.

BENJAMIN WITTES is a senior fellow in Governance Studies at the Brookings Institution and the editor in chief of *Lawfare*. He has written extensively on national security and the law and is codirector of the Hoover Institution's Working Group on National Security, Technology, and Law.

INDEX

Abizaid, John, 200
Adams, Samuel, 296
Adelstein, David, 224
Afghanistan, 43, 66n35
    civilians' attitudes on, 37
    Obama on public support for, 170
    provincial reconstruction teams
        in, 167–68
    Rumsfeld and invasion of, 69,
        198–200, 216n22
    SOA and, 265–67, 269–72, 276–77
    Taliban and, 49–50, 172, 176, 269–70
    YouGov on involvement in, 71, 175,
        177, 178, 237
Afghanistan War
    AVF and, 98–99
    death and wounded, 25
    disagreement over, 170
    Gates strategy on, 171, 176, 204–5
    Jeffersonian and Wilsonian strategic
        culture on, 166–67
    McChrystal resignation and, 70, 92,
        236–37
    Obama strategy lack and, 204
    officers' opposed reduction in, 69–70
    public on, 110, 146, 170, 173, 204
    2009 troop levels debate, 45–48,
        170, 171
    Woodward on strategy for, 205

all-volunteer force (AVF), 1, 16, 73, 138,
        207, 319
    Afghanistan, Iraq War and, 98–99
    competence of, 136–37
    creation of, 212
    Janowitz proposal of, 214
    millennials and, 251
    of post-Vietnam era, 192
    unaffordable and failing veterans,
        316–17
American Enterprise Institute, 15
American Revolution, 164
    civilian military control and, 75–76
American Sniper movie, 18
    Adelstein on, 224
    campus response to, 224–25
    Eastwood as director of, 221–25, 242
    Hedges on, 224
    Moore on, 223
    negative responses to, 223–24, 225
    support of, 224
Amos, James, 279, 285
AQIM. See al Qaeda in the Islamic
        Maghreb
Armed Servants: Agency, Oversight,
        and Civil-Military Relations
        (Feaver), 193
    on military professionalism, 195
    on principal-agent theory, 194–95

Armed Servants: Agency, Oversight, and Civil-Military Relations (continued)
  on soldier and statesmen strategic interactions, 194
Aspin, Les, 191
atrophy, of wartime strategies, 315
authorization to use military force (AUMF), 174
AVF. *See* all-volunteer force

Bacevich, Andrew, 73–74
bases, military
  fewer, larger, 7, 23–24, 34
  relocation policies, 23–24, 34, 35–36
Bellinger, John, 278
Ben-Gurion, David, 189, 195
best and worst paradox, 56, 63
  military change resistance, 61–62
  officer promotions, 60–61
  organization rigidities, 57–58
  recruitment, 57–58
  rigid bureaucratic rules, 61
best tools for wrong problem paradox
  cybersecurity and, 51
  military nontraditional tasks, 50–51, 55–56, 63
  Obama on strong military, 49–50
  terrorism and, 49–50
Betts, Richard, 181–82
Bianco, William, 102–3
Biden, Joe, 205
Billy Lynn's Long Halftime Walk (Johnson, B.), 226
Black Hawk Down mission, in Somalia, 191
Bleeding Talent (Kane), 61
Boot, Max, 212
Bradley, Leigh, 278
Bremer, L. Paul, 200
Budget Control Act, of 2011, 206, 208
Burk, James, 102
Bush, George H. W.
  Gulf War and, 169
  on Somalia humanitarian intervention, 165–66
Bush, George W., 69, 71, 91, 166, 317
  Afghanistan provincial reconstruction teams, 167–68

civil-military relations and, 199–203
Feaver on National Security Council staff of, 193
retired military criticism of, 80
surge strategy, 201, 202–3
wartime actions of, 190
Bush Institute, at George W. Bush Presidential Center, 284
"By Force of Arms, Rape, War and Military Culture" (Morris), 88

calculus of dissent. *See* dissent
Carter, Ashton, 83
Casey, George, 200
casualties
  phobia, 110
  public tolerance for, 116f
Catch-22, 226, 227
CCR 27-14. *See* Central Command Regulation 27-14
CENTCOM. *See* Central Command
Center for Strategic and Budgetary Assessments, 150
Central Command (CENTCOM)
  guidance on SOA, 277–78
  Kyrgyzstan and, 40–42
Central Command Regulation 27-14 (CCR 27-14), 279, 283, 285
Churchill, Winston, 177, 189, 195
civic activism, 318
civic obligation response, by veterans, 315–16
civil liberties support, 31, 101
civilian agencies budget cuts, 50–51
civilian leadership
  lack of military knowledge, 178–79
  military advice dismissal, 299
  in wartime, 195
  YouGov on public trust of, 110–11, 207, 219
  See also political leadership; presidential leadership
civilian military control, 11, 93–95, 191–93, 288, 294–301
  American Revolution and, 75–76
  Bush, G. W., and, 69
  civil-military relations and, 71–74
  Clinton administration and, 69
  Cohen on, 75

command and control issues, 236–38
Congress and, 77, 132, 153, 190, 236, 285, 300
declining budgets, 70
future of, 89–92
history of, 75–76
Huntington on, 75
Janowitz on, 213, 214
military advice and dissent, 71, 79–82, 98
Obama and, 69–70
public attitudes and, 82–89
renegotiation and, 90
theory and practice, 74–79
weakening of, 69–71
civilian-military gap, 16, 18, 27, 39, 97–99, 140–41
AVF impact on, 98
defense budgets and, 37, 149
dissent and, 71, 79–82, 98
drivers of, 125–32
on homosexual military service, 98
medicalized, 190
military effectiveness affect on, 320n2
Mullen on, 36–37
Owens on, 106
partisanship and, 129, 131, 207–8
policy implication and responses, 132–35
post-9/11 studies, 105–8
recommendations, 135–39
TISS on, 100–105, 122, 125
YouGov on, 125, 315–16
See also familiarity gap; grief gap; participation gap
civilians
on civilian leaders military advice dismissal, 299
communication on military, 7
familiarity during WWII, 107, 164, 176, 183
Iraq and Afghanistan attitudes, 32, 37
lack of military knowledge, 21, 295
on military change social nature, 8
military force proponents, 6
military perception of insensitivity by, 8

military support, 21, 22, 226
millennials and, 261
WWII familiarity by, 107, 164, 176, 183
See also elite civilians
civil-military bargain
cold war and, 72, 98
deterrence theory, 72–73
Gulf War and, 73
on homosexual military service, 83, 85
public, government, military establishment in, 72
on women in military, 83, 85, 89
WWII and, 72
civil-military connections
DoD legal and policy barriers for, 276–81
ensuring, 287–326
for informed public and policy, 272–74
Navy SEAL Foundation, 275
Operation Gratitude, 275
Project HOPE, 275–76
recommendations for, 283–85
SOA model of, 15, 19, 266–85, 312–13, 318
social media and, 273–75
uninformed but admiring public, 272–74, 289, 291–94
universal humanitarian principles barriers, 281–83, 284
ways for, 274–76
during WWII, 275
civil-military divergence
changed relationships, 9
cultural differences, 7–8
elite-civilian *versus* civilian-military categories, 10–11
false perceptions of, 1, 3
grief gap, 9–10
military entitlement, 3, 9, 10, 134
nonmilitary purpose, 11–12
strategy differences, 6
undermining military effectiveness, 8
See also civilian-military gap; familiarity gap; ignorance; isolation

civil-military frictions, 18
elite distrust of military, 16, 74
Obama and, 203–6
political partisanship in military, 16, 129, 131, 207–8
WWII and, 78
civil-military paradoxes, 15, 16, 21, 64–68
best and worst, 56–63
best tools for wrong problem, 49–56
enthusiasm and ignorance, 22–39
mistrust and awe, 39–49
civil-military population, in U.S., 1, 2f
civil-military relations, 9, 314–15
Bacevich on, 73–74
Bush, G. W., and, 199–203
civilian military control and, 71–74
Clausewitzian formula for, 196
Clinton and, 100
Cohen on, 73–74, 195–97
extirpation and, 85
Feaver on, 73–74, 193–95
Huntington on, 193–94
institutional lens for, 72
Kohn on, 191–93
liberal administration and, 87
millennials on, 250, 259–60
negotiation in, 300
PME on, 135
post-9/11, 189–218
resentment in, 295
sociological lens for, 72
TISS study under stress of, 320n1
during Truman administration, 77, 79
trust as key to, 18, 74, 91, 319
von Clausewitz, Carl, 53–54
on military strategy, 162
on nature of war, 196, 211–12
Clemenceau, Georges, 189, 195
climate change, 22
Clinton, William "Bill," 69
Feaver on National Security Council staff of, 193
on homosexual recruits, 82–83
military relationship, 100
Somalia troop withdrawal, 166
White House and Pentagon divide, 191

Cobra II: The Inside Story of the Invasion and Occupation of Iraq (Gordon and Trainor), 199
Cohen, Eliot, 73, 75, 189, 295
Cohn, Lindsay, 15, 23
cold war, 176–77
civil-military bargain and, 72, 98
combat occupational categories, 25
command and civilian control issues, 236–38
Congress
civilian military control and, 77, 132, 153, 190, 236, 285, 300
Kohn on Pentagon and, 193
on military pay, 304, 305, 316
military testimony on concerns, 237, 241
Naval Act of 1794 and, 164
presidential requests for AUMF, 174
on sexual assault and PTSD, 208, 209
trust in, 219–20, 251
veterans in, 102–3, 325n49
conservatism, in military, 24, 33, 38, 84, 240, 242
Huntington on, 86
insubordination and, 192
on minorities, 86, 95n41
of officers, 31–32, 82, 83, 85, 104
YouGov on, 84, 292
Council on Foreign Relations, 147
counterinsurgency, 11, 99, 144, 169–70
in Iraq, 200, 202, 204
manual, of 2008, 168
critical perspective, of military
Catch-22, 226, 227
by literary and intellectual culture, 227
YouGov on, 227–28
Crocker, Ryan, 203
Cruz, Ted, 209
cultural differences, 8
military rank structure, 7
military recruitment difficulties, 7
U.S. egalitarian culture, 7
veterans reintegration difficulties, 7, 210
culture
of honor, 321n4
military literary and intellectual, 227

military missions and, 102
U.S. egalitarian, 7
See also strategic culture
cyber attack, 143
Cyber Command (CYBERCOM), 58
cyber domain, 22
cyber threats, 55
CYBERCOM. *See* Cyber Command
cybersecurity, 51

DADT. *See* Don't Ask, Don't Tell
DBB. *See* Defense Business Board
defense budgets
    Budget Control Act of 2011 cuts in,
        206, 208
    civilians ignorance of, 37, 149
    declining, 70
    millennials on, 249–50
    post-9/11, 37–38
    TISS and YouGov on, 122, 124f
Defense Business Board (DBB), of DoD,
    281, 285
Defense Science Board report, 2010, 62
deference and entitlement, 3, 9, 10, 134
Dempsey, Jason
    army personnel social and political
        attitudes, 31
    enlisted personnel liberalism, 32
    on military force and terrorism, 32
    on officers' conservatism, 31–32, 104
Dempsey, Martin, 88
Department of Defense (DoD)
    DBB of, 281
    legal and policy barriers for civil-
        military connections, 276–81
    on military demographics, 27
    on NGO and private sector firms
        collaboration, 277–78
    OGC, CENTCOM guidance on SOA,
        277–78
deployments, 1, 136
    branch statistics on, 25–26
    by Bush, G. H. W., to Somalia,
        165–66
    intangible costs of, 25
Dereliction of Duty (McMaster), 80–81
deterrence theory, civil-military bargain
    and, 72–73
disability benefits, 311

dissent, military advice and, 71, 98
    elite civilians support of, 79, 122, 123f
    Hirschman on, 80
    media use for, 201, 236–38
    Newbold and, 80
    resignations and, 80–82, 122, 123f,
        201
    by Vietnam War officers, 80–81
    YouGov on officers', 115, 122, 201
    YouGov on officers' media use for,
        201, 236–38
diversity
    in military geography, 36, 135–36
    of recruits, 57, 136
DoD. *See* Department of Defense
Donilon, Tom, 205–6
Donnelly, Tom, 14, 310
Don't Ask, Don't Tell (DADT) law,
    246, 250
don't know responses, in YouGov study,
    17, 19, 110, 289, 290t, 291, 321n6
Douglas, Stephen, 89
draft, 17
    cost of, 136
    deployability and capability effect
        from, 136
    peacetime, feasibility of, 137
drones, 40–42
    public on use of, 143, 151, 155
Duty (Gates), 204–5

Eastwood, Clint, 221–25, 242
egalitarian culture, of U.S., 7
Eisenhower, Dwight, 79
electronic communication
    vulnerabilities, 53
elite civilians
    calculus of dissent support, 79,
        122, 123f
    on civilian leaders lack of military
        knowledge, 178–79
    defined, 14, 321n3
    familial military service, 207
    familiarity gap and, 103, 207
    foreign policy attitudes, 105
    on homosexual military service, 102
    improper civil-military norms
        acceptance, 115–16
    on male-dominated military, 306

elite civilians *(continued)*
military distrust, 16, 74
military member
underrepresentation, 28
on political leader values, 322n15
public attitudes compared to, 297–98
Republican Party identification,
32, 105
in TISS, 99, 101, 103
elite military officers, in TISS, 99
civil liberties support, 101
on handgun sales, 101
on homosexual military service, 102
partisan identification, 101–2
on trust, 101
enlistment, in military, 22
Gates on, 23
hereditary profession, 23
immediate family, 23
post-9/11 factors for, 29
reduced numbers of, 23
See also familial military service
enthusiasm and ignorance
paradox, 22–29
geography, 33–39
politics, 30–32
entitlement, military, 3, 9, 10, 134
entrance standards, for military, 295
*Evil Hours: A Biography of Post-
Traumatic Stress Disorder*
(Morris, D.), 210–11
extirpation
civil-military relations and, 85
Huntington on, 82
Obama social change push, 87–88
during peacetime, 87

factions disputes, budget influence on, 78
Fallows, James, 22–23, 147, 225–26
familial military service, 23, 106–7,
125–26, 127, 147, 207, 317
familiarity gap, 12, 20, 127, 129, 206–7
elite civilians and, 103, 207
increase in, 17
leading to pity, 18
military force and, 132–33
millennials and, 252–53
post-9/11, 106–8, 146
on terrorism, 148–51

TISS on, 102–3
See also isolation
FDR. *See* Roosevelt, Franklin Delano
Feaver, Peter, 15, 23, 100
on civil-military relations, 73–74,
193–95
on military force, 110, 133
on military professionalism, 195
on National Security Council
staff, 193
principal-agency theory, 194–95
"Fix the New G.I. Bill" (Hsia and
Ivey), 262
Flournoy, Michele, 45, 189
Flynn, Michael, 70
Foley, James, 158n11
foreign aid misperceptions, 181
Foreign Policy, 21
foreign policy, elite civilians and officers
on, 105
Foreign Policy Leadership Project, 31
Frankel, Rebecca, 147
Franks, Tommy, 198, 199

The Gamble (Ricks), 202
Gates, Robert, 91, 203
Afghanistan strategy, 171, 176, 204–5
on PTSD, 210
on reduced military enlistment, 23
Gelpi, Christopher, 110, 133
geography, military, 102
base relocation, 23–24, 34, 35–36
diversity, 36, 135–36
familiar career paths, 34–35, 135–36
high population density and, 33
large military installations, 34
low population density, 35
southern military population, 24, 33
George W. Bush Presidential Center
Bush Institute, 284
Gerras, Stephen J., 61–62
Gillibrand, Kirsten, 209
Golby, James, 15, 23
on officers' partisan
identification, 105
Goldwater-Nichols Department of
Defense Reorganization Act, in
1986, 77, 90, 192
Gordon, Michael R., 199, 201

government policymakers
  military leadership mistrust, 21,
    39–40, 48–49
  military's capabilities
    overestimation, 21, 39
Green, Brice, 265–66, 273
Greitens, Eric, 315–16
grief gap, 9–10
Groves, Bryan, 133
Guantanamo Bay
  detentions at, 143
  public support for maintaining, 155
Gulf War
  Bush, G. H. W., and, 169
  civil-military bargain and, 73
  disagreement over nature of, 169–70
Gullette, Ethel, 265–66, 273

Hamiltonian school, on economics, 164
handgun sales, 101
Harbaugh, Jim, 224
Harper, E. Royster, 224–25
Harvard University Institute of Politics
  on respect for military, 221
  young American survey, 220–21
Harvard University Pluralism Project, 14
Hedges, Chris, 224
Heritage Foundation, 2008, 28–29
Herndon, William H., 175
*The Heroic Heart: Greatness Ancient
    and Modern* (Lindberg), 15
Hirschman, Albert, 80
Holbrooke, Richard, 45
Holmes, Oliver Wendell, Jr., 297
homelessness, of veterans, 29
homosexual military service, 8, 85,
    98, 100
  Clinton on recruits, 82–83
  DADT law, 246, 250
  Kohn on military service for, 191–92
  millennials support of, 250
  Obama on ban of, 87–88
  Powell on, 191–92
  public inconsistency on, 152
  TISS on, 102, 121f
  YouGov on, 83, 115, 121f, 307
HOPE. *See* Project Health
    Opportunities for People
    Everywhere

"How the Military's 'Bro' Culture
    Turns Women into Targets"
    (Sorcher), 209
Hsia, Tim, 262
Huntington, Samuel, 72, 73, 98
  on civil military control, 75
  civilian supremacy, 190
  on civil-military relations, 193–94
  on extirpation and transmutation, 82
  Feaver on, 193–94
  on functional and societal
    imperative, 82, 85, 87
  Kohn on model of, 192–93
  on liberal administration, 87
  on military conservatism, 86
  subjective control model, 200–202
Hussein, Saddam, 49–50, 169

IED. *See* Improvised Explosive Device
ignorance, civilian, 16–17, 21, 89, 221
  concern for, 289, 291–94. 314–315
  on defense budget, 37, 149
  on degree of military isolation of,
    148–49
  enthusiasm and, 22–39
  Lindberg and Owens on, 308–9
  from military enlistment lack, 22–23
  on military members numbers,
    24, 95n44, 149, 168, 207, 208,
    217n42, 289
  on military pay, 149–50
  by millennials, 247–48
  national security implications, 155
  on NSA, 150–51
  Owens on, 308
  political leaders warfare choices, 5,
    156, 288
  on PTSD, 5–6, 310
  recruitment and, 5
  on terrorism, 154–56, 178
  veterans on post-9/11, 146
  YouGov on, 289, 291–94
  See also enthusiasm and ignorance
    paradox
improper behavior, of military, 17,
    115–16
Improvised Explosive Device (IED), 25
  SOA and, 272
Inbody, Donald, 108

income levels, of military, 28–29, 92
Independence Fund, 317
infantry, women in, 8, 88–89, 115,
    119f, 250
Inman, Bobby Ray, 191
intelligence, surveillance, and
    reconnaissance (ISR)
    assets, 40–41
InterAction, SOA membership
    application to, 282
internal structures, of military, 21
"International Strategy for Cyberspace,"
    U.S., 55
interrogation methods, 143
interventions, quick and massive, 113f,
    169, 174
Iran nuclear program, 179–80
Iraq
    civilian attitudes on, 32, 37
    counterinsurgency, 200, 202, 204
    deaths and wounded in, 25
    Obama position on, 177
    officers' opposed reduction in,
        69–70
    Rumsfeld and invasion of, 69, 198–
        200, 216n22
    SOFA and, 69–70
Iraq War
    absent strategy discussion, 172–73
    AVF and, 98–99
    public opinion on, 158n11
    retired military criticism of, 80
    surge strategy in, 201–3
Islamic State of Iraq and al-Sham (ISIS),
    50, 99, 172, 173–74
    Obama's lack of strategy for, 178
    public opinion on, 144, 158n11,
        177–78
    use of force against, 143, 144
isolation, of military, 6, 67n42, 90, 207
    civilian ignorance on degree
        of, 148–49
    civilians difficult communication, 7
    from fewer, larger bases, 7, 23–24, 34
    perception of public disrespect, 297
    public concern about effects of,
        148, 269
    separation from society, 296–97
    trust and confidence, 145–48

YouGov on, 221
    See also familiarity gap
ISR. *See* intelligence, surveillance,
    and reconnaissance
Ivey, Anna, 262

Jackson, Andrew, 76
Jacksonian tradition, in strategic
    culture, 165–66
Janowitz, Morris, 18, 72, 98
    AVF proposal, 214
    on civilian military control, 213, 214
    constabulary nature of military
        operations, 190
    on military professionalism, 212–14
    on WWII ideological indoctrination,
        212–13, 214
JCS. *See* Joint Chiefs of Staff
Jefferson, Thomas, 318
Jeffersonian school, of strategic culture,
    166–67
JER. *See* Joint Ethics Regulation
Johnson, Ben, 226
Johnson, Jeh, 278
Johnson, Louis, 78
Johnson, Lyndon, 81, 177
Joint Chiefs of Staff (JCS)
    centralization of power, 192
    collaboration cell for, 285
    Vietnam War disagreement, 80–81
Joint Ethics Regulation (JER)
    on NFE support problems, 277
    preferential treatment and
        endorsement prohibition, 280

Kaiser Family Foundation survey, 181
Kane, Tim, 61
Keane, Jack, 202
Kelly, John, 211, 310
Kennan, George, 165
Kennedy, David, 245
Klay, Phil, 295
Kohn, Richard, 100
    "Out of Control: The Crisis in Civil-
        Military Relations," 191–93
    on resignations, 81
    on weakening civilian military
        control, 70, 74
Kohut, Andrew, 14, 321n3

Kyle, Chris, 222–25, 242
Kyrgyzstan, NSS, CENTCOM
    and, 40–42

"left of boom," 56
liberal view, of U.S. military, 219–20,
    239–43
    American Sniper and, 18, 221–25, 242
    command and civilian control
      issues, 236–38
    critical perspective of military,
      225–29
    military as social institution, 18,
      229–33
    wartime issues, 234–36
liberalism, 31, 35, 83
    culture of honor and, 321n4
    of enlisted personnel, 32
    on military values, 85
    of Obama, 87, 90
    officer's conservatism clash with, 82
    in peacetime, 82
    YouGov on, 84, 292
limited war, nuclear arms and, 190
Lincoln, Abraham, 89, 91, 177, 189, 195
Lindberg, Tod, 15, 308
Lippman, Walter, 161, 175
literature, by veterans, 315, 325n48
Lovelace, Douglas, 81

MacArthur, Douglas, 77, 79
Making the Corps (Ricks), 100
male-dominated military, 306
al-Maliki, Nouri, 203
Marion Ware Center for Defense
    Studies, at American Enterprise
    Institute, 15
Markham, Jaime, 102–3
Marshall, George, 79, 91
Mattis, James, 70, 279, 285
McChrystal, Stanley, 46–47, 205
    resignation of, 70, 92, 236–37
McClellan, George B., 77
McKiernan, David, 45–46
McMaster, H. R., 80–81
McNamara, Robert, 80, 177
McRaven, William, 279, 285
Meade, Walter Russell, 163–65, 182
Meals, Ready-to-Eat (MREs), 25

military
    capabilities overestimation, 21, 39,
      40–42, 44–48
    change in, 8, 61–62
    civilians' insensitivity perception
      by, 8
    confidence in, 21, 38, 39–40, 70–71,
      145–48, 219–20
    Congressional testimony on
      concerns, 237, 241
    critical perspective of, 225–29
    culture and missions, 102
    deference and entitlement, 3, 9,
      10, 134
    demographics, 27–28
    economic advancement in, 4
    entrance standards for, 295
    factional debates within, 78
    history, strategy, and civil-military
      relations courses, 259–60
    improper behavior, 17, 115–16
    income levels, 28–29, 92
    less urban population in, 24
    minorities and women opportunities
      in, 86, 95n41, 292, 307
    nontraditional tasks, 50–51,
      55–56, 63
    Obama on strength of, 49–50
    political leaders and public on
      dominance, 309–10
    promotions, 95n41
    rank structure, 7
    as social institution, 18, 229–33
    social issues, 299, 323n20
    social programs, 38
    southern population in, 24
    strength of, 21, 49–50
    trials, 143
    values, 85, 221, 250, 306–10
    See also Pentagon
military advice
    civilian leaders dismissal of, 299
    political leadership distrust of, 319
    See also dissent
military effectiveness, 8, 320n2
    public perception of, 55
military force, 22
    budget cuts, 206, 208
    familiarity gap and, 132–33

military force *(continued)*
    Feaver and Gelpi on, 110, 133
    against ISIS, 143, 144
    presidential AUMF, 174
    public inconsistent attitudes on, 151
    in pursuit of total victory, 169
    terrorism and, 32
    veterans reluctance for, 6
    YouGov and TISS results on, 110,
        112f, 113f, 115
military justice system
    move toward civilian justice system,
        153–54
    public on military jail or court-
        martial, 152–53, 179
military leadership. *See* officers
military members
    age of, 28, 64n4
    civilian ignorance on numbers of,
        24, 95n44, 149, 168, 207, 208,
        217n42, 289
    civilian society respect, 146
    education, 28
    familial ties, 106–7, 125–26, 127, 147,
        207, 317
    millennials respect for, 249
    reason for becoming, 20
    Republican Party and, 107, 204
    sacrifices of, 26
    service obligation fulfillment, 26–27
    socioeconomic status, 28–29
    Teigen on partisan identification
        of, 105
    workplace contact with, 114f, 126,
        147, 206
military officers. *See* officers
military pay
    civilian ignorance on, 149–50
    Congress on, 304, 305, 316
    millennials on, 249–50
    post-9/11, 38
    YouGov on, 273–74, 293
military support, by civilians, 21
    post 9/11, 22
millennials, 18–19, 245, 263, 294
    age of continuous war for, 18, 247
    AVF and, 251
    civilians teaching at military
        institutions, 261

on civil-military relations, 250
DADT law and, 246
on defense budgets, 249–50
exchange programs, 258–59
experiential learning, 254–56
familiarity gap, 252–53
homosexuals military service
    support, 250
ignorance of military, 247–48
on military, political leaders shared
    values with, 250
military history, strategy, and
    civil-military relations courses,
    259–60
on military institution
    skepticism, 249
military members respect by, 249
on military pay, 249–50
on minorities, 251
as 9/11 generation, 247
on officers teaching at civilian
    institutions, 260–61
on ROTC at Stanford University,
    245–46
on service numbers, 252
service obligations fulfillment,
    256–57
technology and, 253
trust of military, 248, 251–52
University fellowships for officers,
    257–58
US Military in International Security
    course, 254–56
veteran scholarships to universities,
    261–62
women in infantry support, 250
minorities
    military opportunities for, 86,
        95n41
    millennials on, 251
The Mission Continues, 316
    Greitens as founder of, 315
mistrust
    of military by elite civilians, 16, 74
    of officers, 21, 39–40, 48–49
mistrust and awe paradox, 49
    Afghanistan 2009 troop levels
        example, 45–48
    Kyrgyzstan example, 40–42

military leaders political
  constraints, 48
military's capabilities
  overestimation, 21, 39,
  40–42, 44–48
political leadership mistrust of
  military, 21, 39–40, 70–71
Sudan example, 42–44
modern warfare, technical skills and, 58
Monroe, James, 76
Moore, Michael, 223
Morris, David J., 210–11
Morris, Madeline, 88
MREs. *See* Meals, Ready-to-Eat
Mullen, Michael, 24
Murray, D. W., 51–52
Myers, Richard, 199

National Academy of Sciences
  academics, 14
National Priorities Project, 2010, 29
National Security Agency (NSA), 58,
  150–51
National Security Staff (NSS), White
  House, 40–42
National Security Strategy
  NSC-68 comparison to, 172
  for public-private partnerships,
  278–79
Naval Act, of 1794, 164
Navy SEAL Foundation, 275
New America Foundation, 21
Newbold, Greg, 80, 199
  on Rumsfeld resignation, 200–201
NFE. *See* non-Federal entity
NGOs. *See* nongovernmental
  organizations
9/11
  millennials as generation of, 247
  strategy differences and, 6
  unrestricted warfare and, 54
  See also post-9/11
non-Federal entity (NFE), 279–80
  JER on support for, 277
nongovernmental organizations
  (NGOs), 14, 279–80
  DoD collaboration with, 277–78
nonmilitary policies and purpose,
  11–12, 323n19

nontraditional tasks, of military, 50–51,
  55–56, 63
NSA. *See* National Security Agency
NSC-68. *See* "United States Objectives
  and Programs for National
  Security"
NSS. *See* National Security Staff
nuclear arms, 179–80, 190

Obama, Barack, 45, 69–70, 71, 317
  on Afghanistan surge, 171
  AUMF of, 174
  civil-military frictions, 203–6
  extirpation social change
  push, 87–88
  on homosexual military service
  ban, 87–88
  insurgency persuasion, 176
  Iraq position, 177
  ISIS lack of strategy, 178
  liberalism of, 87, 90
  on public support for
  Afghanistan, 170
  social policies over military
  objections, 296
  on strong military, 49–50
  on values defense, 165, 176
  wartime actions of, 190
  on women specialties, 88
Occupy movement, 97
Odierno, Raymond, 201–2, 279, 285
Office of General Counsel (OGC), of
  DoD, 278
Office of the Secretary of Defense
  (OSD), 78
officers, 152, 250
  civil liberties support, 31, 101
  on complex security threats, 21
  conservativism, 31–32, 82, 83,
  85, 104
  foreign policy attitudes, 105
  Iraq and Afghanistan reduction
  opposition, 69–70
  male-dominated military and, 306
  media use for dissent, 201, 236–38
  mistrust of, 21, 39–40, 48–49
  partisanship, 105–6, 135
  politicians dismissal of, 39–40,
  70–71, 319

officers *(continued)*
  promotions, 60–61
  Republican Party identification,
    31–32, 84, 101, 105
  role during war, 117f
  teaching at civilian institutions,
    260–61
  on trust, 101
  University fellowships for, 257–58
  WWII recruitment for, 60
  See also elite military officers, in TISS
OGC. *See* Office of General Counsel
O'Hehir, Andrew, 224
Operation Gratitude, 275
OSD. *See* Office of the Secretary of
    Defense
"The Other 1%" (Thompson), 97
"Out of Control: The Crisis in Civil-
    Military Relations" (Kohn)
  on civilian control, 193
  on civil-military relations, 191–93
  on conservatism and
    insubordination, 192
  on Goldwater-Nichols Act
    reforms, 192
  on homosexual military service,
    191–92
  Huntington's model critique, 192–93
  on JCS chairman centralization of
    power, 192
  on military consequences of
    growth, 192
  on military professionalism, 193
Owens, Mackubin Thomas, 15, 300–301
  on civilian ignorance of
    military, 308
  on civilian-military gap, 106

Pace, Peter, 200, 202
Panetta, Leon, 279
  on open women specialties, 88
participation, during WWII, 23,
    133, 136
participation gap, in military, 21–22, 91,
    97, 106, 137, 146–47, 207, 265
partisanship, 85
  civilian-military gap and, 16, 129,
    131, 207–8
  gap, 133–34

officers and, 105–6, 135
  post-9/11 studies on, 105–6
  TISS on, 84, 101–2
Paul, Rand, 209
peacetime
  draft feasibility in, 137
  extirpation during, 87
  liberalism in, 82
Pentagon
  Clinton on White House divide
    with, 191
  Kohn on Congress, president
    and, 193
  Workplace and Gender Relations
    Survey of Active Duty Members
    of, 209
Perry, William, 245
Petraeus, David, 170, 201–2, 302
Pew Research Center, 14
  military members reasons for
    enlisting, 29
  on transition issues, 30
Pew Social Trends survey
  on familial military members ties,
    106–7, 127
  on post-9/11 veteran views, 106
Pluralism Project, at Harvard
    University, 14
PME. *See* professional military
    education
policy
  civilian-military gap implications
    for, 132–35
  for civil-military connections,
    272–74
  DOD barriers for SOA, 276–81
  public on foreign, 175
  veteran advantage in, 6
  YouGov on civil-military gaps and,
    315–16
political leadership
  civilian ignorance of warfare choices,
    5, 156, 288
  lack of military confidence, 21,
    39–40, 70–71
  military advice distrusted by, 319
  military deference to, 9
  military lack of knowledge, 70,
    170–71, 273

public and values of, 115, 118f, 129, 179, 214–15, 218n62, 250, 298, 322n15
public disaffection for, 288, 319
public influence on wartime strategies, 161–62
veterans different values from, 298–99
politicization, 9, 17
politics, military
conservativism, 24, 30–33, 38, 82–86, 240, 242, 292
liberalism, 31, 32, 35, 83–85, 87, 90, 292, 321n4
partisanship, 16, 84–85, 101–2, 105–6, 129, 131, 133–34, 207–8
YouGov on party identification, 111f
Polk, James, 76–77
post-9/11, 99
civilians' military support, 22
civil-military relations, 189–218
defense budgets, 37–38
enlistment factors, 29
familiarity gap, 106–8, 146
military pay, 38
partisan identification studies, 105–6
unemployment, 29, 30
veterans contentment, 30
veterans on civilian ignorance, 146
women veterans, 30
post-traumatic stress disorder (PTSD), 190
civilian ignorance on, 5–6, 310
Congress on, 208, 209
Gates on, 210
VA disability benefits, 311
YouGov survey on crisis of, 206–11, 310–13
post-Vietnam era
AVF after, 192
officers Republican identification, 31–32
Total Force Policy, 137
Powell, Colin, 84, 321n4
on homosexuals military service, 191–92
Powell Doctrine, 129, 130f
presidential leadership, 77, 177–81
AUMF requests to Congress, 174

Kohn on Pentagon and, 193
military recommendations and, 299
Obama insurgency persuasion, 176
public persuasion, 175
role during war, 117f, 200
principal-agent theory, of Feaver, 194–95
professional military education (PME), 135
The Professional Soldier (Janowitz), 98, 212–14
professionalism, military, 21, 134–35, 201, 211
Cohen on, 196
Feaver on, 195
Janowitz on, 212–14
Kohn on, 193
Project Health Opportunities for People Everywhere (HOPE), 275–76
provincial reconstruction teams, in Afghanistan, 167–68
"Psychological Operations" (Klay), 295
PTSD. *See* post-traumatic stress disorder
public
on Afghanistan War, 110, 146, 170, 173, 204
casualty tolerance, 116f
in civil-military bargain, 72
civil-military connections and, 272–74, 289, 291–94
on drones use, 143, 151, 155
on foreign policy, 175
on homosexual military service, 152
improper civil-military norms acceptance, 115
inexperience with veterans, 3
on male-dominated military, 306
military isolation concerns by, 148, 269
on military jail or court-martial, 152–53, 179
political leadership disaffection by, 288, 319
-private partnerships, 278–79
on resignations, 81
response to Syria, 173
TISS on, 99, 101
values of, 115, 118f, 129, 179, 214–15, 218n62, 250, 298, 322n15

public *(continued)*
  veterans on post-9/11 familiarity gap
    from, 146
  wartime strategies influenced by,
    161–62
  YouGov on priorities of, 175, 212
public attitudes
  Brooks on paradoxes of, 15, 16
  civilian military control and, 82–89
  elite civilians compared to, 297–98
  military trust and confidence, 38,
    143–48, 219–20
  volatile and contradictory about
    wars, 17
Public Opinion (Lippman), 161, 175
public opinions
  inconsistent, 151–53, 179–80
  on Iraq War, 158n11
  on ISIS, 144, 158n11, 177–78
  on military unfairness to
    women, 209
  on sexual assault in military, 153,
    208, 209–10
  on spousal abuse, 208
  on terrorism, 143–59, 178, 212
  on wartime strategies, 161–87
public spaces surveillance, 143
public support
  for Afghanistan War, 170
  for maintaining Guantanamo
    Bay, 155
  for torture, 155
  for war, 168

al Qaeda, 45, 49–50
  in the Islamic Maghreb (AQIM), 272
Qiao Liang, 52–53, 54

racial discrimination
  TISS on, 120f
  YouGov on, 115, 120f
radical extremism, 172–73
reconstruction, postconflict, 49, 167–68
recruitment
  Clinton on homosexual, 82–83
  difficulties, 7
  diversity, 57, 136
  ignorance and, 5
  skills and attributes, 59–60

for WWII officers, 60
  young male recruits, 57–58
Reidel, Brice, 45
reintegration difficulties, for veterans,
    7, 210
  See also post-traumatic stress
    disorder
relocation policies, for military bases,
    23–24, 34, 35–36
Republican Party
  familial military members ties, 107
  Golby on, 105
  identification with, 111f
  military members bias for, 204
  officers identification with, 31–32,
    84, 101, 105
  Teigen on, 105, 108
  TISS survey on, 84, 101, 105, 107,
    109, 110
  veterans identification with, 109–10
  YouGov results on, 84, 109, 110
Reserve Officer Training Corps (ROTC),
    at Stanford University, 245–47
resignations, 80, 82
  Kohn on, 81
  of McChrystal, 70, 92, 236–37
  public on, 81
  of Rumsfeld, 200–201
  TISS and YouGov on, 122, 123f, 201
Resilience (Greitens), 315
respect, for military, 4, 314, 321n7
  members, 146
  millennials and, 249
  TISS on, 103, 125
  YouGov on, 211, 221, 288, 289,
    291–94
Rice, Condoleezza, 245
Ricks, Thomas "Tom," 100, 202
Rolling Stone, 70, 92, 223
Roosevelt, Franklin Delano (FDR), 91
  on economic defense, 164
  on values spread, 165
  WWII fireside chats, 164, 176
Roosevelt, Theodore, 320
ROTC. *See* Reserve Officer
    Training Corps
Rumsfeld, Donald, 80, 169–70, 296
  Afghanistan and Iraq invasions, 69,
    198–200, 216n22

Huntington's subjective control
model and, 200
resignation of, 200–201

Sanchez, Ricardo, 200
Scales, Robert, 70
Schafer, Amy, 147
Scott, Winfield, 77
security challenges, world, 21, 22
Segal, David, 106
service members. *See* military members
sexual assault, military, 30, 250
public opinion on, 153, 208, 209–10
Smith, Jay, 267–69
Smith-Richardson Foundation, 15
Snider, Don, 81–82
Snowden, Edward, 144, 145
SOA. *See* Spirit of America
social contact with military, 127,
128t, 129
YouGov on, 133
social institution, military as, 18, 229–33
social issues, of military, 299, 323n20
social media, 273–75
social programs, of military, 38
society
military separation from, 296–97
military values different from, 17, 24,
67n42, 85, 228, 307, 308
veteran support, 3, 146
SOCOM. *See* Special Operations
Command
SOFA. *See* status of forces agreement
The Soldier and the State (Huntington),
82, 98, 193
Somalia, 54
Black Hawk Down mission in, 191
Bush, G. H. W., troop deployment to,
165–66
Clinton troop withdrawal, 166
Sorcher, Sara, 209
southern population, in military, 24, 33
major military bases in, 34
Special Operations Command
(SOCOM), 78
Special Providence (Meade), 163
Spirit of America (SOA), 15, 19, 265,
312–13
AQIM and, 272

CENTCOM CCR 27-14 on, 279,
283, 285
civic involvement and, 318
DOD legal and policy barriers,
276–81
IEDs and, 272
InterAction application by, 282
OGC and CENTCOM guidance on,
277–78
origins of, 266–69
for troop safety and mission success,
269–72
universal humanitarian principles
barriers, 281–83, 284
Windward-Kodoala Drab
videoconference, 269–71
spousal abuse, 208
SSNW. *See* Stanford Says No to War
SSQL. *See* Stanford Students for Queer
Liberation
stabilization, postconflict, 49
Stanford Says No to War (SSNW), 245
Stanford Students for Queer Liberation
(SSQL), 245
Stanford University, 18–19
ROTC and, 245–47
status of forces agreement (SOFA), with
Iraq government, 69–70
Strachan, Hew, 182
strategic culture, 162, 181–82
on economy defense, 164
Hamiltonian school on
economics, 164
Jacksonian tradition, populist
culture, 165
Jeffersonian school, on democracy
protection, 165
Wilsonian tradition, 164–67
strategy differences, 9/11 and, 6
subjective control model, of Huntington
Bush, G. W., and, 201–2
Rumsfeld and, 200
Sudan, 42–44
Sugarman, A. J., 15
suicides, of veterans, 311–12
Supreme Command (Cohen), 189,
197, 207
on civilian leadership in wartime, 195
on military professionalism, 196

surge strategy, of Bush, G. W.,
201, 202–3
surveillance, 40–41, 144
of public spaces, 143
Syria, public response to, 173

Taibbi, Matt, 223
Taliban
Afghanistan and, 49–50, 172, 176,
269–70
propaganda, 269–70
Taylor, Zachary, 77
Team Red, White and Blue, 316
Team Rubicon, 316
technology
millennials and, 253
war and, 53–54, 174
Teigen, Jeremy
on familiarity gap, 108
on military members partisan
identification, 105
terrorism, 49–50, 55, 319–20
civilian ignorance and, 154–56, 178
contradictory attitudes and
expectations, 151–54
Dempsey, J., on military force
and, 32
familiarity gap, 148–51
public opinion and, 143–59, 178, 212
radical extremism and, 172–73
threat reduction, 143–44
trusted but isolated military, 145–48
vacillation and contradictions
on, 144
think tanks, 14
Thompson, Mark, 97
TISS. *See* Triangle Institute for Security
Studies
torture, public support of, 155
Total Force Policy, after Vietnam
War, 137
"The Tragedy of the American Military"
(Fallow), 22–23
Trainor, Bernard E., 199, 201, 316
transmutation, 85, 87
Huntington on, 82
Triangle Institute for Security
Studies (TISS) project, of 1998,
12, 15, 193, 320n1

on civil liberties, 101
on civilian and military values,
104, 118f
on civilian-military gap, 100–105,
122, 125
on civil-military world views,
83–84
on defense budgets, 122, 124f
on dissent, 104, 115, 122
elite civilians in, 99, 101, 103
elite military officers in, 99, 101–2
on familiarity gap, 102–3
on handgun sales, 101
on homosexual military service,
102, 121f
Kohut criticism of, 321n3
on military attitudes, 84–85
on military culture and
missions, 102
on military force, 110, 112f, 113f, 115
on military influence with political
leaders, 104
on partisanship, 84, 101–2
on political leaders and public's
values, 118f
on president's and military's
leadership roles during war, 117f
publications from, 139n4
public's casualty tolerance, 116f
on quick and massive interventions
vs. gradual escalation, 113f
on racial discrimination, 120f
on resignations, 122, 123f, 201
on respect for military, 103, 125
on women in combat jobs, 119f
on workplace contact with military
personnel, 114f
YouGov comparison challenges, 109
Truman, Harry S., 78
civil-military relations and, 77, 79
trust
as civil-military relations key, 18, 74,
91, 319
in Congress, 219–20, 251
elite military officers on, 101
military isolation and, 145–48
millennials military, 248, 251–52
officers on, 101
public attitudes on military, 38, 220

YouGov on civilian leadership,
110–11, 207, 219
See also mistrust; mistrust and awe
paradox

unemployment, for post-9/11 veterans,
29, 30
Uniform Code of Military Justice, on
service obligation, 27
United States (U.S.)
civil-military population in, 1, 2f
continuous war years, 1, 16, 18,
247, 287
egalitarian culture of, 7
"International Strategy for
Cyberspace," 55
liberal view of military in, 18,
219–43
"United States Objectives and
Programs for National Security"
(NSC-68), 172
universal humanitarian efforts,
281–83, 284
universal military service, 136
Unrestricted Warfare (Qiao and
Wang), 52–53
unrestricted warfare, 9/11 and, 54
urban population, 24
Urben, Heidi, 105
U.S. *See* United States
U.S. Agency for International
Development (USAID), 37
US Civil-Military Relations after 9/11
(Owens), 15
USAID. *See* U.S. Agency for
International Development

VA. *See* Veterans Administration
Valkovic, Matt, 269–70, 271
values
military, 85, 221, 250, 306–10
Obama defense of, 165, 176
political leaders and public, 115, 118f,
129, 179, 214–15, 218n62, 250,
298, 322n15
society difference from military, 17,
24, 67n42, 85, 228, 307, 308
TISS on, 104, 118f
veterans on military and society, 308

veterans on political leaders
different, 298–99
YouGov on, 118f, 221, 307
veterans
AVF and, 316–17
civic obligation response, 315–16
civilians Iraq and Afghanistan
attitudes, 32, 37
in Congress, 102–3, 325n49
domestic concerns addressed by, 316
elite, 322n16
groups, 316
homelessness, 29
literature by, 315, 325n48
on military and society values, 308
military force reluctance, 6
millennials on university
scholarships for, 261–62
on nonmilitary policies, 323n19
policy advantage of, 6
on political leaders different values,
298–99
on post-9/11 civilian ignorance, 146
public inexperience with, 3
on public post-9/11 familiarity gap, 146
reintegration difficulties, 7, 210
Republican Party identification,
109–10
society support of, 3, 146
suicides, 311–12
unemployment post-9/11, 29, 30
values, 298–99, 308
Vietnam War return, 314
women post-9/11, 30
Veterans Administration (VA)
disability benefits, 311
practices change, 317
PTSD disability benefits, 311
Vietnam War, 4, 245–46
officers' dissent, 80–81
officers' Republican identification
after, 31–32
veterans return from, 314
See also post-Vietnam era

Wang Xiangsui, 52–53, 54
war, 22, 317
changing soldiers and weapons,
52–53

War *(continued)*
declaration of, 51
electronic technologies and,
53–54, 174
issues of, 234–36
Obama actions of, 190
rituals for, 51–52
shifting battlefield, 54–55
transmutation during, 87
U.S. continuous years of, 1, 16, 18,
247, 287
See also specific wars
war, nature and character of, 17, 167,
175, 190
Afghanistan War disagreement
over, 170
AUMF and, 174
civilian and military views influence
on public, 168, 171
Clausewitzian, 196, 211–12
counterinsurgency operations, 11,
99, 168–70, 200, 202, 204
Gulf War disagreement over, 169–70
ISIS strategy and, 172, 173–74
provincial reconstruction
teams, 167–68
public confusion over strategy,
168–69, 183
public support and, 168
quick and massive interventions,
113f, 169, 174
radical extremism and, 172–73
Syria public response, 173
threats lack of clarity, 171
War Dogs (Frankel), 147
wartime strategies, 301–6
atrophy of, 315
leadership and, 175–81`
public opinion and, 161–87
public volatility and
contradictions on, 17
strategic culture, 162, 163–67,
181–82
Washington, George, 75–76, 167
Watson, Ben, 270–71
Weigley, Russell, 171
Weik, Jesse W., 175
Wilsonian tradition, in strategic
culture, 164–67

Windward-Kodoala Drab, in
Afghanistan, 265–66
videoconference, 269–71, 273
women
civil-military bargain on, 83, 85, 89
public on military unfairness to, 209
veterans post-9/11, 30
YouGov on military opportunities
for, 292, 307
women specialties, 100
Carter on, 83
in infantry, 8, 88–89, 115,
119f, 250
liberals on open, 86
Obama on, 88
Panetta on open, 88
Wong, Leonard, 61–62, 81
Wood, Leonard, 77
Woodward, Bob, 205
workplace, military members contact
in, 114f, 126, 147, 206
Workplace and Gender Relations Survey
of Active Duty Members, of
Pentagon, 209
World War II (WWII), 28, 91, 153,
182, 319
civilian connections during, 275
civil-military bargain and, 72
civil-military frictions and, 78
defense budget, 37
familiarity of civilians during, 107,
164, 176, 183
FDR fireside chats, 164, 176
Janowitz on, 212–13, 214
officer recruitment, 60
participation during, 23, 133, 136
veterans literature after, 235n48

YouGov study, 13–15, 64n6, 99, 217n29,
242n2, 286n1, 321n5
on Afghanistan involvement, 71, 175,
177, 178, 237
casualty-phobia, 110
on civilian ignorance, 289, 291–94
on civilian-military gap, 125, 315–16
on command and civilian control
issues, 236–38
on conservatism/liberalism, 84, 292
country at war during, 241

on critical perspective of military, 227–28
on defense budgets, 122, 124f
don't know responses, 17, 19, 110, 289, 290t, 291, 321n6
on homosexual military service, 83, 115, 121f, 307
on isolation of military, 221
on military and social issues, 299, 323n20
on military as social institution, 229–33
on military force, 110, 112f, 113f, 115
on military pay, 273–74, 293
on military service numbers, 24, 273
on military trust, 220
on military values, 221, 307
on officers' dissent, 115, 122, 201
on officers' media use, 201, 236–38
on political leaders and public's values, 118f
on political leaders lack of military knowledge, 300–301
on political party identification, 111f
on positive military depictions, 226

on president's and military's leadership role during war, 117f, 200
on PTSD crisis, 206–11, 310–13
on public civilian leadership trust, 110–11, 207, 219
on public priorities, 175, 212
public's casualty tolerance, 116f
on quick and massive interventions, 113f, 169, 174
on racial discrimination, 120f
on racial integration, 292
on Republican Party, 84, 109, 110
on resignations, 122, 123f, 201
on respect for military, 211, 221, 288, 289, 291–94
on social contact with military, 133
TISS comparison challenges, 109
on veterans difficult adjustment to civilian life, 210
wartime issues, 234–36
on women in combat jobs, 119f
on women opportunities, 292, 307
on workplace contact with military personnel, 114f, 126, 147, 206